THE PILOT'S GUIDE TO

THE MODERN AIRLINE COCKPIT

THE PILOT'S GUIDE TO

THE MODERN AIRLINE COCKPIT

STEPHEN M. CASNER

IOWA STATE UNIVERSITY PRESS / AMES

STEPHEN M. CASNER is a research scientist at NASA's Ames Research Center in California. Steve holds a Ph.D. degree in Intelligent Systems from the University of Pittsburgh, an M.S. degree in Computer Science from the University of Colorado at Boulder, and a B.S. degree from Millersville University.

Steve holds an Airline Transport Pilot certificate with type ratings in the Boeing 737 and Cessna Citation. Steve is also a Gold Seal Certified Flight Instructor with instrument and multiengine ratings.

Orders: 1-800-862-6657
Office: 1-515-292-0140
Fax: 1-515-292-3348
Web site: www.isupress.com

All illustrations by Stephen Casner and Doug Dupuie.
Cover photograph: Boeing 737 Next Generation, courtesy of The Boeing Company.

∞ Printed on acid-free paper in the United States of America

First edition, 2001

Library of Congress Cataloging-in-Publication Data

Casner, Stephen M.
    The pilot's guide to the modern airline cockpit / Stephen M. Casner
        p.   cm.
    Includes bibliographical reference and index.
    ISBN 0-8138-1011-6 (alk. paper)
        1. Airplanes—Cockpits. I. Title.

TL681.C6 C37 2001
629.135dc21   2001016897

Last digit is the print number: 9 8 7 6 5 4 3 2 1

CONTENTS

v

LIST OF FIGURES AND CAPTIONS

ACKNOWLEDGMENTS

I WOULD LIKE to thank the many pilots and engineers who have taught me many things about cockpit automation. Captains Bill Bulfer, Mike Montalvo, Dave Austin, Jim Irving, Corwin Logsdon, Cliff Bonner, Mark Buzzell, April Gafford, Scott Maclean, Brent Petersen, John Shopland, Ed Szetela, Gavin Tanchuck, and Lisa Wightman, and scores of pilots that I have had the privilege of jump-seating with whose names have been sadly forgotten. Randy Mumaw, Lance Sherry, Mike DeJonge, and Reid Fairburn have shared much of their engineering expertise over the past ten years. Bill Bulfer, Ed Hutchins, Mark Holt, and Eric Villeda took the time to read drafts of this book and provided me with many helpful comments. Kristine Anderson helped choose a title that would make sense to the soon-to-be airline pilot. Doug Dupuie generously offered his graphic arts expertise in the production of several of the technical drawings in the book. The project management was handled by Doug Nalean-Carlson. Dave Rosenbaum at Iowa State University Press provided invaluable support throughout every phase of the project.

INTRODUCTION

Introduction

What's the Difference between a Cessna 172 and a Boeing 737?

When you step into any modern airline cockpit, you will see the colorful glow of the computer screens where round dials and gauges used to be. Whether it is a turboprop, a regional jet, a Boeing, or an Airbus, most every airliner manufactured today contains a suite of high-technology avionics loosely referred to as **cockpit automation.** Few aspiring pilots realize that they will soon have to learn to exercise their multiengine instrument flying skills in this new high-tech environment.

The fast-pace of cockpit technology, together with an accelerated demand for pilots, has created a gap between the skills taught in professional pilot training and the skills that pilots are expected to have when they begin their professional flying careers. During professional pilot training, pilots typically operate piston-engine aircraft with traditional cockpit technology. While this learning environment serves to build an important foundation of instrument flying skills, pilots receive little training or practical experience that helps prepare them to exercise these core skills in a high-technology cockpit. Airline training departments continue to struggle with having to provide "last minute" training to pilots with no prior experience with cockpit automation. One surveyed regional carrier reported that more than one half of all 1,000-hour pilots are unsuccessful during their first pass through regional jet training. How prepared will you be?

It is the aim of this book to provide you with the skills and concepts you will need to confidently begin an initial training program in a modern airline cockpit.

What Is Cockpit Automation?

Despite its intimidating appearance, the technology found in the modern airline cockpit is nothing more than a collection of displays, controls, and computers designed to support the crew in doing its familiar job. Probably the best way to explain what these computers in the cockpit do is in terms of the familiar duties that make up the job of operating a complex multiengine aircraft.

When planning a flight route, the flight crew must gather navigation information about the intended route, the prevailing atmospheric conditions, and the performance characteristics of the airplane. You will learn about a computer that provides you with fast electronic access to this information needed for flight planning. Using entries made by the crew, this computer automatically performs many of the tedious numerical calculations required to create a flight plan.

As the flight plan is set in motion, the crew must guide the aircraft along the planned route. You will learn about other systems in the modern airline cockpit that are capable of performing the laborious task of guiding the aircraft along the planned route. These systems free the flight crew to attend to other duties while you and your crewmate monitor the progress of the flight. As you watch these automated systems perform their assigned duties, you will learn that the automation is, for the most part, "an open book." The modern automated cockpit provides the flight crew with many information displays that allow you to closely follow what the airplane is doing now and what it plans to do next.

As you know from experience, en route changes to a well-planned flight route are inevitable. You will see how the automation provides you with straightforward ways of modifying the flight plan when asked to do so by air traffic control.

As is often the case in busy terminal areas, ATC sometimes decides that the best plan is to have no flight plan at all. In this situation, you must be prepared to quickly respond to short directives that ask you to fly a particular heading, maintain a given speed, or descend to a specified altitude. You will see that the modern airline cockpit offers a collection of simple automated functions that allow you to quickly aim the aircraft at assigned headings, altitudes, and airspeeds.

In short, the automation technologies found in today's cockpit are nothing more than a collection of resources that assist the crew when performing familiar duties. The rest of this book is designed to acquaint you with these new cockpit automation technologies, and show you how they can be integrated into your familiar way of doing business in the cockpit.

Why Is Learning to Use Cockpit Automation Difficult?

Instructors and trainees alike consistently report that the most challenging aspect of learning to operate a modern transport aircraft is learning to use the automated systems found in the cockpit. Why does cockpit automation give pilots so much trouble?

One reason for the difficulty is that cockpit automation is something that most commercial multiengine instrument pilots have never seen before. While many other parts of the modern transport aircraft are common to the piston airplanes you may have flown during flight training, cockpit automation is likely to be something new.

A second reason why learning about cockpit automation is difficult may be that computer systems are harder to learn about than mechanical systems. For example, while mechanical control yokes and control surfaces have moving parts that you can see, the computers in the cockpit have software and logic that can be observed only by reading, hypothesizing, and experimenting. As with the personal computers that you use at home, along with their many quirky behaviors, there is something uncertain about trying to form a solid understanding of a complex system that never really shows its face.

A third reason for the difficulty is that, while cockpit automation can relieve the flight crew of many tedious chores, the automation places new demands on the flight crew. For example, how does the crew decide which automation features to use and when? What are the limits of the automation's capabilities, and how should they be taken into account during real flight situations? How does the flight crew monitor the progress of an automated system? What can the flight crew do to remain "in-the-loop" while the automation performs its duties? These are all new skills that pilots must learn in addition to the technical details of operating the system.

What This Book Teaches You

The purpose of this book is to introduce you to the fundamentals of cockpit automation before you enter training at an airline company. Taking the time to learn the fundamentals of cockpit automation will allow you to make better use of the limited time that you spend studying cockpit automa-

tion during company training. By the time you leave company training, your understanding of the modern automated cockpit will undoubtedly be greater than that of the pilot who had to devote precious training time to understanding the very purpose of cockpit automation or memorizing simple knobs-and-dials procedures. The benefit of having a deeper understanding of cockpit automation is founded on the belief that a truly competent, safe, and conscientious pilot has to know more than the simple button-pushing procedures. Pilots should know enough to be able to intelligently follow the procedures they learn. Even more important, pilots need to have a depth of understanding that can guide them in unexpected situations that differ from the ones they practiced in training.

After understanding the fundamentals of cockpit automation, the problem of becoming proficient in a particular airplane at a particular company becomes a matter of differences training. You won't have to start at the beginning because all cockpit automation systems are fundamentally the same. You will have to commit to learning only the details of the particular system that you are learning to operate and the standard operating procedures your company uses.

This book does not begin with system diagrams and technical diatribes as many technical manuals often do. This book explains cockpit automation in terms of what you already know as a commercial multiengine instrument pilot. One thing I have learned from the engineers who design cockpit automation is that the automation is built to support the flight crew in performing their familiar flight duties. This book teaches you cockpit automation in terms of these duties and how the automation was designed to help you perform them. Through every phase of flight, this book begins with a review of the duties that the flight crew must perform. Cockpit automation systems are introduced as resources that the crew has available to help them when performing these duties. You will learn how to make informed decisions about which system features, if any, to use in which situations. You will learn how to assume the role of supervisor when delegating control of the aircraft to the automation: how to solicit information from the automation about what it is doing and what it plans to do next.

How to Practice What You Are Learning

PC-Based Simulators

The cockpit automation systems described throughout the book are based on the ones found in the cockpit of the next-generation Boeing 737. Although several computer-based training systems are available for this airplane, most are developed for the airline training department market and cost up to several hundred thousand dollars. A more practical choice for individual pilots looking to get a head start on cockpit automation is an inexpensive PC-based Boeing 747-400 simulator made by Aerowinx. The Aerowinx 747-400 simulator sells for about $250 and offers most of the cockpit automation systems discussed in the book. More information about this PC-based simulator is available on the WWW at: www.aerowinx.com

For the purposes of the material covered in this book, the differences between the Boeing 737 and the Boeing 747-400 are minor. The last chapter of the book points out the differences that will allow you to get started using this simulator immediately.

IFR GPS Units

Another excellent way to get hands-on experience working with computers in the cockpit is by using what are referred to as IFR GPS units. These computers are now common in airplanes used for primary instrument training. You will find that the basic concepts and skills presented in this book can be applied to planning, following, and modifying an instrument flight plan using any one of the popular IFR GPS units. Garmin, one of the leading manufacturers of these units, makes available desktop simulations of their products for free on the WWW at: www.garmin.com

THE PILOT'S GUIDE TO

THE MODERN AIRLINE COCKPIT

Cockpit Overview

CHAPTER 1

The Quick Tour

THIS CHAPTER TAKES you on a quick tour of the modern airline cockpit. You will see that the intimidating-looking computers in the cockpit are nothing more than a collection of tools designed to lend a helping hand as you perform the same flight duties that are required when operating any aircraft. These include the familiar chores of: (1) planning a flight route; (2) guiding the aircraft along the planned flight route; (3) making en route modifications to the flight route; (4) flying off the flight route to comply with simple ATC clearances; and (5) sometimes rejoining the flight route when cleared by ATC.

You will see how using cockpit automation changes the way you do your job. The automation is capable of handling some of the dirty work while you and your crewmate assume the role of supervisors who must intelligently manage the automation as it performs its duties.

Planning the Flight Route

Back at the gate, the flight crew works together with a device called a flight management computer to plan a highly tuned flight route that makes optimum use of time and fuel. You and your crewmate must first provide the flight management computer with information about the assigned route, aircraft, and expected conditions. The flight management computer then calculates the details of the route based on your inputs and displays this information to you. The flight crew must then review the route to ensure it meets all requirements.

Prior to departure, the flight crew works together with a powerful component of the modern automated cockpit to plan the ideal flight route. The component is known as the **flight management computer** (FMC). The route created by the combination of you and the flight management computer will do more than simply maneuver the aircraft among the waypoints and airways that make up the assigned route. This route will be highly tuned with respect to both time and fuel. The computed takeoff thrust will be just right for atmospheric conditions. The climb, cruise, and descent speeds chosen will reflect a near-perfect trade-off between time enroute and fuel burned. The FMC will calculate the point at which the aircraft will reach the assigned cruise altitude with remarkable accuracy. Finally, the FMC will choose a top-of-descent point that will allow the aircraft to perform a whispering idle-thrust glide that delivers the aircraft on speed and altitude at the assigned descent crossing restriction.

How does this ideal flight route get built? The flight crew and the FMC work together to accomplish this in three simple steps.

The Flight Crew Enters Information about the Assigned Route, Aircraft, and Expected Atmospheric Conditions

The first step in creating a flight route requires the flight crew to enter a variety of pertinent information that will help the FMC do its part.

Like every other computer, the flight management computer has a keyboard and monitor that allow the flight crew to view information contained in the computer and to input

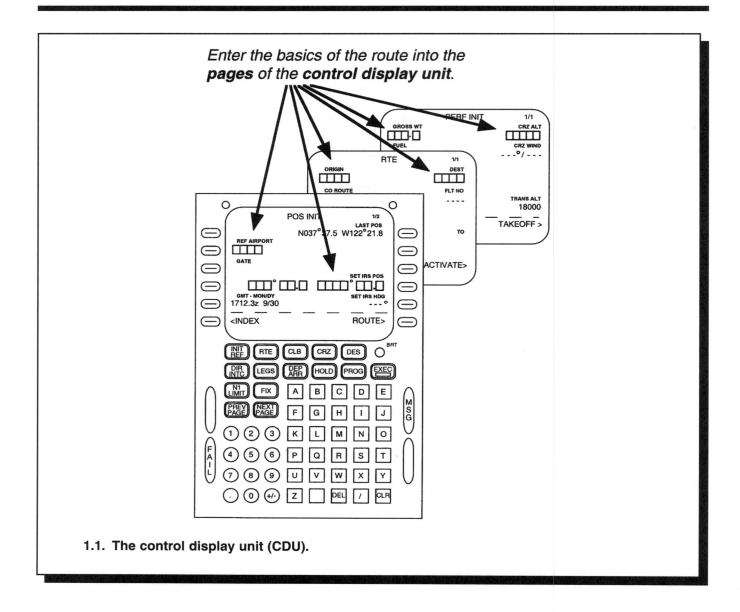

1.1. The control display unit (CDU).

information into it. The **control display unit** (CDU) serves as the keyboard and monitor for the FMC. Shown in Figure 1.1, the CDU displays information about the route on the **CDU screen.** Since the FMC contains far more information than could fit on one small screen, information stored in the FMC appears on a collection of **CDU pages.** Each CDU page displays information related to one particular aspect of the flight route. Only one CDU page can appear on the CDU screen at a time. The alphanumeric buttons allow the crew to enter information the FMC needs to perform its part in building the flight route.

The CDU pages shown in Figure 1.1 allow you to enter information such as the initial position of the aircraft, the origin and destination airports, the gross weight of the aircraft, and the planned cruising altitude.

Using the CDU keypad to enter this information into each of the CDU pages is the first step in the flight crew's part in building the flight route.

The FMC Uses the Crew Entries to Calculate the Flight Route

After you and your crewmate have entered the basic information about the route and aircraft, the FMC constructs a detailed flight route. The FMC draws on two extensive databases to accomplish this step. A **navigation database** electronically stores the same navigational information contained in your aeronautical charts. A **performance database** details the performance characteristics of the aircraft and engines. It tells the FMC how the aircraft will perform in a variety of configurations and atmospheric conditions.

Using the information you have entered, the FMC performs all of the calculations that you had to perform in the past using your hand-held flight computer. In addition to figuring the tracks, distances, times, and fuel remaining at each waypoint, the FMC also calculates the most fuel-efficient speeds to fly and the ideal point at which to start your descent as you approach your destination airport.

The flight plan created by you and the FMC can take you all the way from your departure runway to the missed-approach point at your destination airport.

The Crew Reviews the Flight Route

Once the FMC has done its job, the crew must review the finished product. Why is it so important for you and your crewmate to check the flight route? You will soon learn that modern cockpit automation offers you the capability to auto-matically guide the aircraft along the route. With that in mind, it's a good idea to make sure the FMC's plan is the right one!

How do you review the route that the FMC has devised? Two displays help you and your crewmate check the flight route that is now programmed into the FMC.

A variety of CDU pages list the many details of the planned route. For example, the **Route Legs page,** shown in Figure 1.2, lists the succession of waypoints that make up the route, along with the altitude and airspeed at which the aircraft is expected to cross each waypoint.

Another cockpit display called the **electronic horizontal situation indicator** (EHSI), shown in Figure 1.3, provides the "big picture" presented in a graphical format. The waypoint symbols and lines sketch the lateral track of the aircraft along the programmed route. The T/C and T/D symbols show the points at which the aircraft is predicted to reach the assigned cruising altitude and the planned top-of-descent point.

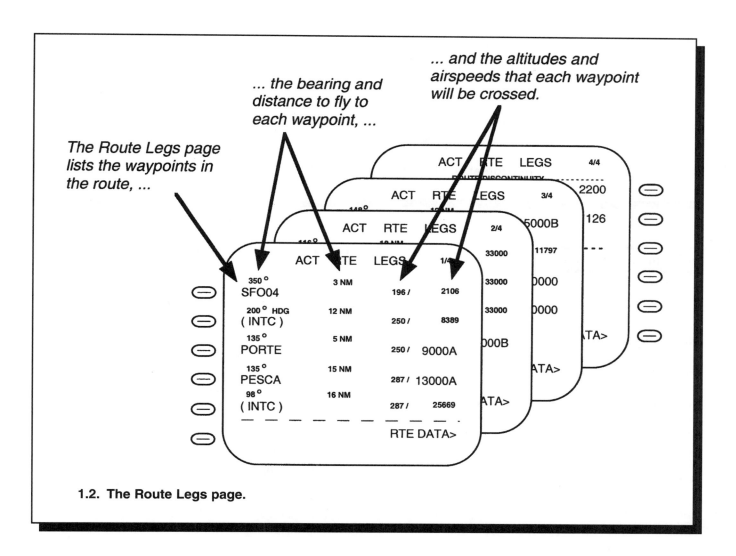

1.2. The Route Legs page.

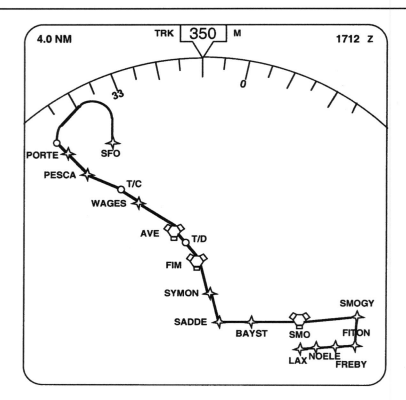

*The **electronic horizontal situation indicator** (EHSI) presents the "big picture."*

1.3. The electronic horizontal situation indicator (EHSI).

Following the Flight Route

The modern airline cockpit also supports the flight crew in accurately guiding the aircraft along the flight route that has been planned. Guidance is provided not only along the lateral portion of the route but also along the vertical trajectory as well. In one mode of operation, the pilot flying must manipulate the control yoke and thrust levers in response to roll, pitch, and power commands that are generated by the automation. In another mode of operation, the control yoke and thrust levers are automatically manipulated while other computers track the progress of the airplane through the air.

Now that the flight route has been built, the next step is to fly it. As you will see, the automation found in the modern airline cockpit not only helps you plan a flight route, it also helps you follow it.

The Crew Engages Two Powerful Guidance Functions: LNAV and VNAV

Aside from the flight management computer that helps you plan a flight route, most modern airliners contain an **autoflight system** that assists the flight crew in guiding the airplane along the route stored in the flight management computer. The autoflight system offers powerful **guidance functions** that help guide the airplane along the programmed route. The **lateral navigation** (LNAV) guidance function automatically manages the roll of the aircraft to guide the aircraft between the waypoints listed on the Route Legs page shown in Figure 1.2. LNAV does not manage the speed or vertical trajectory of the aircraft. To handle that job, the crew can engage a second guidance function called **vertical navigation** (VNAV). VNAV automatically manages pitch and thrust to help ensure that the aircraft crosses each waypoint at the speed and altitude shown on the Route Legs

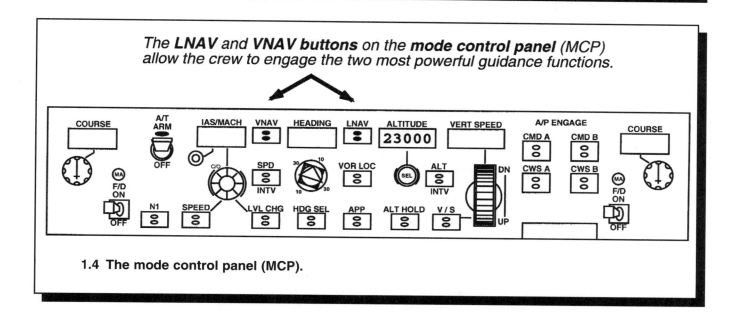

The **LNAV** and **VNAV** buttons on the **mode control panel** (MCP) allow the crew to engage the two most powerful guidance functions.

1.4 The mode control panel (MCP).

page. You can engage the LNAV and VNAV functions just after takeoff and use them all the way to the missed-approach point at the destination airport.

LNAV and VNAV can be engaged by pressing the LNAV and VNAV buttons on the **mode control panel** (MCP) shown in Figure 1.4.

Guidance functions such as LNAV and VNAV can be used in two basic ways. In one mode of operation, the pitch and roll commands that are necessary to guide the aircraft along the programmed route are presented to the crew using a set of command bars that appear on each pilot's **electronic attitude director indicator** (EADI). Together, these command bars are referred to as the **flight director** and resemble the glide slope and localizer needles you have seen in smaller aircraft. An EADI with flight directors is shown in Figure 1.5.

Commands presented on the **engine indicators** show the pilot flying how to manipulate the thrust levers. The arrows that appear beside the needles on the N1 gauges shown in Figure 1.6 are called **cursors** or **bugs** and show the crew the thrust settings that the FMC has calculated.

In this mode of operation, the flight crew is able to receive guidance information from the autoflight system, yet remain in close contact with the controls of the aircraft.

In another mode of operation, an autoflight system component called an **autopilot** automatically manipulates the control yoke, while another autoflight system component called an **autothrottle** automatically manipulates the thrust levers. Together, these components work the controls of the airplane as if it were being flown by an invisible pilot.

If the flight management computer stores the sequence of waypoints that make up the flight route and the autoflight system guides the airplane between the waypoints, how does

the airplane keep track of where it is? Every modern airliner contains a collection of technologies that keeps all of the cockpit automation systems informed about the present position of the airplane at all times. Conventional **radio navigation receivers** use VOR stations to track position. **Inertial reference systems** sense the airplane's movements in space. **Global positioning system receivers** use satellites to determine the aircraft's position. Working together, these systems provide an answer to the important question: Where are we?

The Crew Closely Monitors the Progress of the Aircraft

Although the cockpit automation systems we have discussed can do many things that save you time and effort, like any other computer system, they don't always work the way you want them to. For this reason the flight crew remains in a leadership role in the cockpit. You and your crewmate are at all times responsible for evaluating your situation, deciding how best to fly the aircraft, and closely supervising and monitoring the automation. For the flight crew who is now placed in a supervisory role, cockpit automation provides plentiful information about what it's doing and what it plans to do next.

The **Route Legs page,** shown in Figure 1.7, lists the waypoints in the planned route along with the planned speed, altitude, and distance remaining to each waypoint. Of particular importance is the first waypoint in the list, known as the **active waypoint.** The active waypoint is the one that the automation is always working to achieve when LNAV and VNAV are engaged.

The **Progress page,** shown in Figure 1.8, displays the planned time of arrival and fuel remaining at each waypoint

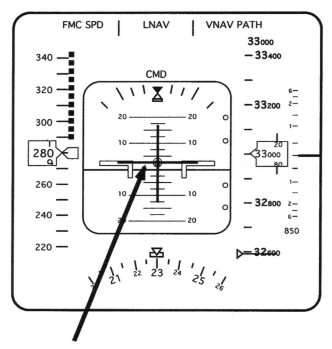

The **flight director** shows the pitch and roll commands generated by the FMC.

1.5. The electronic attitude director indicator (EADI) and flight director.

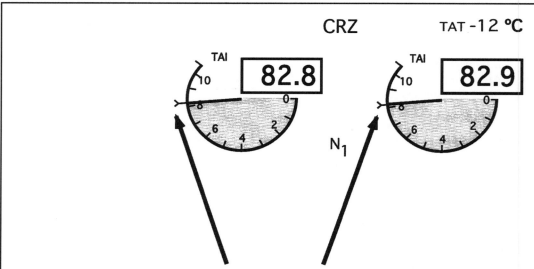

The **cursors** on the engine indicators show the thrust settings calculated by the FMC.

1.6. Engine indicators.

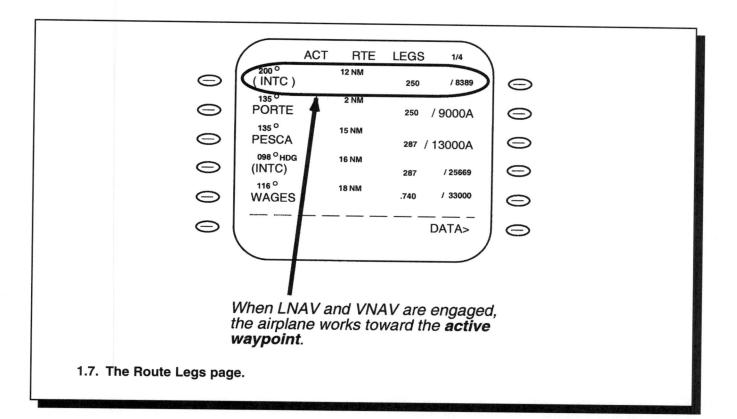

*When LNAV and VNAV are engaged, the airplane works toward the **active waypoint**.*

1.7. The Route Legs page.

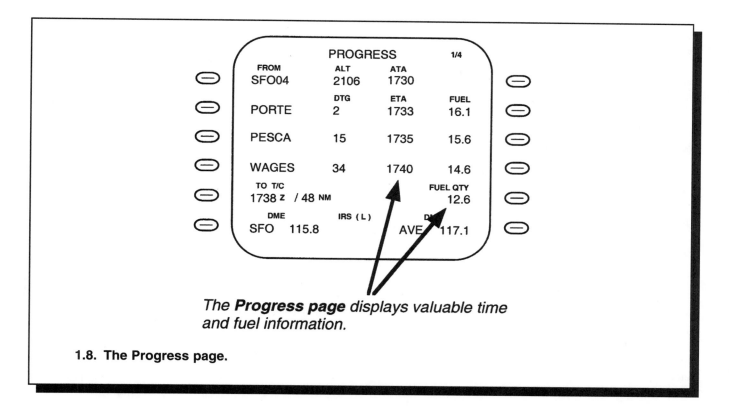

*The **Progress page** displays valuable time and fuel information.*

1.8. The Progress page.

along with the actual time and fuel remaining for the way-point you have just passed.

Modifying the Flight Route

The flight management computer allows the flight crew to make simple modifications to the flight route when instructed to do so by air traffic control.

It is often the case that, somewhere along the way, ATC will call and make a modification to this time- and fuel-efficient flight route that you have taken the trouble to build prior to departure. Fortunately, the flight management computer provides simple ways of modifying the planned route and instructing the aircraft to follow the modified route. The CDU offers special pages that allow the flight crew to quickly carry out several of the more popular route modifications. Using these pages to modify the planned route typically amounts to filling in a few prompts that ask for the details of the clearance and then activating the modification by pressing the **execute button** (EXEC) that appears on the front of the CDU.

For example, the **Direct To page** shown in Figure 1.9 allows you to proceed directly to an assigned waypoint. Suppose you have been instructed to proceed directly to Avenal. Entering AVE into the DIRECT TO prompt on the Direct To page causes Avenal to become the new active waypoint. The FMC then builds a direct course from the aircraft's present position to Avenal.

All of the waypoints that appeared between the aircraft's present position and Avenal are deleted.

Flying off the Flight Route

The flight crew always has the option to turn off the highly automated LNAV and VNAV functions and fly the aircraft in a more direct and simple way. The autoflight system offers a collection of simpler guidance functions that allow you to quickly respond to ATC directives that differ significantly from the flight route stored in the FMC or to maintain closer control of the aircraft whenever you determine it is best to do so.

Aside from the highly automated LNAV and VNAV guidance functions, the autoflight system offers a few more simple-to-use guidance functions. These functions allow you to quickly respond to simple and direct ATC clearances. Figure 1.10 illustrates a guidance function called **Heading Select.** For example, suppose ATC calls and instructs you to fly a heading of 220 degrees for spacing. You can dial 220 into the Heading window on the mode control panel (MCP)

and then push the Heading Select button. The airplane then turns to a heading of 220 degrees.

Suppose ATC now instructs you to descend and maintain 17,000 feet. Figure 1.11 illustrates another simple guidance function, called **Level Change,** that allows you to dial an assigned altitude into the Altitude window on the mode control and press the Level Change button. The aircraft will immediately commence a descent to 17,000 feet.

The interesting thing to note about these simple guidance functions is that they do not guide the airplane to the route stored in the FMC but rather to headings, speeds, and altitudes that you can quickly dial using the mode control panel.

The Crew Keeps Track of Which Guidance Functions Are Engaged at All Times

A display called a **flight mode annunciator** (FMA), shown in Figure 1.12, helps you and your crewmate keep track of which guidance functions are engaged at all times.

The flight mode annunciator requires a bit of study to learn to interpret correctly but is an important means of determining what the airplane is currently doing and is planning to do next.

Rejoining the Flight Route

The position sensors in the modern airliner track the position of the aircraft with respect to the route stored in the FMC at all times. If the crew is asked to leave the planned route and is then cleared to return to it, the automation provides a simple way of aiming the aircraft back toward the route and eventually recapturing it.

After vectoring you around for a while, ATC sometimes allows you to go back to what you were doing: flying efficiently on the route that the crew and the FMC built. It turns out that if the aircraft leaves the FMC route, the flight management computer does not discard it. The route is still in the FMC whether it is being followed or not. If ATC does allow you to resume your own navigation, the FMC provides a handy way of rejoining the route.

Rejoining the FMC route takes place in two steps. After diverting off course, you can aim the aircraft back toward the FMC route using a simple guidance function such as Heading Select. When the aircraft approaches the vicinity of the FMC route, you can then reengage LNAV and VNAV. Engaging LNAV and VNAV will cause the aircraft to recapture the FMC route and follow the route as before. Figure 1.13 illustrates a typical scenario in which ATC vectors the aircraft off the planned route and then allows you to rejoin it later.

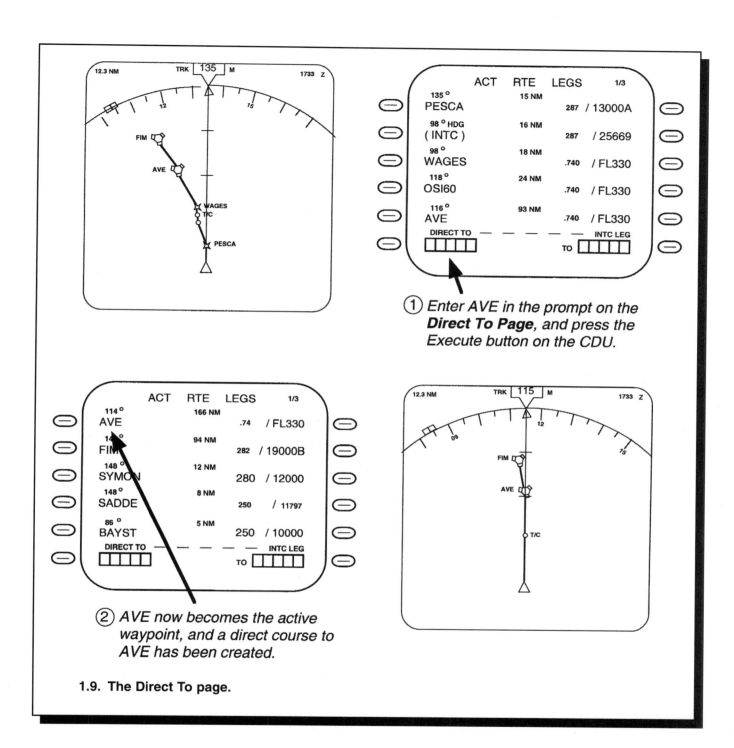

① Enter AVE in the prompt on the **Direct To Page**, and press the Execute button on the CDU.

② AVE now becomes the active waypoint, and a direct course to AVE has been created.

1.9. The Direct To page.

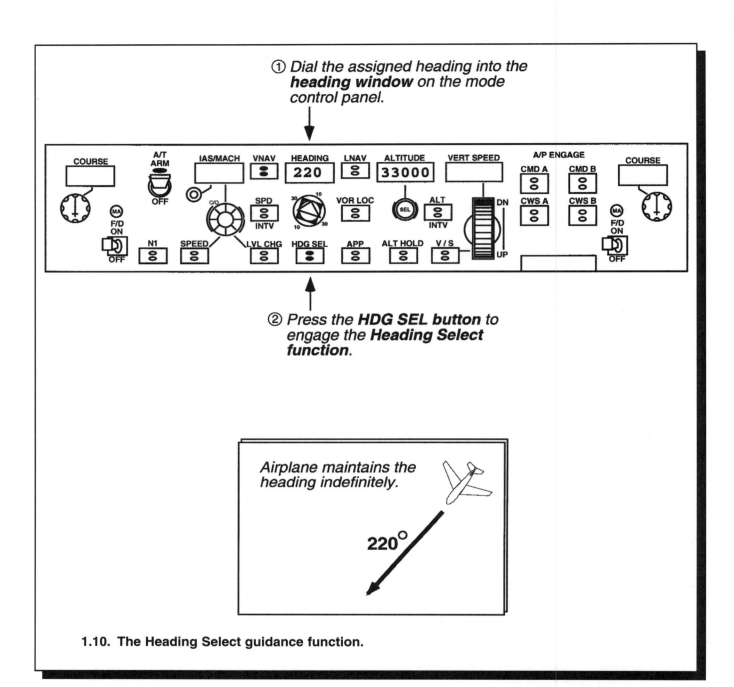

① Dial the assigned heading into the **heading window** on the mode control panel.

② Press the **HDG SEL button** to engage the **Heading Select function**.

Airplane maintains the heading indefinitely.

220°

1.10. The Heading Select guidance function.

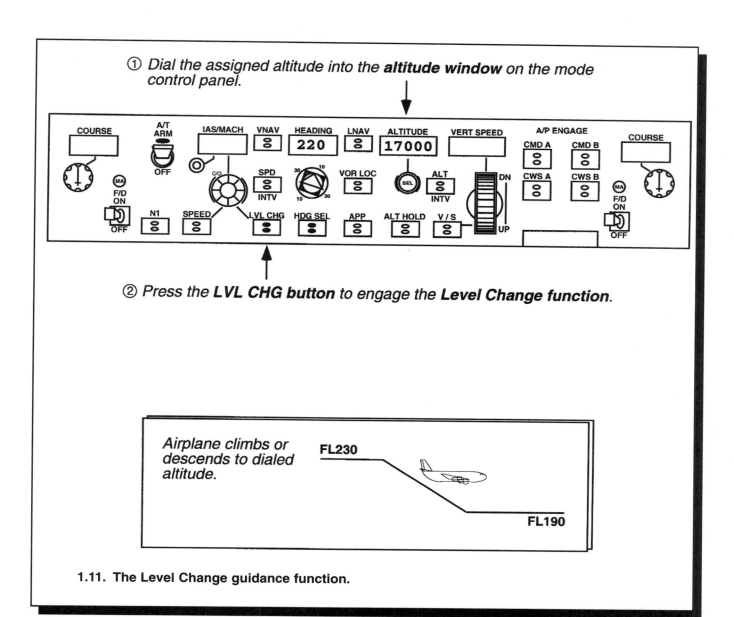

① *Dial the assigned altitude into the **altitude window** on the mode control panel.*

② *Press the **LVL CHG button** to engage the **Level Change function**.*

Airplane climbs or descends to dialed altitude.

FL230

FL190

1.11. The Level Change guidance function.

Check the **flight mode annunciator** to remain aware of which guidance functions are engaged.

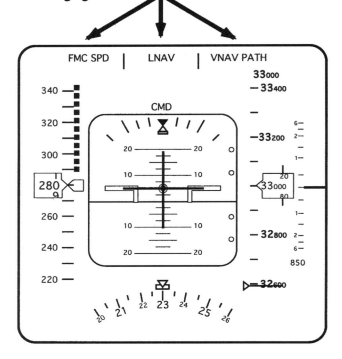

1.12. The flight mode annunciator (FMA).

Use Heading Select to turn off of the programmed route.

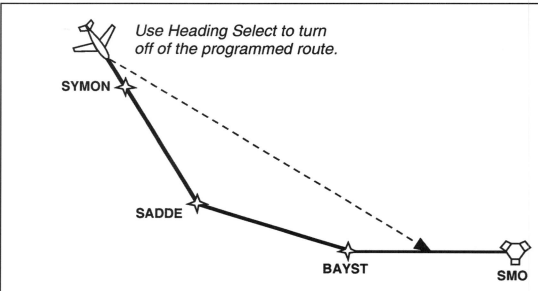

Re-engage LNAV once the aircraft re-intercepts the programmed route.

1.13 Departing and rejoining the flight route.

Human Factors of Cockpit Automation

As you may have noticed, using the automated systems in the cockpit changes the way you fly the airplane. Gone are the days of donning your scarf and goggles and getting there on two wings and a prayer. The introduction of powerful cockpit automation systems has had many unexpected consequences, some beneficial, some not. Cockpit automation can sometimes save you time and reduce your workload. But at the same time, by automating many chores traditionally performed by human pilots, automated systems expose you to many potential pitfalls. Using cockpit automation can sometimes challenge your ability to pay attention and remain "in the loop." The complex nature of cockpit automation can also confuse the flight crew. Why did the airplane do that? What's it doing now? What's it going to do next? Throughout the book we discuss these issues and show how the informed flight crew can remain one step ahead of the airplane at all times.

Chapter Summary

In this chapter you took a quick tour of the process of flying in a modern airline cockpit. You learned that cockpit automation supports you in performing specific pilot duties. The flight management computer supports you in planning a good flight route. The autoflight system offers powerful automated guidance functions, LNAV and VNAV, that generate guidance commands that help guide the aircraft along the planned route. The pilot flying can choose to follow these guidance commands and steer the aircraft manually or allow two other autoflight system components, called the autopilot and autothrottle, to steer the aircraft automatically while both crew members supervise the automation. You learned how several kinds of sensors track the position of the airplane along the planned route. Because change is always a part of every flight, you learned that you are able to make en route changes to the planned flight route. The crew also has the option of putting aside the planned route and the automated guidance functions LNAV and VNAV. In these situations a collection of simpler guidance functions can be used to fly the aircraft in a much simpler and more responsive way.

CHAPTER 2

Planning the Flight Route

IN THIS CHAPTER you take a closer look at the process of planning a flight route in the modern airline cockpit. You will learn that planning a flight route using cockpit automation is really no different from the way you have planned flight routes in the past. To create a flight plan such as the one shown in Figure 2.1, you must gather navigation charts and aircraft performance data, list the sequence of waypoints that make up the route, and then "do the math." As you know from experience, the mathematical calculations required to determine distances, tracks, estimated times of arrival, fuel burned, and ground speed at each waypoint are quite tedious and prone to error.

You will see how using cockpit automation to create the same flight plan greatly simplifies the process. Not only does the automation provide all of the information needed to create the route at the push of a button, it also performs all of the calculations.

Building a flight plan in the modern airline cockpit proceeds in three simple steps.

In the first step, the flight crew uses a device called a **control display unit** (CDU) to input basic information about the assigned route, aircraft, and expected conditions. The control display unit serves as the keyboard and monitor for a powerful device called the **flight management computer** (FMC). Together, the CDU and FMC are sometimes referred to as the **flight management system** (FMS) or the **flight management computer system** (FMCS).

In the second step, the FMC accepts the pilot inputs and uses its detailed navigation and performance databases to construct a detailed flight route that takes the aircraft from runway to runway. The FMC calculates optimum lateral tracks, vertical trajectories, thrusts, and speeds along every phase of the flight.

In the third step, you and your crewmate must carefully review the route that the FMC has created to ensure that it meets all of the requirements for the flight. The details of the flight route are presented on different displays that the flight crew can call up on the CDU. Another display called an **electronic horizontal situation indicator** (EHSI) provides a pictorial summary of the flight route.

These three steps will be illustrated in the context of planning a flight route from San Francisco (KSFO) to Los Angeles (KLAX) International Airport.

The Crew Enters Information about the Assigned Route, Aircraft, and Expected Conditions

The first step in planning a flight route is for the flight crew to provide the FMC with the basic information that it needs to do its part in constructing the flight route. You need to only enter a few essential details about the assigned route, aircraft, and expected conditions. This information is entered using the control display unit (CDU). Let's take a moment to learn our way around this important device that you will use many times throughout the flight.

The Control Display Unit (CDU)

Shown in Figure 2.2, the control display unit (CDU) is your principal means of communicating with the flight management computer.

Flight Plan								KSFO to KLAX	
Waypoints	Ident.	A i r w a y	A l t i t u d e	C o u r s e	Fuel	Dist.	GS	Dept. Time	
	Freq.				Leg	Leg	Est.		
					Rem.	Rem.		ETE	ETA
SFO	115.8				16.6	320	Act.	ATE	ATA
PORTE	113.7	PORTE3	9000	135	.51 / 16.1	18 / 302	244	5:22	5:22
PESCA	113.7	PORTE3	13000	135	.48 / 15.6	15 / 287	249	3:49	9:11
WAGES	116.8	PORTE3	FL330	090	.98 / 14.6	34 / 253	282	7:21	16:32
AVE	117.1	J1	FL330	118	2.48 / 12.2	116 / 137	452	14:40	31:12
FIM	112.5	J1	FL330	130	2.1 / 10.0	94 / 43	452	12:41	43:56
SYMON	112.5	SADDE6	12000	148	.23 / 9.8	12 / 31	282	2:55	46:51
SADDE	112.5	SADDE6		148	.18 / 9.6	8 / 23	282	1:36	48:27
BAYST	110.8	SADDE6	10000	081	.11 / 9.5	5 / 18	248	1:12	49:39
SMO	110.8	SADDE6		081	.21 / 9.3	10 / 8	248	2:38	52:17
LAX	108.5			249	.24 / 9.4	8 /	182	4:32	56:49

2.1. A conventional flight plan.

At the top of the CDU is the **CDU screen.** Since the FMC contains far more information than could be presented on a single CDU screen, information is presented using a collection of separate displays called **CDU pages.** Each CDU page displays information relevant to one particular aspect of your flight route. Every CDU page has a **title** that is always shown at the top of the CDU screen.

Data appearing on every CDU page is broken up into twelve **page lines:** six lines on the left and six on the right. For convenience, the page lines are named. The six page lines on the left are called **1L, 2L, 3L, 4L, 5L,** and **6L.** The page lines on the right are referred to as **1R, 2R, 3R, 4R, 5R,** and **6R.** The twelve page lines are used to both display

information to the flight crew as well as accept inputs from them. For example, the CDU page shown in Figure 2.2 displays the fuel on board the aircraft at line 2L.

Box prompts indicate a required entry that the flight crew must make. Entering information into the CDU is accomplished using the **number** and **letter keys** found on the bottom portion of the CDU. When numbers and letters are typed using the keys, the characters appear in a special area near the bottom of the CDU screen called the **scratch pad.** The scratch pad temporarily stores the characters until the pilot entering the data decides at which page line to insert the characters. After all characters have been entered into the scratch pad, the entire entry can be moved up to one

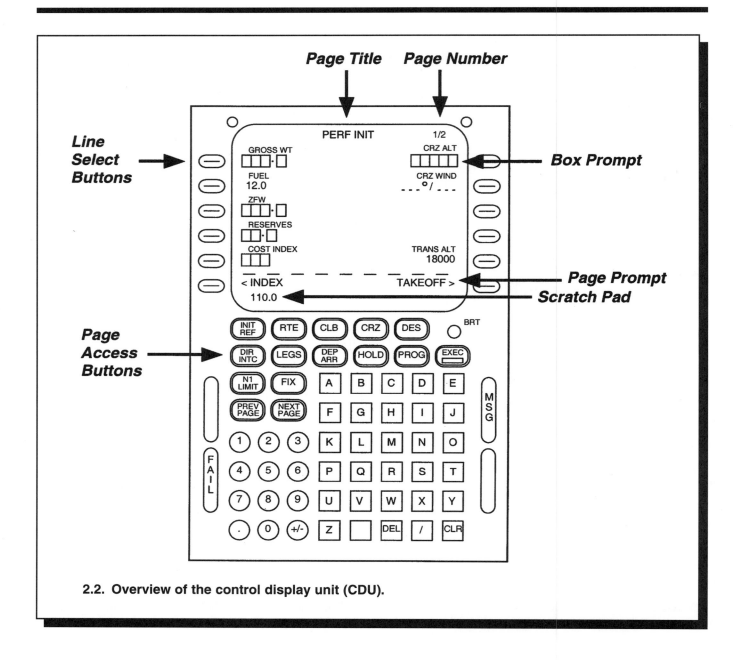

2.2. Overview of the control display unit (CDU).

of the page lines by pushing the **line select button** that is located next to each page line. This process is illustrated in Figure 2.3.

Some CDU pages can be accessed by pressing one of the **page access buttons** that appear on the front of the CDU. All other CDU pages can be accessed using **page access prompts** that appear on other CDU pages. For example, line 6R on the CDU page in Figure 2.3 contains a page access prompt for the CDU page called the Takeoff page.

Since many pages contain more related information than can fit onto one CDU screen, some pages are broken up into **extended pages.** You can recognize an extended page by

looking at the **page number** shown in the upper right corner of the CDU. The 1/2 indication means that there is a total of two extended pages for this page and that the first of the two extended pages is currently shown on the screen. You can move between extended pages by pressing the NEXT PAGE and PREV PAGE buttons on the front of the CDU.

Now that you know your way around the control display unit, let's look at the process of entering the information needed by the FMC in order to create the flight route. To keep things simple, the engineers created a series of CDU pages that must be reviewed and filled out when creating a flight route. These pages are shown in Figure 2.4.

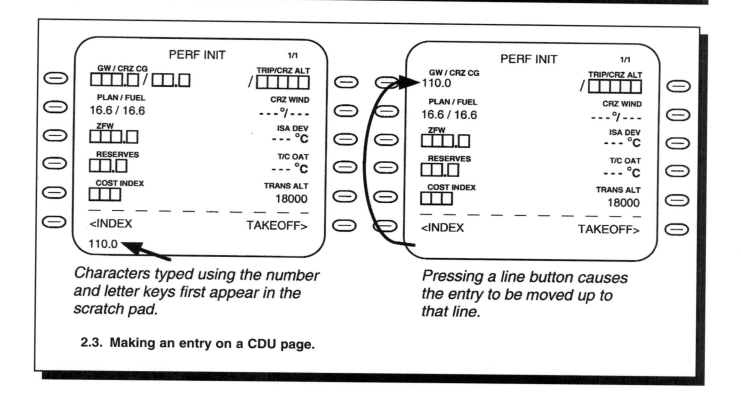

Characters typed using the number and letter keys first appear in the scratch pad.

Pressing a line button causes the entry to be moved up to that line.

2.3. Making an entry on a CDU page.

Most pages contain box prompts that indicate where the flight crew must make entries. To get to the next page in the route-planning sequence, a page access prompt is usually provided at line 6R. Just press the line select button beside this prompt, and the next page in the sequence will appear.

Another way to get around between pages is to use an index page that lists each of the pages and provides a page access prompt that allows you to access each page. The Init Ref Index page is shown in Figure 2.5.

Let's take a closer look at each of the CDU pages that you and your crewmate must consider when planning a flight route using the flight management computer.

The Ident Page: Selecting the Current Navigation Database

This first action performed by the flight crew takes place on a CDU page called the **Ident page.** Shown in Figure 2.6, the Ident page allows you to review what software is currently loaded into the FMC.

The most important software is the **navigation database** that the FMC uses when helping to plan a flight route. The navigation database contains the same information about fixes, navigation aids, airways, and terminal area procedures that is contained in your paper charts, only in an electronic format that the FMC can access. Electronic navi-

gation databases are published on the same schedule as paper charts and are valid for a period of 28 days. Just as you do not want to depart with expired en route charts and terminal area procedure plates, you don't want the FMC to be using expired navigation information.

You can determine whether the FMC's navigation database is current by comparing today's date to the effective dates for the active navigation database shown on line 2R. Let's assume that today's date is September 29, 2001. As we can see in Figure 2.6, the active navigation database expired yesterday. Before departing, you must update the navigation database. Since the new database appears to be shown at line 3R, one possibility would be to type in SEP29OCT27/01 and press the line 2R line select button. Fortunately, the CDU provides you with a shortcut technique that allows you to copy entries from one line to another. This technique is illustrated in Figure 2.7. Pressing the 3R line select button causes the SEP29OCT27/01 entry that appears at line 3R to be moved down to the scratch pad. Pressing the line 2R line select button now causes the scratch pad entry to be moved up to line 2R, and the job is finished. The expired database has now been replaced with the updated database.

To continue to the next page in our route-planning sequence, you can simply follow the page access prompt at line 6R: POS INIT>.

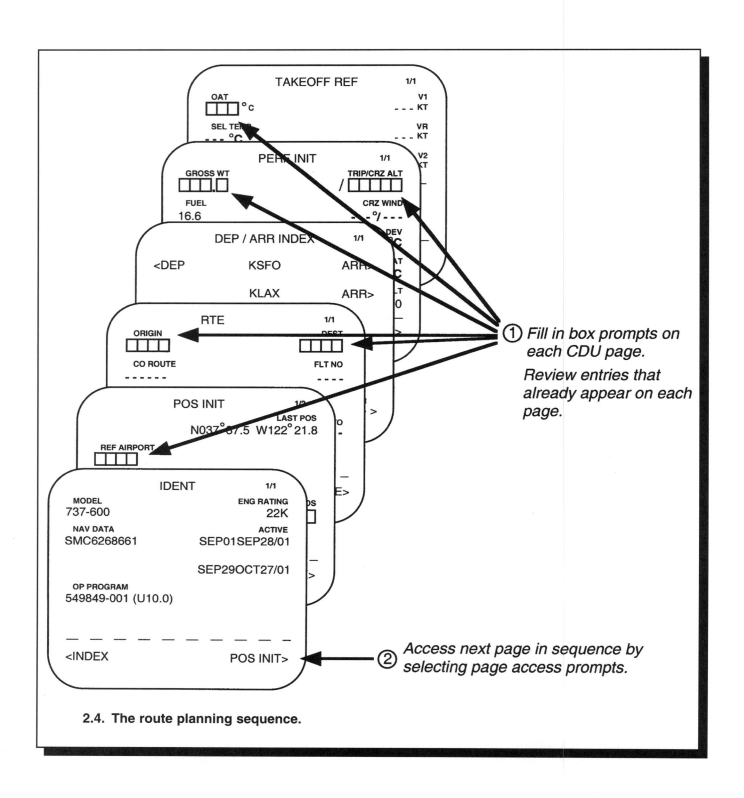

TAKEOFF REF 1/1

OAT
[ ][ ][ ]°C

SEL TEMP
- - - °C

V1
- - - KT

VR
- - - KT

V2
- - KT

PERF INIT 1/1

GROSS WT
[ ][ ][ ].[ ]

FUEL
16.6

TRIP/CRZ ALT
/ [ ][ ][ ][ ]

CRZ WIND
- - °/ - - -

DEP / ARR INDEX 1/1

<DEP   KSFO   ARR>

              KLAX   ARR>

RTE 1/1

ORIGIN
[ ][ ][ ][ ]

CO ROUTE
- - - - - -

DEST
[ ][ ][ ][ ]

FLT NO
- - - -

POS INIT 1/2

LAST POS
N037°67.5 W122°21.8

REF AIRPORT
[ ][ ][ ][ ]

IDENT 1/1

MODEL
737-600

NAV DATA
SMC6268661

OP PROGRAM
549849-001 (U10.0)

ENG RATING
22K

ACTIVE
SEP01SEP28/01

SEP29OCT27/01

— — — — — — —

<INDEX   POS INIT>

① Fill in box prompts on
   each CDU page.

   Review entries that
   already appear on each
   page.

② Access next page in sequence by
   selecting page access prompts.

2.4. The route planning sequence.

20

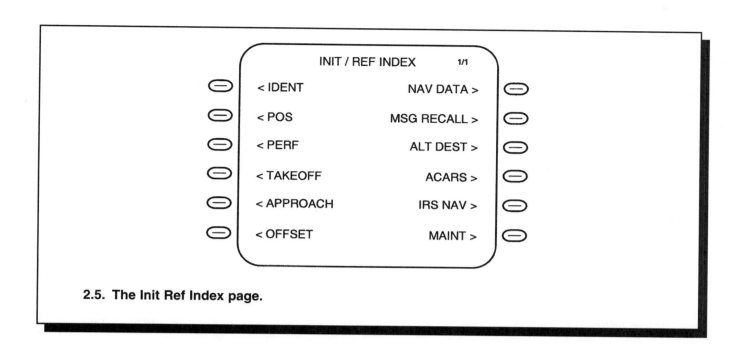

2.5. The Init Ref Index page.

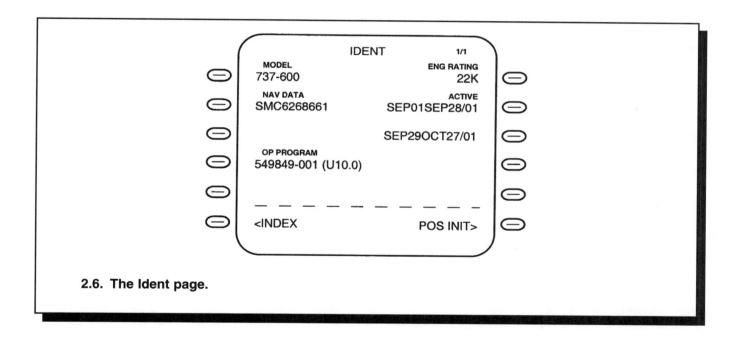

2.6. The Ident page.

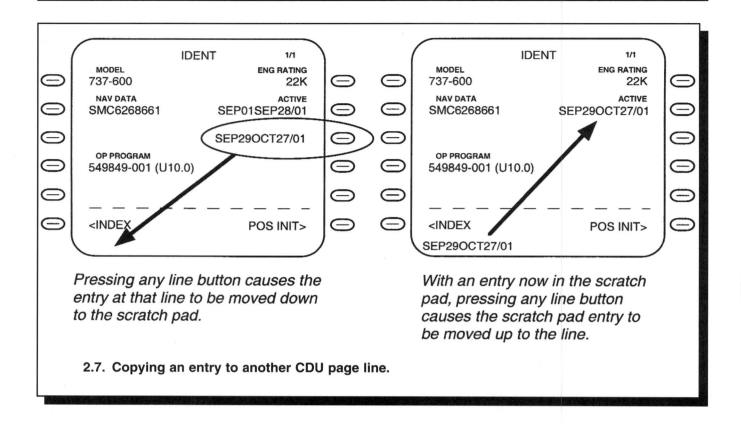

Pressing any line button causes the entry at that line to be moved down to the scratch pad.

With an entry now in the scratch pad, pressing any line button causes the scratch pad entry to be moved up to the line.

2.7. Copying an entry to another CDU page line.

The Pos Init Page: Telling the FMC Where the Aircraft Is Located

In order to build a flight route from here to there, the FMC must first be told where "here" is. That is, you must provide the FMC with an accurate estimate of the aircraft's initial position. This is accomplished by using a CDU page called the **Pos Init page,** shown in Figure 2.8.

The Pos Init page requires the flight crew to enter the present position of the aircraft at line 4R. It seems that the FMC is asking you to input a set of latitude and longitude coordinates for your present position. How do you determine your lat/long? There are several ways of determining an accurate estimation of your present position.

Line 1R on the Pos Init page displays the last known position of the aircraft. The latitude and longitude coordinates of this position are always displayed at line 1R; no pilot input is required to retrieve it.

The second line of the Pos Init page allows you to retrieve the latitude and longitude coordinates of any airport in the navigation database. To search for the position of an airport, simply enter the four-letter ICAO identifier for the airport at line 2L. Since you are preparing to depart from San Francisco International (KSFO) Airport, you enter the four-letter identifier "KSFO" into line 2L. When you enter an airport identifier into line 2L, the FMC searches its navigation database for an entry matching the airport you typed. If found, the latitude and longitude coordinates for the airport are retrieved and written to line 2R, as shown in Figure 2.9.

Looking at the page number for the Pos Init page, you can see that it reads 1/2. This means that there is a second page to the Pos Init page. You can access this page by pressing the NEXT PAGE button on the front of the CDU. Doing this produces the page shown in Figure 2.10.

This page reveals all of the sensors that the airplane uses to determine its position. This airplane contains two **inertial reference systems** (IRS), two **global positioning systems** (GPS), and **navigation radio receivers.** Each one of these sensors seems to have an opinion about where the aircraft is presently located. Comparing the GPS position to the airport coordinates suggests that the GPS has a reliable estimate of the airplane's present position. Pressing the 4L line select button copies the GPS L position down to the scratch pad. Flipping back to the first page of the Pos Init page, you can now submit the GPS position as your official position. The completed Pos Init page is shown in Figure 2.11.

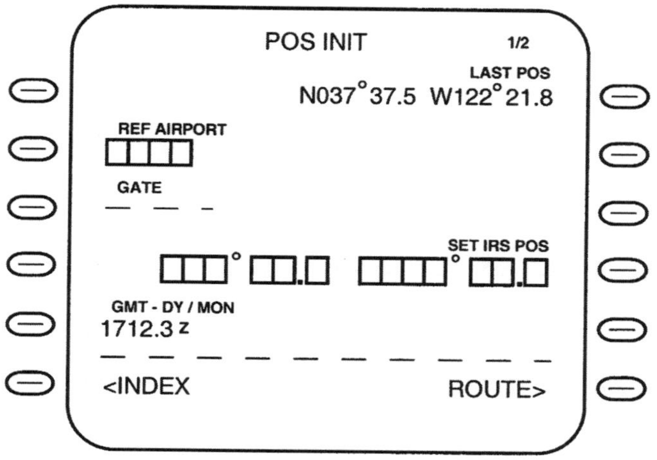

POS INIT   1/2
                   LAST POS
           N037°37.5 W122°21.8

REF AIRPORT
▢▢▢▢

GATE
_ _ _

                            SET IRS POS
  ▢▢▢° ▢▢.▢   ▢▢▢▢° ▢▢.▢
GMT - DY / MON
1712.3 z
_ _ _ _ _ _ _ _ _ _

<INDEX   ROUTE>

2.8. The Pos Init Page.

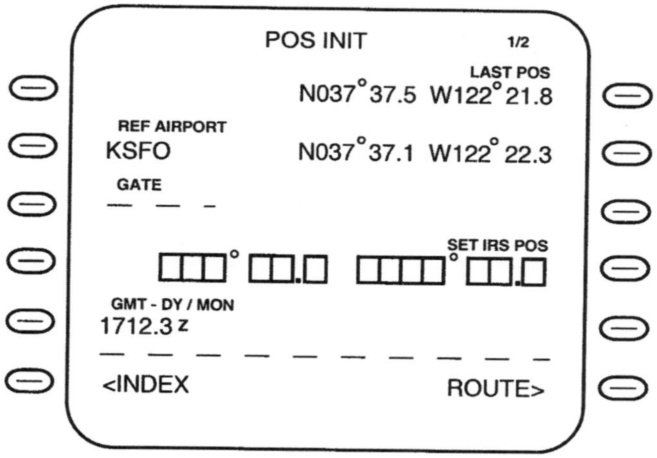

POS INIT   1/2
                   LAST POS
           N037°37.5 W122°21.8
REF AIRPORT
KSFO   N037°37.1 W122°22.3
GATE
_ _ _

                            SET IRS POS
  ▢▢▢° ▢▢.▢   ▢▢▢▢° ▢▢.▢
GMT - DY / MON
1712.3 z
_ _ _ _ _ _ _ _ _ _

<INDEX   ROUTE>

2.9. Searching the navigation database for airport coordinates.

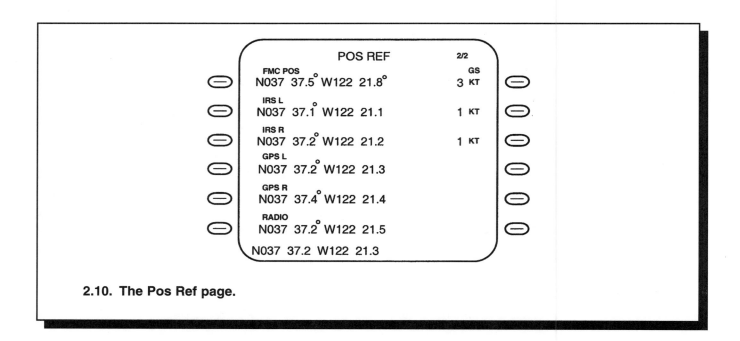

2.10. The Pos Ref page.

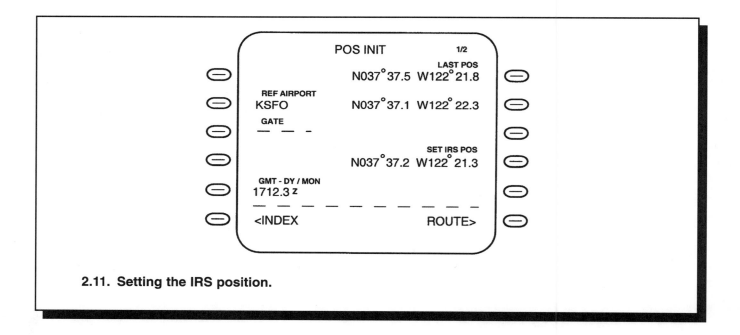

2.11. Setting the IRS position.

The Route Page: Telling the FMC Where You Want to Go

Once you have told the FMC where the aircraft is currently located, the next step is to tell the FMC where you want to go. Let's suppose you have been instructed to follow the Porte Three departure procedure out of San Francisco via the Avenal transition. Furthermore, you have been told to expect the Sadde Six Descent Profile into Los Angeles and the VOR or GPS runway 25R approach.

Your next step is to use the FMC to start planning your route based on what ATC has instructed you to do. This process starts on the **Route page,** which is shown in Figure 2.12. Again, you can get to the Route page from the Pos Init page by simply following the prompt at line 6R.

Entering a Company Route

Note that the Route page prompts the flight crew to enter the origin and destination airports, a departure runway, and a series of waypoints that make up the planned lateral track. Rather than entering this information by hand, many FMCs sometimes make available a database of prepared **company routes** that package together all of this required information. Entering the name of a company route causes the FMC to automatically fill in the prompts you see on the Route page. Figure 2.13 shows the Route page after the name of a company route has been entered.

Note that the origin and destination airports have been filled in. Starting at line 4, you can see that the airways and fixes that make up the company route are listed. Routes are summarized on the Route page using combinations of VIA and TO entries. VIA entries typically describe airways or terminal area procedures. The entries describe waypoints and fixes that are the endpoints for the jet routes and terminal area procedures. The Route page reflects that the company route that you have entered proceeds directly to Wages intersection. Then J1 is followed until Avenal intersection.

Manually Entering a Route

The Route page also allows you to enter a route by filling in all of the entries that appear on the Route page by hand. This process is not only tedious but also prone to common typing errors.

The Departures and Arrivals Pages: Selecting Terminal Area Procedures

You can see on the Route page that several important details of your assigned flight route are missing. For example, your programmed route indicates that you will fly directly to Wages intersection. This is clearly not what you have been instructed to do. Your programmed route does not yet contain the details of the Porte Three departure that you have been instructed to follow. Finally, there is no mention of the Sadde Six arrival procedure into Los Angeles or the VOR or GPS runway 25R approach on the Route page.

The CDU offers a collection of pages that allows you to select runways and departure, arrival, and approach

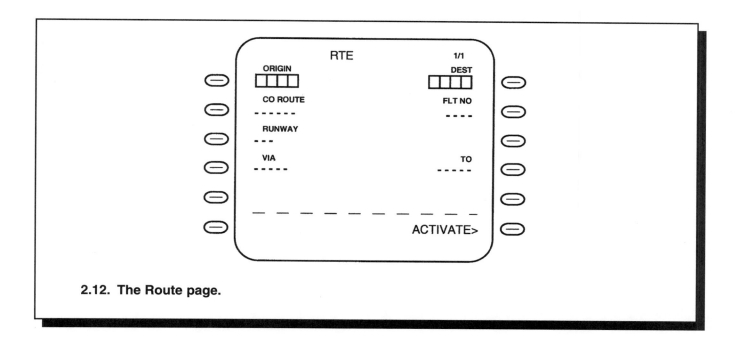

2.12. The Route page.

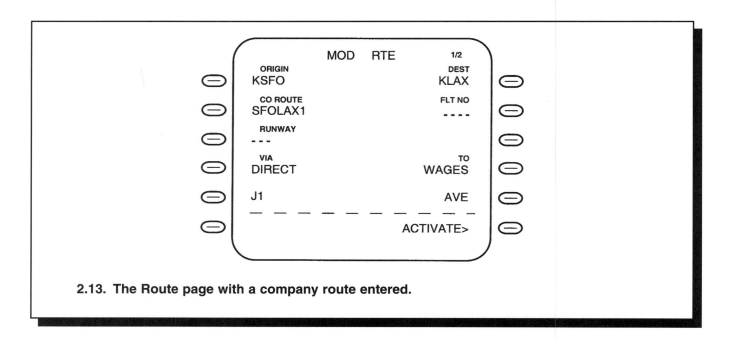

2.13. The Route page with a company route entered.

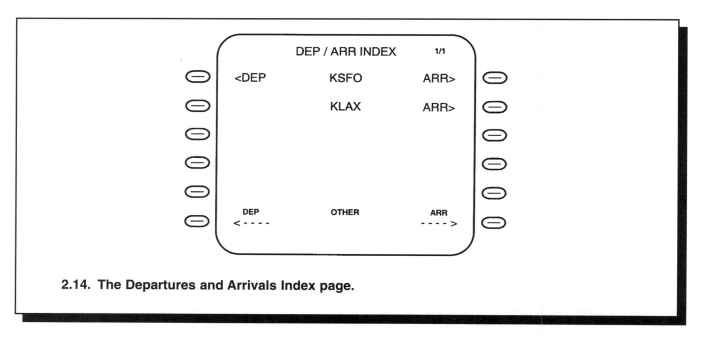

2.14. The Departures and Arrivals Index page.

procedures. You can access these pages by pushing the DEP/ARR button on the front of the CDU. This takes you to the Departures and Arrivals Index page shown in Figure 2.14.

The Departures and Arrivals page presents a menu that allows you to select the departures, arrivals, and approaches from the origin and destination airports you designated back on the Route page. Arrivals for KSFO are made available to you in case you need to cut your flight short and return to your originating airport.

Selecting a Departure Procedure and Runway

You can access a list of departure procedures for KSFO by pushing the 1L line select button. This takes you to the Departures page shown in Figure 2.15. The purpose of the Departures page is to present you with a list of all departure procedures for your origin airport.

On the Departures page, you see a list of departure procedures for KSFO. Selecting PORTE3 causes the page to change as shown in Figure 2.16.

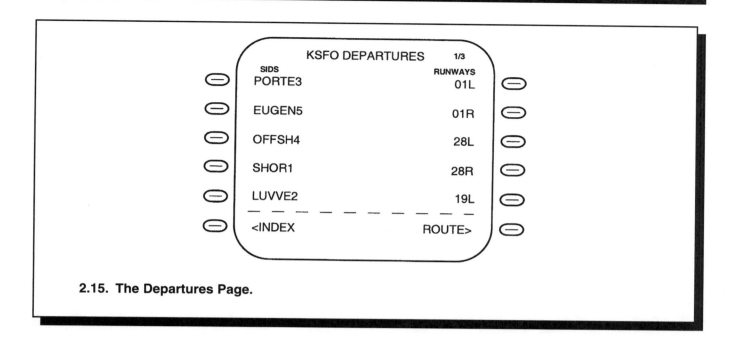

2.15. The Departures Page.

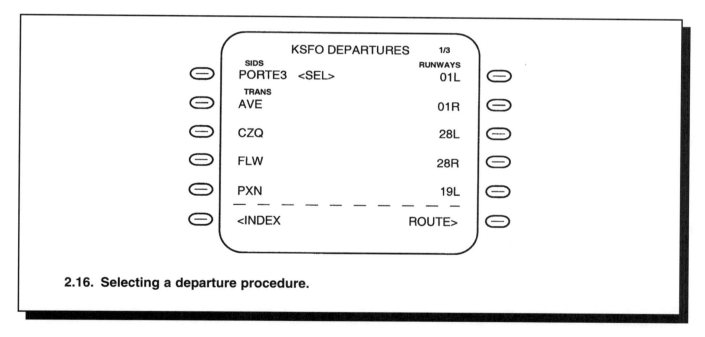

2.16. Selecting a departure procedure.

The <SEL> marker beside the PORTE3 entry indicates that the Porte Three departure has been chosen. Below PORTE3, you see that the other departure procedures have been removed. In their place appear the four transitions for the Porte Three departure. Since you have been instructed to follow the Avenal transition, you press the line select button next to the AVE entry. Figure 2.17 shows that the Avenal transition has now been selected and you now have to choose a runway.

Pressing the line select button beside the runway 1L prompt causes runway 1L to be selected as shown in Figure 2.18.

You can now return to the Route page. On the Route page in Figure 2.19, you can see that your choice of runway is reflected at line 3L.

If we switch to the second page of the Route page, shown in Figure 2.20, you can see that your programmed route extends all the way down to KLAX.

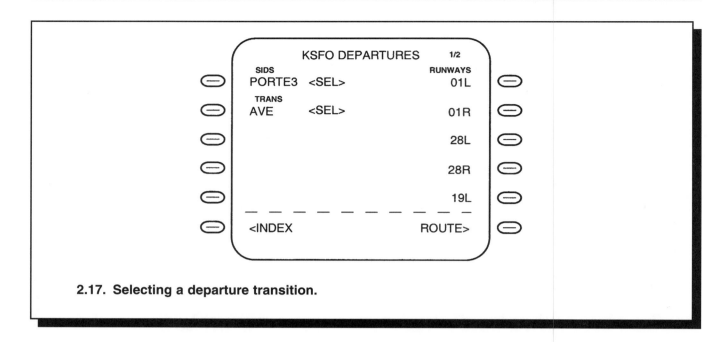

2.17. Selecting a departure transition.

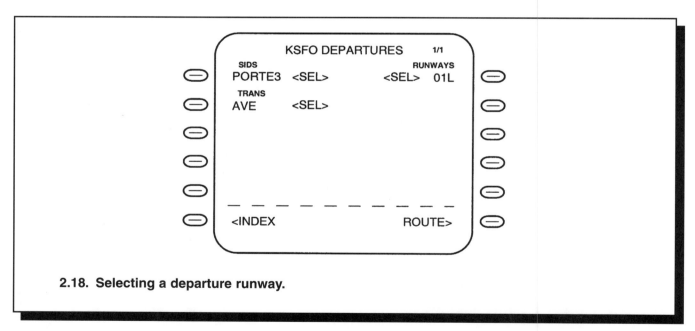

2.18. Selecting a departure runway.

However, just before the KLAX waypoint, the Route page shows a kind of entry that you have not seen before. Instead of the name of an airway, waypoint, or terminal area procedure, you see ROUTE DISCONTINUITY. A **route discontinuity** (or **route disco** as many pilots call them) appears whenever there is a gap in the route that you have entered into the CDU. Note that you have entered the origin and destination airports, a departure procedure, and much of the en route portion of your route. The route discontinuity reflects the fact that you have not yet told the FMC how to

get from AVE intersection to LAX. A route discontinuity is the FMC's way of letting you know that there is a break or uncertainty in the programmed route.

Selecting an Arrival and Approach Procedure

You can now add to your route and extend it all the way down to the LAX airport by choosing an arrival and approach procedure. Arrivals and approaches are selected using the **Arrivals page,** which works just like the Depar-

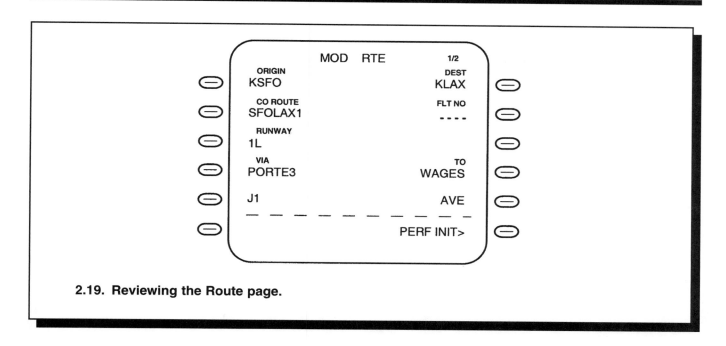

2.19. Reviewing the Route page.

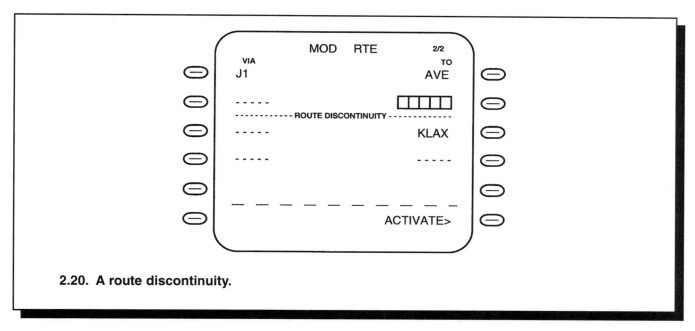

2.20. A route discontinuity.

tures page. Pressing the DEP/ARR button on the front of the CDU takes you back to the Departures/Arrivals Index page. Pressing the KLAX Arrivals button this time takes you to the KLAX Arrival page, where a list of arrival and approach procedures is presented, just as a list of departure procedures was presented on the KSFO Departures page. Since you have been advised to expect the Sadde Six arrival procedure with the Avenal transition into LAX, you can choose that one and get the page shown in Figure 2.21.

You have also been advised to expect the VOR or GPS runway 25R approach procedure. When you make that selection, the page changes as in Figure 2.22.

Executing Your Route

The final step is to execute your route. None of the entries that you make using the CDU will ever become part of the active flight route unless you first execute them. You

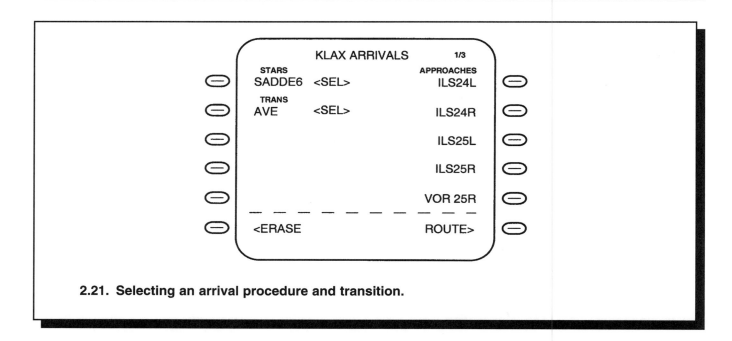

2.21. Selecting an arrival procedure and transition.

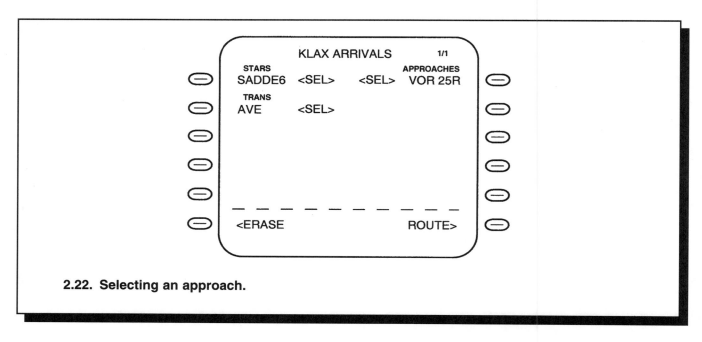

2.22. Selecting an approach.

can execute your route by pressing the **execute button** on the front of the CDU. You can always tell whether or not your route has been executed by looking at the title of the Route page. If it reads MOD RTE, then your entries are still considered modifications in progress. If the title reads ACT RTE, then your entries have now become part of the active flight route. Figure 2.23 illustrates the process of executing a route.

The Perf Init Page: Telling the FMC about the Aircraft and Prevailing Atmospheric Conditions

The next step in the procedure is to provide the FMC with some information about your planned cruising altitude, aircraft characteristics, and the atmospheric conditions you are likely to encounter. The **Perf Init page,** shown in Figure 2.24, was designed for this purpose.

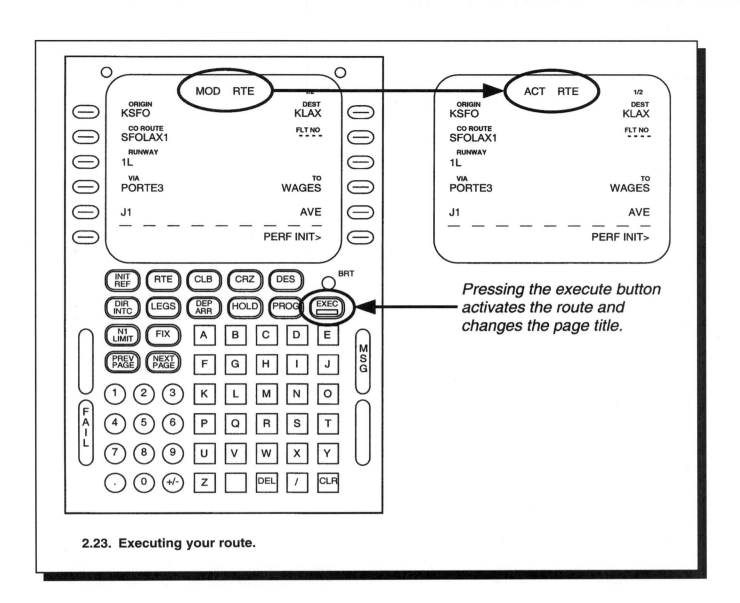

Pressing the execute button activates the route and changes the page title.

2.23. Executing your route.

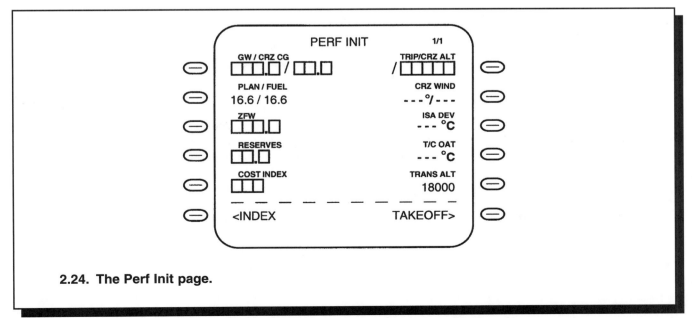

2.24. The Perf Init page.

Telling the FMC about Weight and Balance

To perform calculations about the performance of the aircraft along the programmed route, the FMC must know the weight and balance of the airplane. Entering weight information can be done in either of two ways.

ENTERING GROSS WEIGHT

Line 1L on the Perf Init page allows you to enter the gross weight of the aircraft. If you enter a gross weight in line 1L, the zero fuel weight (ZFW) displayed at line 3L will be automatically filled in. The zero fuel weight will be calculated to be gross weight minus the measured weight of the fuel on board.

ENTERING ZERO FUEL WEIGHT

Line 3L allows you to enter the zero fuel weight of the aircraft. If you enter a ZFW at 3L, the gross weight will be automatically filled in. The gross weight will be calculated to be zero fuel weight plus the measured weight of the fuel on board.

ENTERING CENTER OF GRAVITY

Line 1L on the Perf Init page also allows you to enter the center of gravity of the airplane. This information helps the FMC calculate optimum altitudes and maneuvering speeds.

Checking Fuel

The next step is to determine how much fuel has been put on the aircraft. The purpose of this check is to ensure that the fuel truck has indeed loaded the amount that you ordered. Line 2L allows you to check the measured amount of fuel on board.

Designating Reserve Fuel

Some of the fuel that has been put on board will always be considered reserve fuel. Entering the reserve fuel at line 4L tells the FMC how much of the boarded fuel is to be considered reserve.

Telling the FMC How to Balance Time and Fuel

Probably the most interesting form of control that operators have over the way the FMC works is that you can tell it how fuel or time-efficient you would like it to be when planning the route. Line 5L on the Perf Init page allows you to enter a value into a line called **cost index.** The cost index is nothing more than a number along a scale that tells the FMC how to trade between time and fuel during your flight.

Entering a low cost index causes the FMC to focus on fuel efficiency. To save fuel, the FMC will choose slower climb, cruise, and descent speeds. Although these slow speeds will reduce the costs associated with fuel, they raise the costs associated with longer flight time such as aircraft usage and crew wages.

Entering a high cost index has the opposite effect. Fast speeds are chosen to reduce time-related costs at the expense of fuel efficiency. With a high cost index, you'll get there quicker but burn more fuel in the process.

Companies typically have a standard value for cost index that they require you to enter. It is interesting to compare how different kinds of carrier companies think differently about the importance of time and fuel costs. The popular overnight delivery companies tend to place heavy emphasis on time costs and use high cost indices. For these companies, nothing could be more costly than being late. On the other hand, passenger airlines tend to choose cost indices that lean more toward fuel savings.

Entering Your Planned Cruising Altitude

Another important piece of information related to aircraft performance is your planned cruising altitude. In order for the FMC to construct the vertical portion of your flight route, it will certainly need to know how high you intend to fly. Line 1R on the Perf Init page is the place to enter your planned cruise altitude.

Telling the FMC about the Prevailing Winds

The last performance-related information you need to provide to the FMC are the details of the atmospheric conditions that will prevail through out your flight. This information helps the FMC fine-tune its calculations and predictions. Line 2R allows you to enter the anticipated wind direction and velocity at your cruising altitude. To do this, you must enter the wind direction and velocity, separated by the "/" character. You might be thinking already that it is rather unlikely that this one entry is going to accurately describe the wind conditions all along your route. You know that not only are the winds aloft different all over the country, but they also change over time. You will see that other CDU pages allow you to enter wind information for each waypoint along your route, much in the way they are given to you on your dispatch paperwork. So what's the point of line 2R? You can use line 2R to enter the winds aloft for the vicinity in which you will reach your cruising altitude. This one entry will allow the FMC to have a good chance of predicting aircraft performance up until assigned cruising altitude. The point at which the airplane reaches the assigned cruising altitude is called the **top-of-climb point.** You will learn how to enter winds for each waypoint along your route, when the airplane has reached the top-of-climb point.

The completed Perf Init page is shown in Figure 2.25.

Entering Outside Air Temperature

The final step in planning a flight route using the FMC is to provide the FMC with the outside air temperature,

which can be entered at line 1L on the **Takeoff Ref page** shown in Figure 2.26.

The OAT is used by the FMC to calculate takeoff thrust as well as the takeoff V-speeds. The FMC computes the takeoff thrust and V-speeds once you have entered the OAT as shown in Figure 2.27. The V-speeds computed by the FMC can be displayed on each pilot's airspeed indicator so that they can be easily referenced during the takeoff procedure.

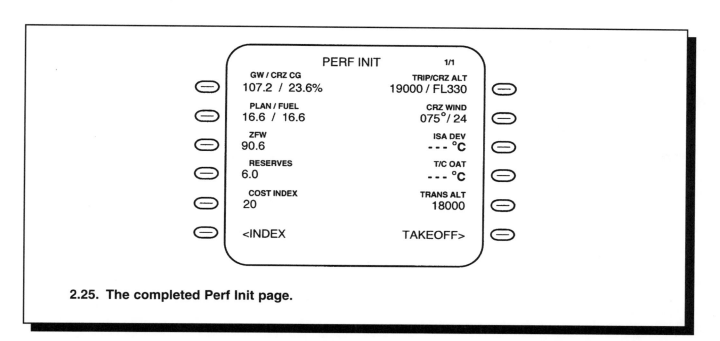

2.25. The completed Perf Init page.

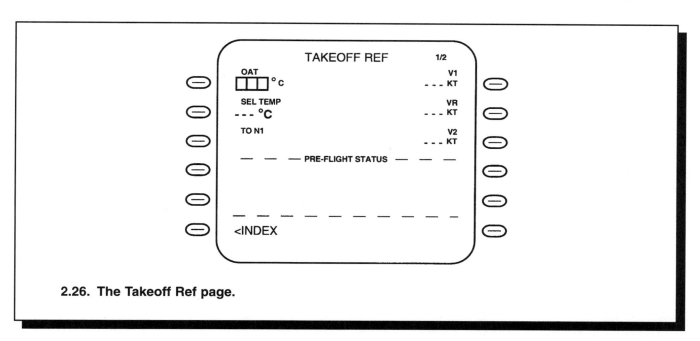

2.26. The Takeoff Ref page.

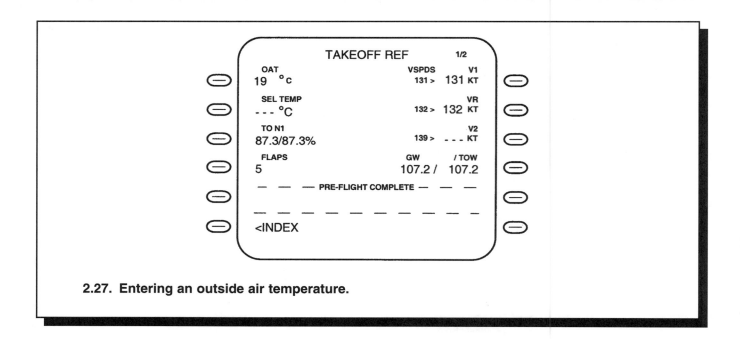

2.27. Entering an outside air temperature.

Checking the Predeparture Checklist

The Takeoff Ref page also offers another handy feature. Lines 4 and 5 provide a checklist for the entire process of planning an FMC route. If upon arriving at the Takeoff Ref page, you have omitted any required entries, prompts will appear indicating the name of the CDU pages on which the missing entries must be made. Figure 2.28 shows the situation in which we have neglected to make any entries into the CDU.

The FMC Uses the Crew Entries to Calculate the Flight Route

Now that you have finished making all of the required entries, the FMC takes over and performs the tedious calculations required to fill in the details of the flight route. The FMC calculates the following things:

1. The lateral tracks between the waypoints along the route
2. The distances between the waypoints along the route
3. The most economical climb, cruise, and descent speeds
4. The point at which the aircraft is predicted to reach the assigned cruise altitude
5. The point at which the airplane should start its descent
6. The altitudes and airspeeds at which the aircraft is predicted to cross each waypoint during climb and descent

7. The estimated time of arrival at each waypoint
8. The estimated fuel remaining at each waypoint

Although fully understanding the methods that the FMC uses to perform these calculations might require a few years of graduate study, you can certainly get the gist of it without too much effort. Let's go through the FMC's calculations one by one.

Calculating the Lateral Tracks between Waypoints

A first step in constructing the flight route is to determine the lateral tracks that the airplane must fly in order to travel between the waypoints along the route. To do this, the FMC plays a game of "connect the waypoints." For each pair of successive waypoints that appear on the Route Legs page, the FMC figures the shortest track between the two waypoints.

Contrary to the old saying, the shortest distance between two points on the earth is not a straight line; it is an arc, as shown in Figure 2.29.

The arc that defines the shortest route between two points on the surface of the earth is called a **great circle route.** To visualize the great circle route between two points on the earth, imagine a plane cutting through the earth that passes through three points: your point of origin, your point of destination, and the center of the earth. If your proposed route doesn't lie on the arc along which this plane intersects the earth, you are taking the long way there.

Consider the route from San Francisco to New York in the illustration shown in Figure 2.29. What is the bearing on

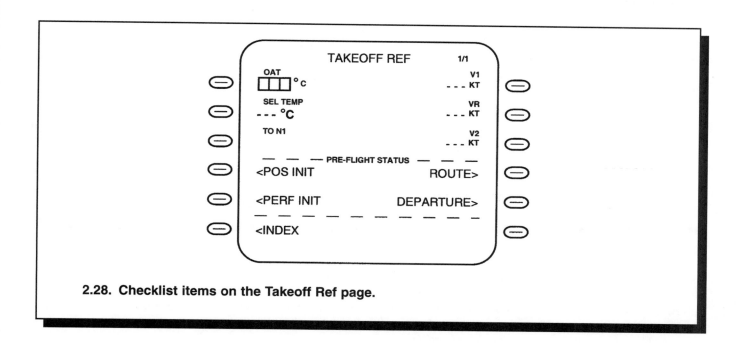

2.28. Checklist items on the Takeoff Ref page.

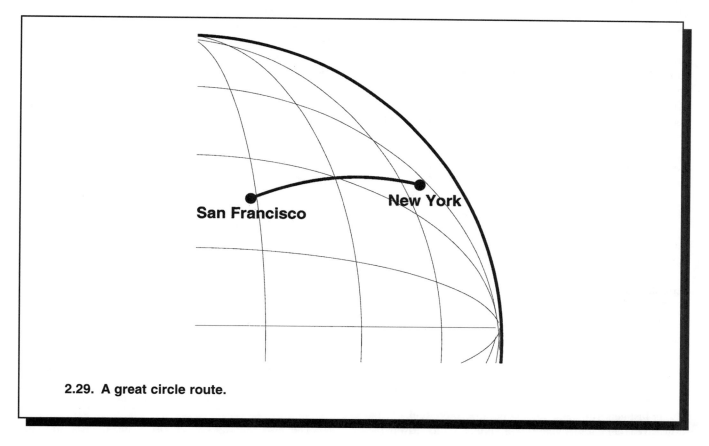

2.29. A great circle route.

COST INDEX	CLIMB SPEED	CRUISE SPEED	DESCENT SPEED
0	271/.73	.70	230/.69
20	283/.74	.74	266/.74
200	335/.78	.79	330/.79

2.30. Speeds computed by the FMC when three different cost indices are entered.

course as you depart San Francisco? It looks like it is a little less than 90 degrees. How about the course as you arrive in New York? It looks like it is a little more than 90 degrees. The interesting thing to learn from this exercise is that there is no one bearing to a destination along a great circle route. The farther you go along the great circle, the more the track changes.

The FMC knows how to do the complex spherical trigonometry needed to calculate the lateral tracks between pairs of waypoints along the planned route. The FMC looks up the latitude and longitude for each waypoint in its navigation database. A few sines and cosines later, the FMC now knows what track to fly to take the aircraft from waypoint to waypoint.

Calculating the Distances between Waypoints

The FMC also needs to know the distances between all of the waypoints in the route. Using the latitude and longitude of the waypoints in the navigation database, the FMC does the same spherical trigonometry to calculate the distances between each of the waypoints in the route.

Calculating the Most Economical Speeds

The FMC's ability to calculate economical climb, cruise, and descent speeds is one of the main reasons that airline companies buy flight management computers. Calculating economical speeds is one way the FMC saves the airline company money. As you already know, there is a trade-off between time costs and fuel costs when choosing speeds. Flying fast gets you there quickly but uses more fuel. Flying slow saves fuel but sets you back in time. For this reason, the engineers created the cost index entry that you entered back on the Perf Init page. The cost index tells the FMC how to trade off between time and fuel expenses when calculating speeds.

It is an interesting exercise to change the cost index and see the difference in the speeds produced by the FMC. Figure 2.30 shows the climb, cruise, and descent speeds generated by the FMC when a cost index of 0, 20, and 200 is entered.

Notice how changing the cost index causes a corresponding change in the speeds produced by the FMC. Entering a cost index of 0 causes the FMC to choose an economy cruise speed that provides maximum range. Entering a cost index of 200 causes the FMC to choose an economy cruise speed that provides a minimum-time flight.

Calculating the Most Economical Thrust Settings

Since the speed of an airplane is determined in part by the thrust setting used, the FMC must compute the thrust settings that will help achieve the planned climb, cruise, and descent speeds.

Predicting the Top-of-Climb Point

The FMC also predicts the point at which the aircraft will reach its assigned cruising altitude. The factors that are important for the FMC's prediction of the top-of-climb point are the items that you entered on the Perf Init page: (1) the planned cruising altitude; (2) the gross weight of the aircraft; (3) the outside air temperature; and (4) the planned climb speed, which was determined by the cost index you entered.

Calculating the Most Economical Top-of-Descent Point

The FMC attempts to choose a **top-of-descent point** such that, if the thrust levers are set at idle, the aircraft will execute an idle-thrust glide and end up at the assigned crossing restriction, called the **bottom-of-descent point,** at exactly the right altitude and airspeed.

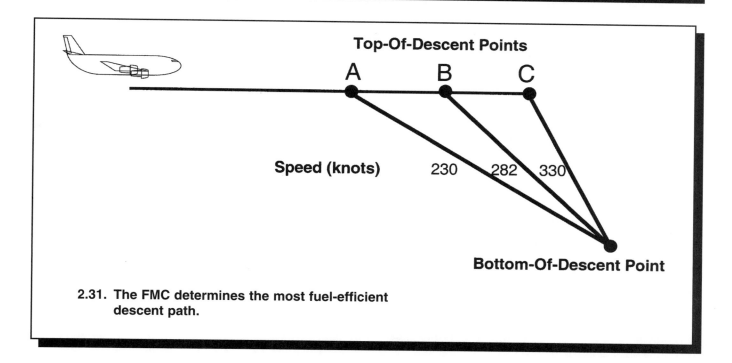

Top-Of-Descent Points

A   B   C

Speed (knots)   230   282   330

Bottom-Of-Descent Point

2.31. **The FMC determines the most fuel-efficient descent path.**

Looking at the diagram in Figure 2.31, you can see that there are several top-of-descent points that satisfy the FMC's goal of meeting a crossing restriction after an idle-thrust glide. You could start down at top-of-descent point A and glide down at a speed of 230 knots, the approximate best glide speed of the airplane. Top-of-descent point A allows you to pull the thrust levers back to idle the soonest and thus is the most fuel-efficient descent. The slow descent speed, however, means that top-of-descent point A requires the most time to reach your crossing restriction. Top-of-descent point C requires that you burn more fuel getting to point C but then shortens the time required to get to your crossing restriction due to the faster speed. To summarize, top-of-descent point A is fuel-efficient and slow, whereas top-of-descent point C is fast but uses more fuel. Top-of-descent point B is a compromise between the two.

How does the FMC choose among these top-of-descent points? It all depends on the cost index you enter on the Perf Init page. If you enter a low cost index, the FMC will favor a top-of-descent point like point A in Figure 2.31. This descent minimizes the amount of fuel burned. On the other hand, if you enter a high cost index, the FMC will favor a top-of-descent point like point C. This descent uses more fuel and gets you there quicker. Once again we see that the FMC responds to the entries the flight crew made.

The line that connects the top-of-descent point and the bottom-of-descent point is called the **descent path.** Note that once a top-of-descent point has been chosen, following the planned descent path is the only simple way of reaching the bottom-of-descent point.

Predicting the Altitudes and Airspeeds at Each Waypoint

Now that the top-of-climb and top-of-descent points are established, the next step for the FMC is to calculate the altitudes and airspeeds for the waypoints that will be crossed on the way up to the final cruising altitude and on the way down to the final descent restriction. Although more complicated, this process is related to the notion of **interpolation** that you learned in high school algebra. Figure 2.32 illustrates this idea. For example, if an airplane is cruising at FL330 and is descending to 12,000 feet at a point 80 nautical miles away, we can interpolate that the airplane will pass a point 40 nautical miles away at an altitude of 22,500 feet.

It is important to understand that the altitudes and speeds calculated for in-between waypoints are indeed predictions. Many factors such as engine performance and unexpected atmospheric conditions can make these predictions less accurate than expected. Why does the FMC bother to make predictions at all? The FMC gives the crew predicted performance against which actual performance can be compared.

Estimating the Time of Arrival at Each Waypoint

The FMC also estimates the time that the aircraft will arrive at each waypoint. To accomplish this, the FMC uses its performance database, which contains detailed information about the performance of the aircraft. The FMC also considers the winds that the aircraft will likely encounter

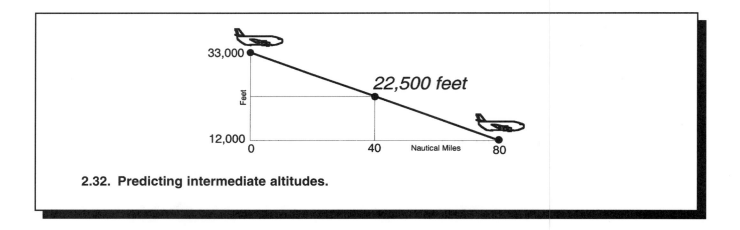

2.32. Predicting intermediate altitudes.

along the way. Where does the FMC get wind information? Remember entering a wind direction and velocity back on the Perf Init page? The FMC assumes that this wind direction and velocity will prevail throughout the flight. You will see in the next chapter that the FMC allows you to update these wind predictions en route as you get more information. The updates will help the FMC refine its estimates for arrival times at each waypoint.

Estimating the Fuel Remaining at Each Waypoint

A final part of constructing the flight route is to estimate how much fuel will be remaining at each waypoint along the route. These calculations are based on the FMC's performance database and the anticipated winds.

The Crew Reviews the Flight Route

Now that the flight management computer has done its part, you must review the flight route. Remember, the FMC is a tool that helps you plan and execute flight routes. It is your responsibility to ensure that the tool is working correctly. One airline captain with a good sense of humor likes to carry a sign in his flight bag that reads "Our policy is to always blame the computer." Although this sign is always good for a few laughs, we know that the FAA will not allow anyone to blame a computer if a pilot misses a crossing restriction. The crew is responsible for the operation of the aircraft at all times.

To ensure that you and the FMC have the same flight plan in mind, the flight crew must consult two important information sources.

CDU Pages

The first source of information available to you when reviewing the route that you have built using the FMC is the

control display unit (CDU). Several pages of the CDU provide the details of the route you have built.

The Route Legs Page

The Route Legs page provides much of the information you need to review the route that the FMC has built. The Route Legs page, shown in Figure 2.33, lists each waypoint in the order that it occurs along the route.

Each line on the Route Legs page represents a single waypoint. Note that the FMC has generated five things for each waypoint in the route:

1. The waypoint name
2. The great circle course to the waypoint
3. The distance to the waypoint
4. The predicted airspeed at the waypoint
5. The predicted altitude at the waypoint

Several interesting things about the waypoints appear on the Route Legs page.

CONDITIONAL WAYPOINTS

Some waypoints have names that agree with the waypoint names appearing on our charts, while others do not. The waypoints that have strange-looking names such as (INTC) are called **conditional waypoints.** Unlike waypoints such as Porte and Pesca, conditional waypoints do not have fixed geographical positions. Conditional waypoints describe events rather than places. Conditional waypoints allow the FMC to track events that are prescribed in the terminal area procedures you must fly. The second waypoint in Figure 2.33 is a good example of a conditional waypoint. The Porte Three departure procedure states that you must fly a heading of 200 degrees until intercepting the 135-degree radial from the Point Reyes VOR. Note that this event can happen at a variety of geographic positions. If you experi-

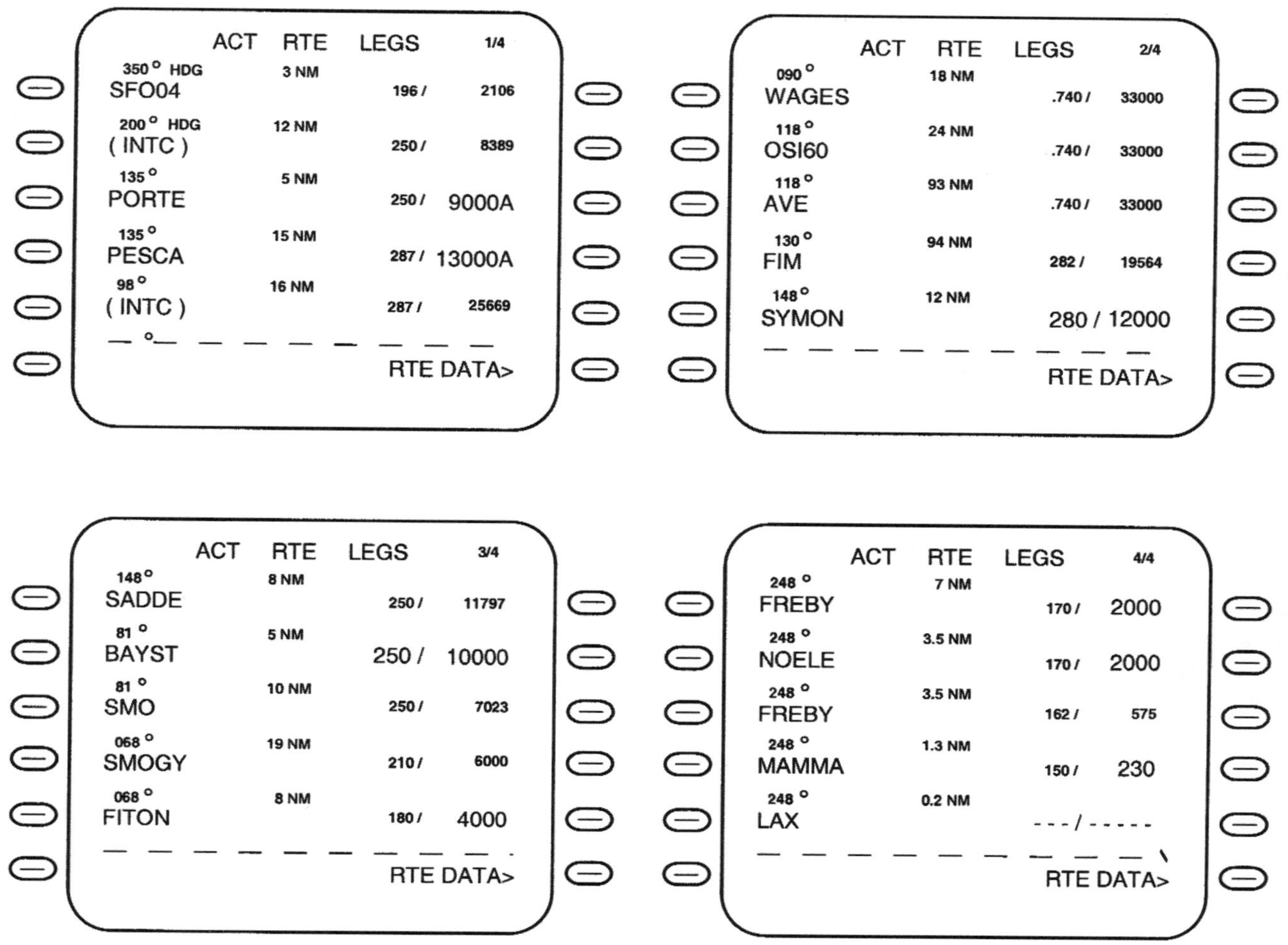

2.33. Reviewing the Route Legs page.

ence calm winds, you might intercept the radial at a different location than you would if we were flying through strong crosswinds. Conditional waypoints are easy to recognize. Conditional waypoints are always enclosed in parentheses. You cannot enter a conditional waypoint yourself. Conditional waypoints are created by the FMC and appear only as part of published terminal area procedures.

SPEED AND ALTITUDE RESTRICTIONS

The Route Legs page also reflects the **speed** and **altitude restrictions** that are part of your terminal area procedures. Speed and altitude restrictions are depicted in a large font. For example, the altitudes associated with Porte and Pesca intersections appear in large font indicating that these are required altitudes. The letter *A* appearing after the altitude indicates that you are required to cross the waypoint "at or above" the designated altitude. The letter *B* indicates an "at or below" crossing restriction. If no letter appears next to the altitude, you are required to cross that waypoint at the designated altitude.

The second page of the Route Legs page shows an example of a speed restriction. The large font for the speed at Symon indicates that you are required to cross Symon at 280 knots.

You now know that the Route Legs page indicates the requirement to cross certain waypoints at required speeds and altitudes, but how do you know that the FMC plans to obey these restrictions? Looking around at surrounding waypoints helps you be sure that the FMC is planning to do the right thing. For example, the Porte Three departure procedure requires you to cross Porte intersection at or above

9,000 feet and to cross Pesca intersection at or above 13,000 feet. As you can see from neighboring waypoints on the Route Legs page, the FMC plans to take you well above these restrictions. The bottom of page 1/4 of the Route Legs page indicates that you will pass through 25,669 feet at the conditional waypoint that is just 16 NM past the at-or-above restriction of 13,000 at Pesca. This suggests that the aircraft will be well above 13,000 feet when crossing Pesca intersection.

Speeds and altitudes that appear in a smaller font indicate that they have been computed by the FMC.

PHANTOM WAYPOINTS

Sometimes as scary as their name suggests, your FMC route also contains **phantom waypoints.** A phantom waypoint is one that is stored in the flight plan but is not shown to the flight crew on the Route Legs page. For example, phantom waypoints occur in your route to mark important events such as (1) the point at which takeoff thrust is reduced to climb thrust; (2) the point at which the aircraft is predicted to reach the planned cruising altitude; (3) the point at which the FMC is planning to commence its descent; and (4) the point at which the aircraft will begin its deceleration to a speed restriction. Fortunately, information about some of these important events is available on other pages of the CDU.

The Climb Page

On the **Climb page,** shown in Figure 2.34, you see a summary of your climb. The planned cruise altitude is reflected at line 1L, while the target climb speed is shown at 2L. Line 1R shows the first crossing restriction along your departure: Cross Porte at or above 9,000 feet. You can also see at Line 3L that the FMC is planning to obey the speed restriction of 250 knots below 10,000 feet. Finally, you can see the planned climb thrust setting at line 4R.

The Cruise Page

On the **Cruise page,** shown in Figure 2.35, you see a similar summary of your cruise.

The planned cruise altitude is reflected at line 1L and the target cruise speed at 2L. The Cruise page also provides you with a number of additional features that help you determine what flight level is the most cost-efficient at any given time. You will use these features, which we discuss in the next chapter, once you are airborne.

The Descent Page

The **Descent page,** shown in Figure 2.36, summarizes the details of your descent. Line 1L shows you the target altitude at the last crossing restriction in the route. Line 1R shows the first crossing restriction that was used by the FMC when constructing the descent. Line 2L shows the target descent speed. Recall that this speed changes with the cost index you entered on the Perf Init page. Line 3L indicates that the FMC is planning to obey the speed restriction in the terminal area. The other lines on the Descent page are used when you are flying your descent and are discussed in the next chapter.

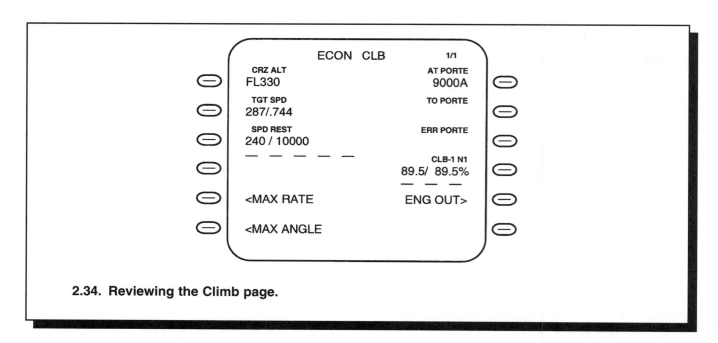

2.34. Reviewing the Climb page.

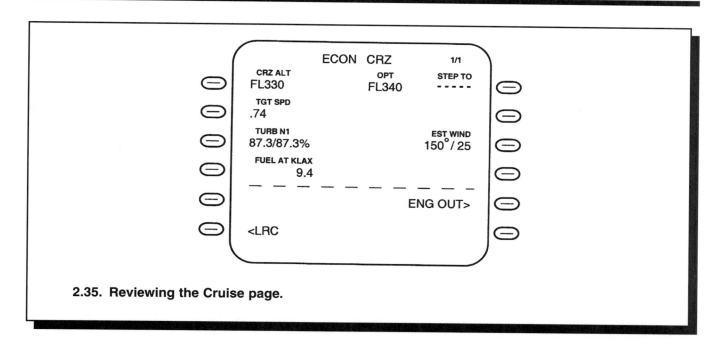

2.35. Reviewing the Cruise page.

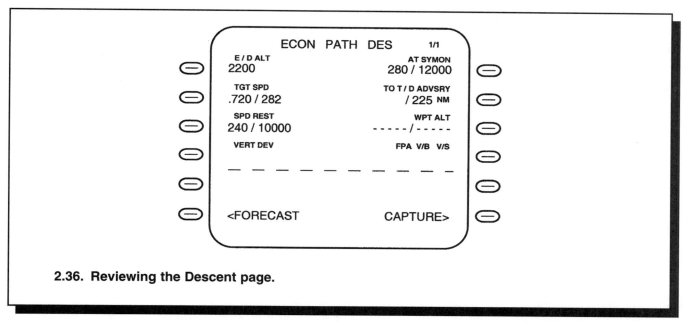

2.36. Reviewing the Descent page.

The N1 Limit Page

The **N1 Limit page,** shown in Figure 2.37, summarizes the thrust settings that the FMC plans to use during climb, cruise, and descent.

The Electronic Horizontal Situation Indicator (EHSI)

The second source of information available to the flight crew when reviewing the flight route is a display called the electronic horizontal situation indicator (EHSI). The EHSI provides a "big picture" display of the route that the FMC has built. The EHSI in Figure 2.38 shows the flight route you have just built from KSFO to KLAX. The symbology used on the EHSI is similar to that used on aeronautical charts: Familiar icons depict VOR stations and intersections, while lines depict the airways that run between them.

The EHSI offers several display modes that present the flight route in different ways. You can switch between these

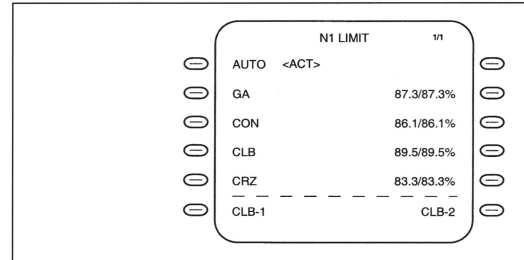

2.37. Reviewing the N1 Limit page.

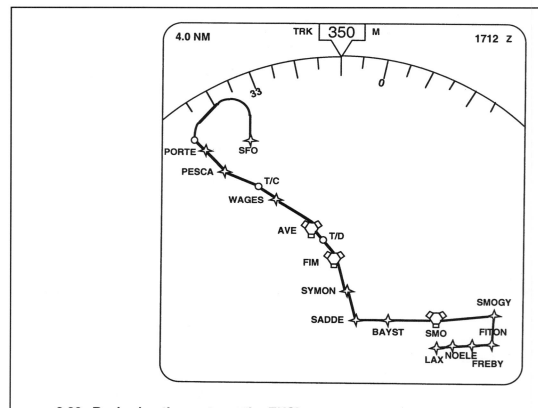

2.38. Reviewing the route on the EHSI.

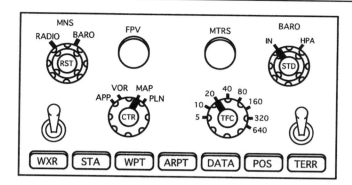

2.39. The electronic flight instrument control panel (EFCP).

modes using another device called the **electronic flight instrument control panel,** shown in Figure 2.39.

The EHSI in Figure 2.38 is set to **plan mode.** Plan mode shows your route from beginning to end and allows you and your crewmate to review what you have built. Using plan mode, you can see the waypoints lined up along the way from KSFO to KLAX. Note that there are no breaks in the route, indicating that the FMC was able to construct a lateral route between each waypoint. The T/C symbol indicates the point at which the FMC predicts the aircraft will reach the assigned cruising altitude. The T/D symbol indicates the point at which the aircraft will commence its descent down to the crossing restriction of 12,000 feet at Symon intersection.

route prior to the departure of every flight. In planning a flight route from KSFO to KLAX, you learned how to use the control display unit (CDU) to input vital information about the assigned flight route, the aircraft, and the expected atmospheric conditions. You learned how the FMC uses its detailed navigation and performance databases together with its powerful computing capabilities to calculate a highly tuned flight route based on the entries the flight crew made. Finally, you learned how to use the pages of the CDU and a display called an electronic horizontal situation indicator (EHSI) to review the created flight route to ensure that it meets all of the requirements for the flight.

Chapter Summary

In this chapter you learned how the flight crew and flight management computer work together to create a flight

CHAPTER 3

Following the Flight Route

IN THIS CHAPTER you take a closer look at the process of guiding the airplane along the flight route you have planned. You learn the fundamentals of the airplane's **autoflight system** that provides automated assistance to the flight crew when guiding the airplane along the planned route.

In the first section you are introduced to the basics of two powerful functions offered by the autoflight system: **lateral navigation** (LNAV) and **vertical navigation** (VNAV). You will see that LNAV and VNAV are capable of generating the roll, pitch, and power commands necessary to guide the aircraft along the flight route that is stored in the flight management computer.

In the second section you will learn two different ways to make use of the roll, pitch, and power commands that are generated when LNAV and VNAV are used. In one mode of operation, the roll, pitch, and power commands are presented to the flight crew, while the pilot flying manually carries them out using the control yoke and thrust levers. In another mode of operation, the autoflight system carries out the roll, pitch, and power commands and steers the airplane automatically.

In the third section, you will see how using LNAV and VNAV combines the powerful capabilities of the flight management computer that stores the flight route and the autoflight system that guides the airplane along that route. You will see how the airplane can be flown almost automatically along the planned flight route from SFO to LAX. With many of the traditional piloting responsibilities now delegated to the automation, you will experience what it is like to manage the automation while it does its job. You will learn how the flight crew must at all times remain aware of what the automation is doing and what it plans to do next.

The Basics of LNAV and VNAV

Probably the easiest way to understand what LNAV and VNAV do is to look at the route you have programmed into the flight management computer prior to departure. Look at the Route Legs page shown in Figure 3.1 to see a summary of your programmed route.

Each line on the Route Legs page displays a waypoint along with an altitude and a speed at which the waypoint is to be crossed. The purpose of LNAV and VNAV is to generate roll, pitch, and power guidance commands that help ensure that the aircraft reaches each waypoint at the predicted altitude and speed.

LNAV

The job of LNAV is to generate the roll commands that will guide the airplane between the waypoints that are listed along the left-hand side of the Route Legs page. For the route shown in Figure 3.1, LNAV will guide the aircraft along a heading of 350 degrees until reaching a waypoint that lies 4 nautical miles from the San Francisco VOR. After reaching this waypoint, the aircraft will follow a heading of 200 degrees until reaching the conditional waypoint at which the airplane will intercept a course of 135 degrees to Porte intersection.

How does the airplane know when it reaches each waypoint? Modern autoflight systems use a variety of components that help track the position of the aircraft as it moves through space. First, conventional **navigation radios** automatically tune and identify nearby VOR stations and trian-

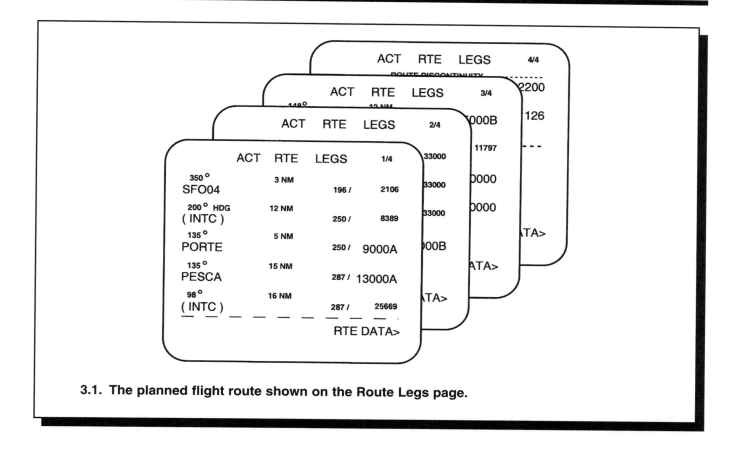

3.1. The planned flight route shown on the Route Legs page.

gulate the position of the aircraft. Second, most airplanes contain one or more **inertial reference units** (IRU) that use gyroscopic principles to sense the lateral and vertical movements of the aircraft. Inertial reference units must be aligned, or set to reflect an accurate initial position prior to departure. Finally, many new airplanes feature **global positioning system** (GPS) receivers that determine position by detecting signals from a group of satellites orbiting the earth. All of these systems work together to provide the airplane with a committee of opinions about where it is located at all times.

How do you engage LNAV? All guidance functions are engaged by the flight crew using a device called the **mode control panel** (MCP) shown in Figure 3.2. LNAV can be engaged by pressing the LNAV button located on the MCP.

VNAV

VNAV provides guidance along the vertical trajectory of the planned flight route. Looking at the right-hand side of the Route Legs page in Figure 3.1 you see an altitude and airspeed target associated with each waypoint. The VNAV generates the pitch and power commands that help ensure that the aircraft reaches each waypoint in the route at the tar-

get altitude and airspeed. For example, VNAV will generate the pitch and power commands that help guide the aircraft to Porte intersection at or above 9,000 feet and at a speed of 250 knots.

How does the airplane track its altitude and airspeed as it makes its way along the route? Modern airliners contain another component called a **digital air data computer** (DADC) that continuously provides information about the aircraft's present altitude as well as its indicated and true airspeed.

VNAV can be engaged following two simple steps illustrated in Figure 3.2. The first step is to dial the altitude to which the flight has been cleared into the altitude window on the mode control panel. VNAV will never climb or descend beyond the altitude dialed into the **altitude window.** For example, even though you have entered FL330 as your planned cruising altitude into the FMC, and this is reflected on the Climb page, the airplane will not climb beyond the 23,000 feet that is dialed into the altitude window. The same is true in a descent: VNAV will not descend below the altitude that has been dialed into the altitude window even if the Descent page reflects a lower altitude. The second step is to press the VNAV button located on the mode control panel.

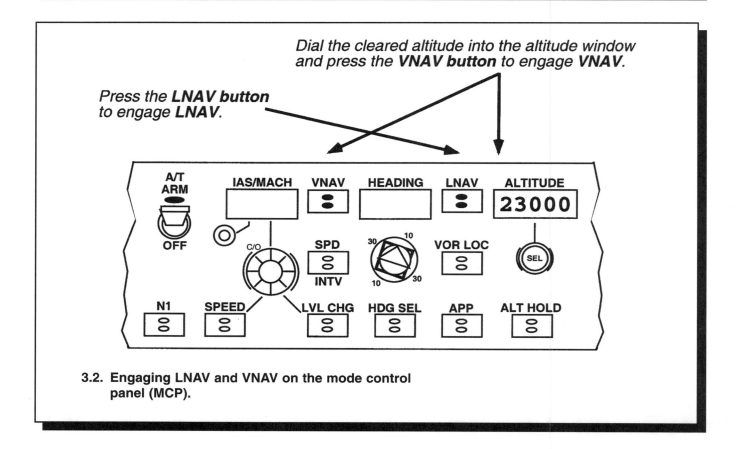

3.2. Engaging LNAV and VNAV on the mode control panel (MCP).

Two Ways to Use LNAV and VNAV

You have just learned that LNAV and VNAV generate the roll, pitch, and power commands that are necessary to guide the aircraft along the route stored in the FMC. You will now see that the crew has two choices about how the aircraft can be steered in response to these guidance commands.

Manual Control with LNAV and VNAV

The first way to use the guidance commands generated by LNAV and VNAV is to have them displayed to the flight crew, while the pilot flying manually manipulates the yoke and thrust levers to obey the guidance commands. Using this method, the pitch and roll commands that are necessary to guide the aircraft along the programmed route are presented to the flight crew using a set of command bars that appear on each crew member's **electronic attitude director indicator** (EADI). Together, these command bars are referred to as the **flight director** and resemble the localizer and glide slope needles you have seen in smaller aircraft. An electronic attitude director indicator with flight director command bars appears in Figure 3.3.

Commands presented on the **engine indicators** show the pilot flying how to manipulate the thrust levers. The **cursors** appearing on each engine indicator show the thrust settings required to achieve the thrust and speed targets stored in the flight management computer. Figure 3.4 shows cursors appearing on the N1 engine indicators.

This mode of operation allows the crew to receive guidance support offered by LNAV and VNAV, yet remain in close contact with the controls of the aircraft.

You may have noticed that the instruments in the modern airline cockpit seem to be presented on computer screens rather than on round dials and gauges that you have most likely used in the past. The electronic attitude director indicator (EADI) and electronic horizontal situation indicator (EHSI) replace the standard six-pack of flight instruments with which you are familiar. Always eager to back up the invention of new technology with the invention of new terminology, avionics manufacturers have given these new computerized instruments the name **electronic flight instrument system** (EFIS). Similarly, the computer displays and associated systems that take the place of round-dial engine instruments and warning systems have been given the even longer moniker **engine indicating and crew alerting system** (EICAS).

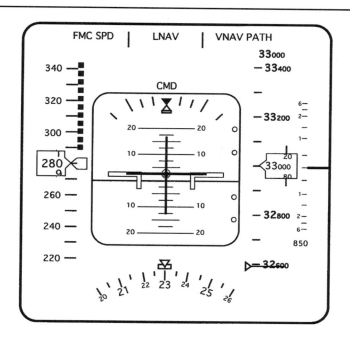

3.3. Roll and pitch guidance commands presented on the electronic attitude director indicator (EADI).

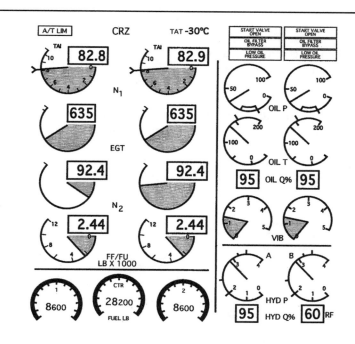

3.4. Thrust guidance commands presented on the engine indicators.

Automatic Control with LNAV and VNAV

The second way to use the guidance commands generated by LNAV and VNAV is to allow the autoflight system to carry them out automatically. Using this method, the control yoke and thrust levers are manipulated automatically in response to the roll, pitch, and power commands as if controlled by an invisible pilot. The autoflight system relies on two important components to accomplish this form of automated guidance. An **autopilot** accepts roll and pitch guidance commands and automatically manipulates the aircraft's ailerons and elevators. The **autothrottle** accepts thrust guidance commands and automatically manipulates the thrust levers.

Choosing between Manual and Automated Control

When LNAV and VNAV are engaged, the use of both manual and automated guidance is fairly standard among operators. When operating in the vicinity of an airport terminal area, it is customary to turn on the flight directors and autothrottle but to leave the autopilot turned off. In this semimanual configuration, the pilot flying must operate the control yoke to obey the pitch and roll commands that are presented on the flight director. The autothrottle is automatically manipulated in response to the thrust guidance commands generated by VNAV.

During the cruise and descent phases of flight, it is customary to turn on the autopilot and allow the control yoke to be automatically manipulated as well. This is the highest level of automation, in which all flight controls are automatically manipulated to guide the airplane along the route stored in the FMC.

Turning the flight directors, autopilot, and autothrottle on or off is accomplished using the switches found on the mode control panel shown in Figure 3.5.

Since most transport airplanes contain redundant autopilot systems, an autopilot can be engaged by pressing either of the two CMD buttons located on the MCP.

Flying the Route Using LNAV and VNAV

You now know that LNAV and VNAV are capable of providing guidance support along the flight route that you built prior to departure. While LNAV and VNAV are engaged, the combination of flight management computer and autoflight system will certainly aim to do all the right things at all the right times. But what if the crew made a mistake in programming the route? What if LNAV and VNAV malfunction in some small way or the airplane performs differently from what you expected? What if ATC intervenes and modifies your flight route or the winds you encounter are different from those forecasted? The answer to these questions is why airplanes still have human pilots in the cockpit. Cockpit automation technologies are far from perfect. At best, they are tools designed to support skilled pilots who are at all times responsible for the outcome of the flight.

What are the responsibilities of the flight crew when using guidance functions such as LNAV and VNAV? The answer is simple: The flight crew has all of the responsibilities that you would have if the automation didn't exist. You and your crewmate are ultimately responsible for all of the familiar chores associated with operating a complex aircraft on an IFR flight. When LNAV and VNAV are used, the flight crew must serve as watchful monitors of the automation to which you have delegated certain responsibilities.

In this chapter you learn to continually ask yourself three questions:

1. What are the responsibilities associated with the current phase of flight?
2. Who (or what) is assigned to the job of fulfilling them?
3. How are they doing?

We ask these three questions during every phase of flight along your route. We spell out the responsibilities of the flight crew during each phase of flight, illustrate how the automation helps carry out these responsibilities, and show how to use important cockpit displays to closely follow the progress of the aircraft.

Takeoff

Since takeoff is fundamentally different from flying a climb, cruise, and descent, a special guidance function is used during this critical phase of flight. This guidance function is discussed in Chapter 5. In this chapter you will make use of LNAV and VNAV once you are just off of the ground. So let's assume that you have gotten the aircraft off of the ground, are just passing through 1,000 feet, and have reduced to climb power.

Climb

You are now airborne and have achieved a positive rate of climb. You have at least the following responsibilities during your climb out of San Francisco:

1. Laterally guide the aircraft between the waypoints that make up your departure procedure.
2. Achieve the desired climb speed, obeying any speed restrictions along the way.

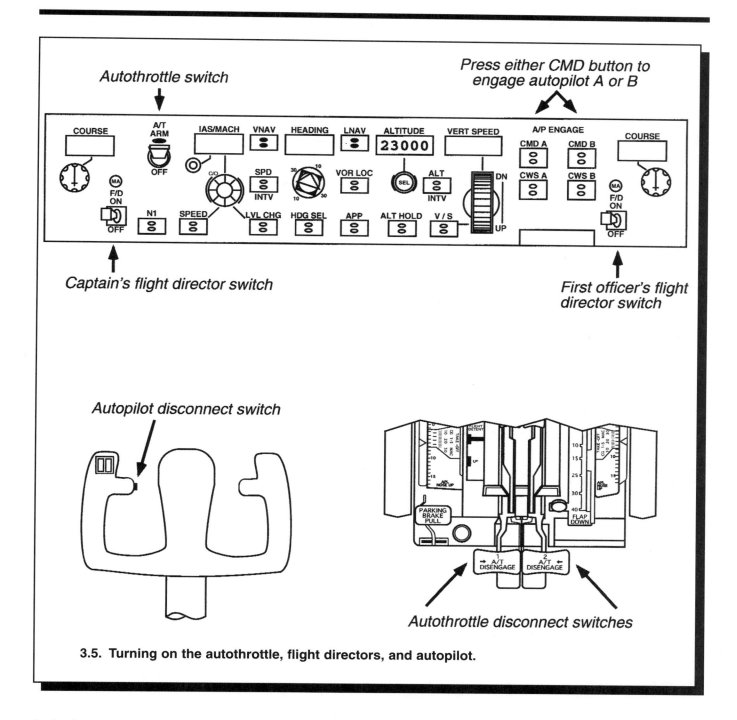

3.5. Turning on the autothrottle, flight directors, and autopilot.

3. Achieve the assigned cruising altitude, obeying any altitude restrictions along the way.
4. Maintain awareness of surrounding traffic and terrain.

You will now see how the combination of the automation together with an informed and watchful flight crew handles these responsibilities.

The first step is to engage LNAV and VNAV. This is accomplished by pressing the LNAV and VNAV buttons located on the mode control panel. Back on the ground, you configured the airplane to present the roll and pitch guidance commands on the flight directors so that the pilot flying can manually follow them by manipulating the control yoke. You also turned on the autothrottle so that it will automatically carry out the power guidance commands. Your job now is to follow the flight director commands and also to keep track of the overall plan that the guidance commands represent.

Follow Lateral Portion of Departure Procedure

As soon as you engage LNAV, it begins to guide you between the waypoints that make up the lateral portion of your route. Aside from following the roll commands presented on the flight director, you can use two additional displays to monitor your progress as you make your way along the lateral track.

At any given time, the commands generated by LNAV guide you toward the first waypoint that appears on the Route Legs page. This waypoint is referred to as the **active waypoint.** The active waypoint can be seen on line 1 of the Route Legs page at any time. For the active waypoint shown in Figure 3.6, the guidance commands generated by the LNAV function keep you on a track of 350 degrees until you reach the active waypoint.

The initial portion of your route is displayed on the electronic horizontal situation indicator (EHSI). The EHSI in Figure 3.7 is set to a different display mode than the one you used to review your route prior to departure. When set to **center map mode,** the EHSI displays your route with respect to the present position of the aircraft. In center map mode, the aircraft symbol always appears at the center of the display in a track-up orientation, while the route is shown issuing from the nose of the aircraft. You can see the early portion of your route on the EHSI: the 350-degree heading until reaching the first waypoint, followed by a turn to the left to the conditional waypoint where you intercept the 135-degree course to Porte intersection.

After a minute or so, you can refer to the Route Legs page shown in Figure 3.8 and see that you have passed the first waypoint and the intercept conditional waypoint is now the active waypoint.

Achieve Climb Speed and Obey Speed Restrictions

Now established in your climb, the airplane prepares to achieve your planned climb speed. You have to be sure to obey any speed restrictions that apply. The 250-knot restriction below 10,000 feet is one you don't want to miss. Referring again to the Route Legs page in Figure 3.8, you can see that speed management is part of the plan as long as VNAV is engaged. Note that the speeds that are associated with any waypoint that will be crossed at or below 10,000 feet all obey the 250-knot restriction. Any waypoint that will be crossed above 10,000 feet reflects the economy climb speed that has been computed by the FMC prior to takeoff.

Achieve Assigned Altitude and Obey Altitude Restrictions

VNAV is also responsible for the problem of getting the airplane up to the assigned cruising altitude and obeying any crossing restrictions along the way. On the Climb page shown in Figure 3.9, you see that the crossing Porte intersection at or above 9,000 feet is part of the FMC's plan. As

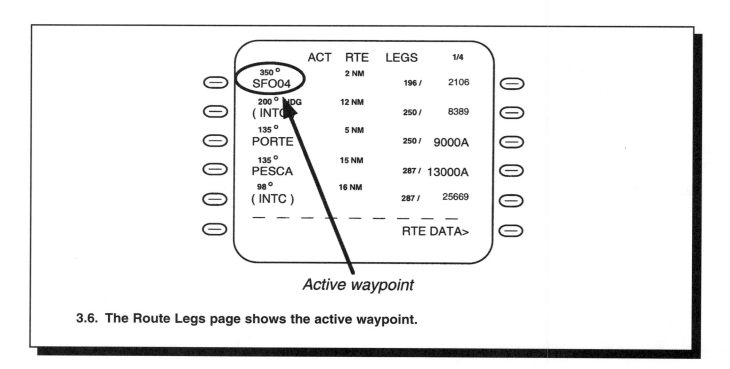

Active waypoint

3.6. The Route Legs page shows the active waypoint.

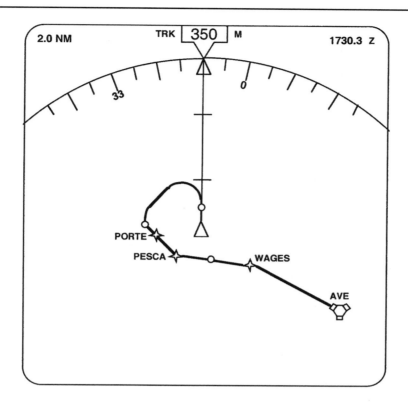

3.7. The electronic horizontal situation indicator (EHSI) in map mode.

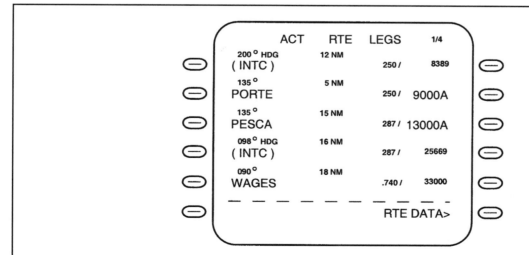

3.8. The Route Legs page shows the new active waypoint.

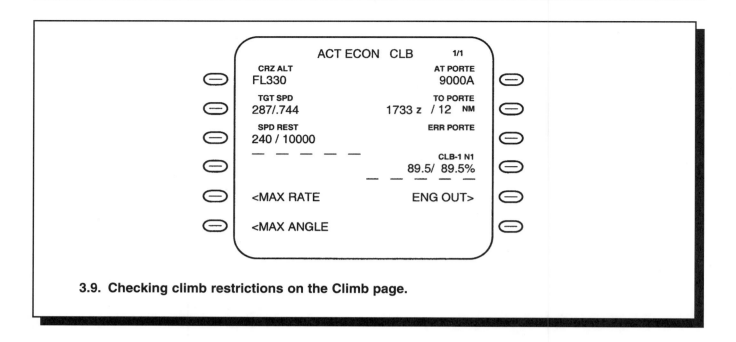

3.9. Checking climb restrictions on the Climb page.

long as VNAV is engaged, the airplane will follow the route stored in the FMC.

Looking at line 2R on the Climb page, you can see that you are now 12 miles away from Porte intersection. A glance at the altitude tape on the electronic attitude director indicator (EADI) reveals that you are comfortably above this crossing restriction altitude already.

TURN ON AUTOPILOT

Thus far along your route, you have had LNAV and VNAV engaged and have been working the control yoke to follow the roll and pitch commands that the flight director has indicated. The FMC has been doing much of the thinking, while you have been doing the actual steering. You and your crewmate have also been carefully monitoring what the FMC has had in store for you, making sure that you don't blindly follow any flight director commands that lead you astray.

You can now move to the highest level of automation and turn on an autopilot. Once you do that, the autopilot will automatically carry out the roll and pitch commands. They will still appear on the flight director, but the control yoke will move automatically. It will look like an invisible pilot is watching the flight director and working the control yoke to follow it. You reach up to either one of the CMD buttons located on the mode control panel (see Figure 3.5) and push it.

You have now achieved the highest degree of flight path automation. All of the automation is turned on, and you are now in the role of manager. Like good managers, you need

to remain in the loop about what the automation just did, is currently doing, and plans to do next.

CHECKING WHEN THE AIRCRAFT WILL REACH THE ASSIGNED CRUISING ALTITUDE

When will the aircraft reach its planned cruising altitude of FL330? You can find this information in a variety of places. Looking at the electronic horizontal situation indicator in Figure 3.10, you can see the top-of-climb symbol. The EHSI in Figure 3.10 is set to map mode. Map mode shows the route with respect to the present position of the airplane, which always appears at the bottom of the display.

You can get a more precise estimate of when you will reach your top-of-climb point by referring to the Progress page shown in Figure 3.11. Line 5L on the Progress page shows you an estimate of the time you will arrive at the top-of-climb point, as well as the distance remaining to the top-of-climb point.

The aircraft continues to climb, crossing Porte at 10,330 feet and Pesca at 17,222. At Pesca, LNAV commands a left turn toward Wages intersection.

Continuing your climb, you will eventually be cleared up to your planned cruising altitude of FL330. Upon receiving this clearance, you must dial 33000 into the altitude window on the mode control panel as shown in Figure 3.12.

Recall that the airplane will never climb above or descend below the altitude that has been entered into the altitude window even if you have programmed a different altitude into the FMC.

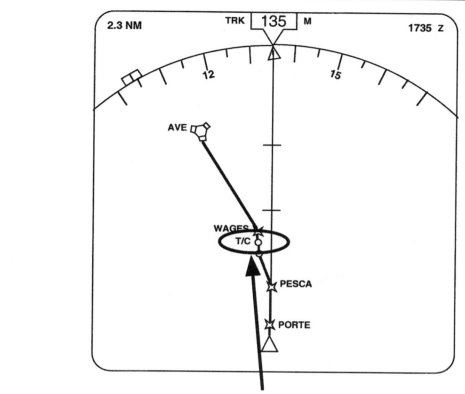

Top-of-climb point

3.10. Checking the top-of-climb point on the EHSI.

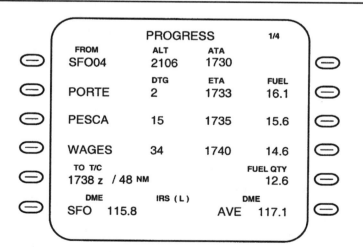

3.11. Checking the top-of-climb point on the Progress page.

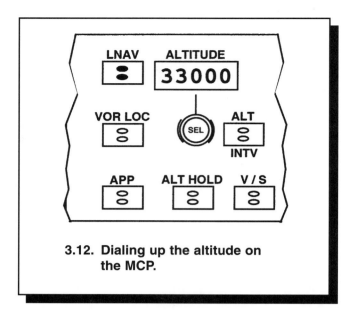

3.12. Dialing up the altitude on the MCP.

Maintain Awareness of Surrounding Traffic and Terrain

As you monitor the activities of the flight management computer and autoflight system, it is also important to maintain an awareness of what is happening outside of the cockpit. The flight crew is at all times required to "see and avoid" other traffic even if ATC is providing separation services. Your first line of defense against encroaching traffic is to wisely divide your attention between monitoring cockpit displays and looking out the window. Coordinating your efforts with the other members of the flight crew makes best use of all available resources in the cockpit.

As a last line of defense against collisions with traffic and terrain, modern airliners feature two systems that help track the position of the airplane with respect to surrounding traffic and terrain.

TRAFFIC ALERT AND COLLISION AVOIDANCE SYSTEM (TCAS)

The **traffic alert and collision avoidance system** (TCAS) alerts the flight crew to surrounding traffic that presents a collision hazard. Popularly referred to as the "fish finder" or the "metal detector," TCAS actually works by querying the transponders of nearby aircraft to determine their distance, altitude, and bearing. TCAS issues two types of advisories to the flight crew when a nearby aircraft is considered a threat. A **traffic advisory** (TA) is issued to the crew in the form of the aural alert "Traffic! Traffic!" when an aircraft appears to be within a 40-second range of your airplane. If the nearby aircraft closes to within a 25-second range, TCAS will issue a **resolution advisory** (RA).

A resolution advisory takes the form of an avoidance command that instructs the flight crew to climb or descend to avoid the encroaching traffic. Typical resolution advisories are "Climb! Climb!" or "Descend! Descend!" Your company training will likely emphasize the many limitations of TCAS. For example, TCAS cannot detect aircraft that do not have transponders. As another example, TCAS is known to sometimes issue unwanted resolution advisories in situations in which operations in proximity to other aircraft are normal, such as simultaneous approaches to parallel runways.

In addition to aural alerts, TCAS can also display surrounding aircraft on the airplane's EHSI, making the EHSI in some ways similar to the radar scope used by the controllers who are directing the traffic. The symbols used to depict traffic detected by TCAS are shown in Figure 3.13.

For resolution advisories, TCAS can also display vertical avoidance information on each pilot's attitude indicator. These displays typically show which pitch attitudes to avoid in order to resolve the traffic conflict.

GROUND PROXIMITY WARNING SYSTEM (GPWS)

The **ground proximity warning system** (GPWS) alerts the crew to a variety of situations in which the airplane is about to enter a potentially unsafe situation with respect to surrounding terrain. A complicated judgement to make, GPWS must take into consideration not only the distance of the airplane from the terrain but also the phase of flight and the likely intentions of the flight crew. For example, a warning that the airplane is about to impact terrain would be inappropriate during a normal landing flare.

The GPWS system takes inputs from a variety of airplane instruments and systems including the airplane's **radio altimeter.** The radio altimeter measures the airplane's absolute distance above the ground by transmitting radio signals at the ground and sensing changes in their reflections.

At the present time, there are seven types of GPWS warnings that are delivered to the flight crew in the form of aural announcements.

1. Excessive descent rate
2. Excessive terrain closure
3. Altitude loss after takeoff or go-around
4. Unsafe terrain clearance when not in the landing configuration
5. Excessive deviation below an ILS glide slope
6. Descent below specific radio altimeter altitudes
7. Windshear conditions

GPWS is also capable of displaying surrounding terrain on the airplane's EHSI as shown in Figure 3.13. It is likely

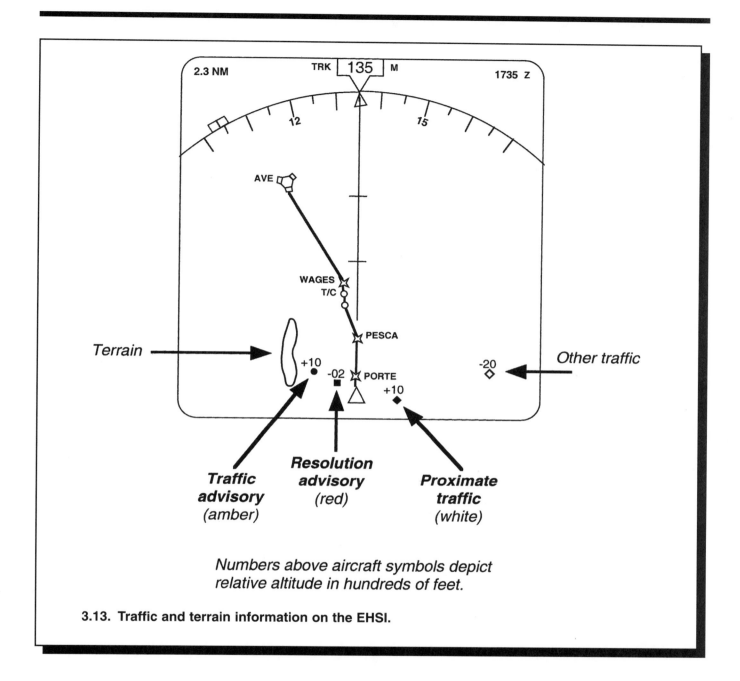

Numbers above aircraft symbols depict
relative altitude in hundreds of feet.

3.13. Traffic and terrain information on the EHSI.

that future cockpit automation technologies will feature databases of the topographical features of the earth to help reduce the risk of the far-too-common **controlled flight into terrain** (CFIT) accident.

THE ALTITUDE ALERTER

Soon you begin to approach your planned cruising altitude of FL330. Passing through 32,000 feet, you and your crewmate call out "32 for 33." This standard call-out ensures that everyone in the cockpit is aware of where the airplane is and where it is going. Passing through 32,300 feet, the **altitude alerter** sounds. The altitude alerter is an automated system designed as a back-up to the crew that has lost awareness of their altitude. The altitude alerter is a last line of defense against climbing or descending to an undesired altitude. The point of the "1,000 feet to go" call-out made by every aware flight crew is to never allow the altitude alerter to tell you anything that you don't already know.

Upon reaching the planned cruising altitude of FL330, VNAV commands the thrust levers to come back, and the aircraft levels off.

Cruise

Now that you have reached your assigned cruising altitude of FL330, your job is straightforward. LNAV and VNAV are engaged and the autopilot and autothrottle are both turned on. The aircraft will be guided along the programmed route in a fully automated manner. As supervisor of the automation, some of your most important tasks are the following:

1. Navigating from waypoint to waypoint along the route
2. Keeping track of time en route and fuel burned
3. Maintaining the desired cruise speed
4. Maintaining the assigned cruising altitude

Navigating from Waypoint to Waypoint

As long as LNAV is engaged, it will continue to issue roll commands to the autopilot that cause the aircraft to be steered from waypoint to waypoint. Your job is to ensure that the airplane remains on the intended route. You can keep track of what LNAV is doing and intends to do by using two displays. The electronic horizontal situation indicator (EHSI) presents you with the "big picture." In the EHSI shown in Figure 3.14, you can see the waypoints along your route mapped out. Since the EHSI is a "track-up" display, you can quickly see that the aircraft is aimed at the next waypoint in the sequence. The numerical display of the track and the distance to the active waypoint at the top of the EHSI lets you know your position more precisely.

On the Route Legs page shown in Figure 3.15, you see a different representation of the same route. The courses and distances that appear above the waypoint names provide the same information shown on the EHSI, only in a numerical format. It is interesting to note that the numerical representation offers great precision but doesn't offer the "quick glance" that the EHSI provides. Different displays suit different purposes; that's why the engineers gave you more than one.

Keeping Track of Time En Route and Fuel Burned

As you make your way between the waypoints along your route, you must also keep track of what time you arrive

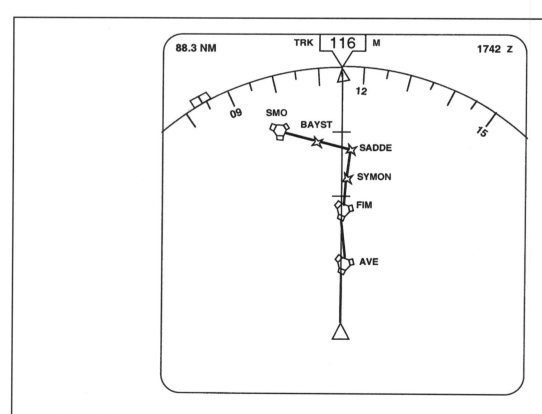

3.14. Following your progress on the EHSI.

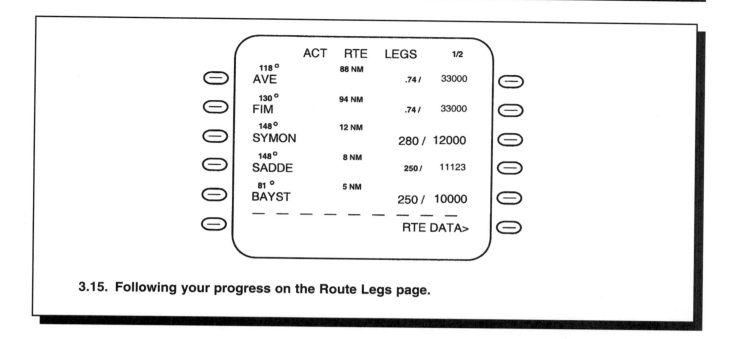

3.15. Following your progress on the Route Legs page.

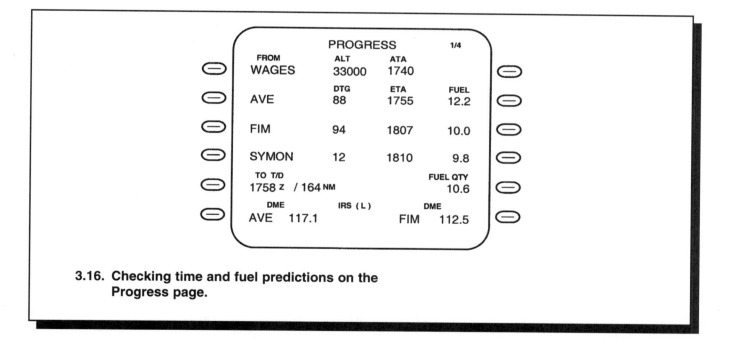

3.16. Checking time and fuel predictions on the Progress page.

at each waypoint and whether your estimates of how much fuel you are burning are accurate.

Toward this end, the Progress page, shown in Figure 3.16, provides you with a different display of your route. The Progress page shows the same list of waypoints shown on the Route Legs page but also provides estimates of the time at which the aircraft will arrive at each waypoint as

well as the fuel remaining. On your flight plan that was distributed with your dispatch papers, a predicted fuel burn was listed for each waypoint along your route. These estimates are what the dispatch office would like you to achieve. The Progress page lets you keep track of how you are doing.

Naturally, the accuracy of the time and fuel estimates depends on the winds that you encounter along your way.

When you created your FMC route back at SFO, you used the Perf Init page to enter a cruise wind. Recall that entering this value helped the FMC to predict the aircraft's performance in the climb and to make a more accurate prediction of when the aircraft would reach its top-of-climb point. If this information helped the FMC predict climb performance, then it should come as no surprise that wind information will also help the FMC predict cruise performance. After all, the stronger the headwinds, the longer it will take to get there, and the more fuel you will burn along the way.

Fortunately, the FMC also allows the crew to enter wind information for the cruise phase of flight. Following the RTE DATA prompt at line 6R of the Route Legs page takes you to another page called the **Route Data page** shown in Figure 3.17. The purpose of the Route Data is to allow the crew to provide the FMC with up-to-date information about cruise winds.

Using the same format as the Route Legs and Progress page, the Route Data page lists the waypoints that make up your route. To the right of each waypoint name is an estimated time of arrival at that waypoint along with a prediction for the winds at that waypoint. You note that the wind prediction at every waypoint is the same in Figure 3.17. Why is this? Remember entering a prediction for the top-of-climb winds back on the Perf Init page prior to departure? In the absence of any new information from you, the FMC is assuming that the winds all along your route will be the same as those predicted for your top-of-climb point. As you all know, the winds do change. What happens if the FMC assumes that the winds will be the same throughout the flight and then the aircraft encounters different winds during the flight? The answer is simple. All of the FMC predictions about estimated times of arrival and fuel burn will be inaccurate. What can you do about it? Get the latest information about the winds aloft at each waypoint and type it into the Route Data page. Once you do, the FMC will recalculate all of its ETA and fuel estimates and they will be more accurate. Remember, the CDU is not there only to give you information but also to get valuable information from you. The automation and the flight crew make a team. It is important that each team member share its information with the other. Figure 3.18 shows the Route Data page after updated wind information has been entered. Note the effect on the estimated arrival times at each waypoint.

The astute reader may have noticed the REQUEST> prompt that appears on the Route Data page. Some airplanes are equipped to receive up-linked weather information from the dispatch office. The system that facilitates this sort of data transmission between airplane and company is called an **ARINC communications and addressing system** (ACARS). Although the details of ACARS is beyond the scope of this book, pressing the line button beside the REQUEST> prompt sends a message to company dispatch, who can then transmit wind information directly to the FMC. After accepting the transmission, wind information will appear on the Route Data page.

Maintaining the Desired Cruise Speed

Once established in cruise, VNAV handles the job of maintaining the planned cruise speed. Recall that back on the ground, the FMC calculated the most economical cruise

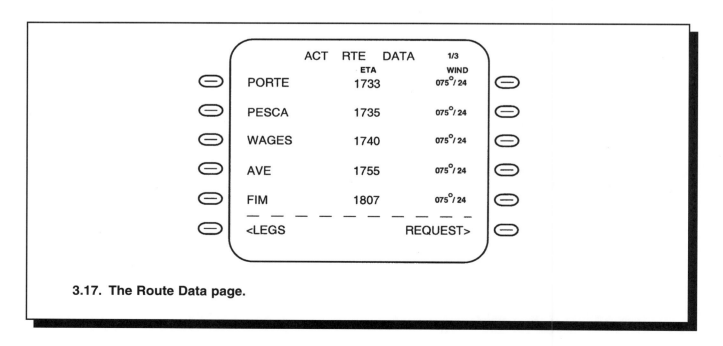

3.17. The Route Data page.

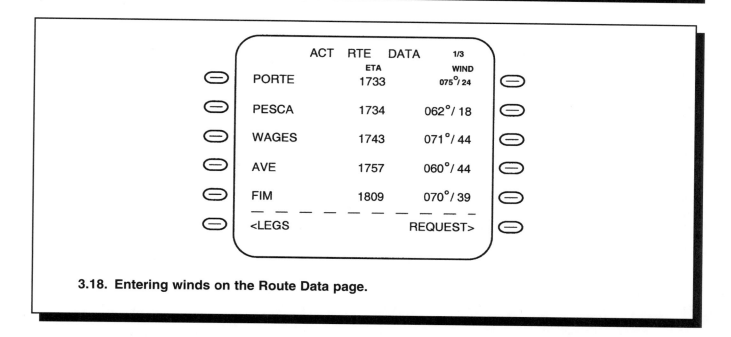

3.18. Entering winds on the Route Data page.

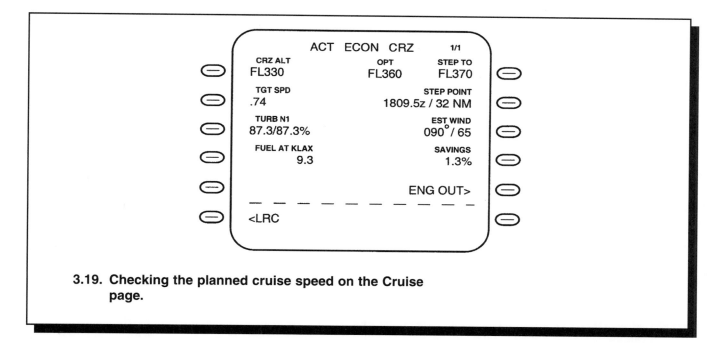

3.19. Checking the planned cruise speed on the Cruise page.

speed based on the entries made on the Perf Init page. With VNAV engaged, the FMC is controlling the aircraft to the planned cruise speed. You can see the planned cruise speed at any time by looking at line 2L on the Cruise page shown in Figure 3.19.

Note that the title of the Cruise page reads ACT ECON CRZ. This means that the speed being pursued by the FMC and shown at line 2L is the one calculated to be the most

economical by the FMC, given the cost index that the crew has entered on the Perf Init page.

Maintaining the Assigned Cruising Altitude

VNAV is also assuming the job of maintaining the aircraft at the assigned cruising altitude. When VNAV is engaged during cruise phase, the FMC will issue guidance commands that maintain the aircraft at the cruise altitude that you have entered into the CDU.

The Cruise page on the CDU is an important information resource during cruise phase. Line 1L of the Cruise page echoes the assigned cruise altitude, while line 2L does the same for the economical cruise speed calculated by the FMC.

For the economy-minded flight crew, line 1R on the Cruise page provides an interesting piece of information. As you know, as the aircraft makes its way along its route, it burns fuel. And as the aircraft burns fuel, it gets lighter. And as the aircraft gets lighter, it is able to operate more cost-efficiently at a higher altitude. The Cruise page allows the flight crew to ask "what if" questions about flying at higher altitudes and reducing costs. Line 1R shows you the optimum altitude for the aircraft at all times and allows you to enter a proposed altitude. For example, Figure 3.19 indicates that the optimum altitude for the aircraft is FL360. Clearly, ATC is not going to let you fly at FL360. But what about FL370? Even though FL370 is not the optimum altitude, it might be more efficient than flying at FL330, your current altitude. Line 1R allows the crew to type in a proposed altitude and see how

efficiently the aircraft would fly. When you enter a proposed altitude at line 1R, the cost savings or penalty is displayed at line 4R. This percentage reflects the gain or loss in time and fuel associated with flying at the proposed altitude.

As you make your way down toward Avenal intersection, the aircraft symbol on your EHSI gets closer and closer to the next important milestone along your route. Shown on the EHSI in Figure 3.20, the T/D symbol indicates the point at which the FMC plans to commence the descent out of FL330.

Descent

The descent phase is probably the hardest phase of flight to do well. Descent provides an opportunity to take advantage of the aircraft's glide capabilities. If timed right, the thrust levers can be moved back to idle while the aircraft performs a whispering descent down to the target altitude. To perform this ideal descent, you must do the following:

1. Check to make sure that the planned top-of-descent point is a sensible one.

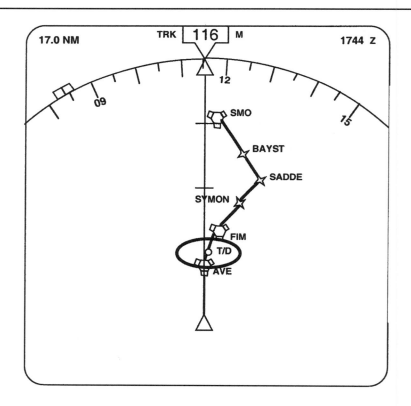

3.20. Checking the planned top-of-descent on the EHSI.

2. Maintain aircraft on the descent path.
3. Control airspeed.

Check the Planned Top-of-Descent Point

As you learned in Chapter 2, one of the FMC's most impressive capabilities is that of calculating top-of-descent points. The FMC uses complex methods to make its best guess at a descent point that will allow the airplane to perform an idle thrust descent to the assigned crossing restriction.

If you look at the EHSI shown in Figure 3.20, you see that the FMC has already decided on a top-of-descent point. Before arriving at the FMC-planned top-of-descent point, the flight crew's job is to figure their own descent and compare it to what the FMC has calculated. Clearly, you couldn't hope to arrive at a top-of-descent point that is more optimized than what the FMC is able to calculate. Rather, your purpose here is to make sure that the FMC hasn't come up with something that is way off base due to a mistaken entry made by the flight crew, a problem with the FMC itself, or a problem with the databases that the FMC uses to do its work. There are a number of "reality checks" that the crew can do to ensure that the FMC's descent plan is a viable one.

The first check is to see that the FMC is shooting for the right crossing restriction. From your Sadde Six arrival procedure chart, you can see that the first descent restriction is 12,000 feet at Symon. To determine whether the FMC plans to meet this restriction, you consult the Descent page, an important information resource both before and during a descent. Line 1R on the Descent page in Figure 3.21 shows the next crossing restriction to be Symon at 12,000 feet. You can also see that the FMC is programmed to comply with the 250 knots below 10,000 feet restriction.

A second check is to determine whether the FMC-planned top-of-descent point is reasonable. A good rule of thumb is the "3 NM per 1,000 feet" rule. This rule states that airplanes of this type typically traverse about 3 nautical miles for every 1,000 feet of descent. Begin with the first crossing restriction along your descent. In your case, it is Symon at 12,000 feet. If you subtract 12,000 feet from your cruising altitude of 33,000 feet, you get 21,000. This is how far you have to descend: 21,000 feet. Following your rule, you will need about 3 NM for every 1,000 you hope to descend. Multiplying 21 by 3, you get 63. In other words, you need about 63 NM to descend from FL330 down to 12,000 feet. Now let's compare this with what the FMC has computed. You can see the top-of-descent point on the EHSI, but in this case you need some hard numbers. Recall that the Progress page is full of useful information like this. Pushing the PROG button on the front of the CDU calls up the page shown in Figure 3.22.

Line 5L shows the distance to the top-of-descent point. You see that it is 46 NM. Adding up the distances between waypoints until you reach Symon gives you 120 NM. Subtracting the 46 NM you have to travel from the total distance of 120 NM gives you 74 NM. In other words, the top-of-descent point is 74 NM before Symon. Comparing this to your rough estimate of 63 NM, you can see that the FMC-calculated top-of-descent point seems reasonable.

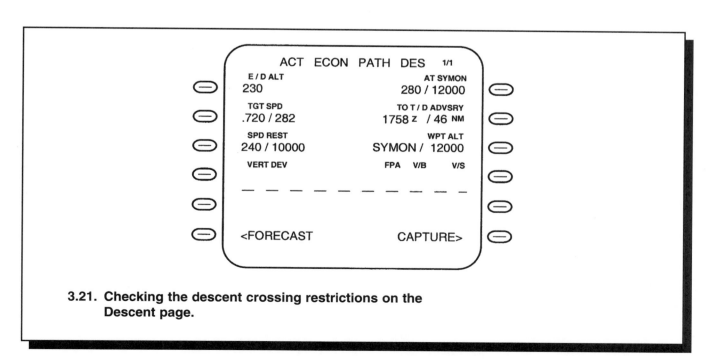

3.21. Checking the descent crossing restrictions on the Descent page.

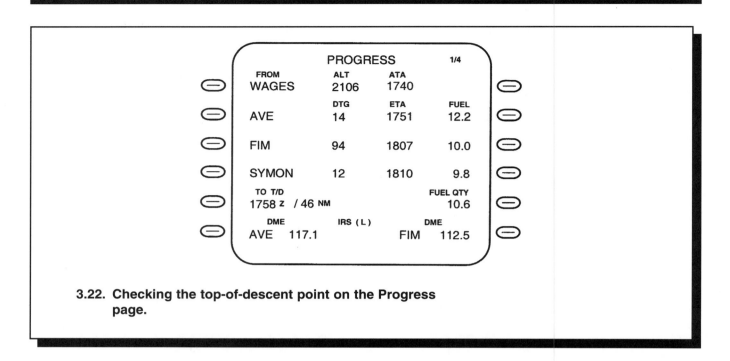

3.22. Checking the top-of-descent point on the Progress page.

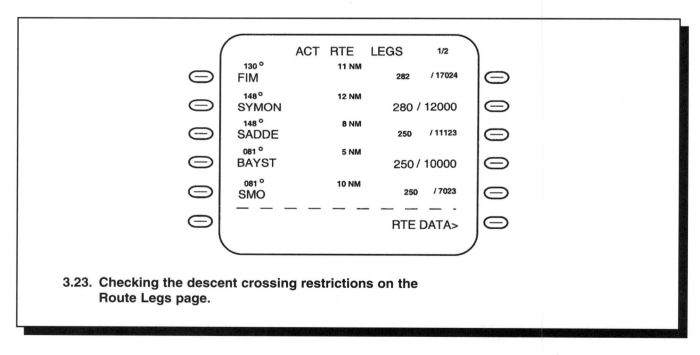

3.23. Checking the descent crossing restrictions on the Route Legs page.

A third check is to make sure that the FMC's descent path satisfies all of the other restrictions that are part of your clearance. In the case of the Sadde Six arrival procedure, you have crossing restrictions at Fillmore, Symon, and Sadde. Looking at the Route Legs page in Figure 3.23, you can see the predicted altitudes and speeds for each of these waypoints. From the Route Legs page, you can see that all of the altitude and speed restrictions are met.

About 20 NM short of the FMC-planned top-of-descent, ATC clears you to descend pilot's discretion to FL240. The pilot's discretion clearance allows you to start your descent any time you like. This allows you to let the

FMC start the airplane down at the planned top-of-descent point. The clearance clears you to only FL240, but hopefully you will get cleared to a lower altitude prior to reaching FL240. You can now wait patiently as the top-of-descent symbol approaches the bottom of the EHSI. A few miles short of the top-of-descent point, the message shown in Figure 3.24 appears in the scratch pad of the CDU.

Keep in mind that the airplane will never descend below the altitude that has been entered into the altitude window on the mode control panel. Prior to reaching the top-of-descent point, you dial down the altitude to 24,000 feet. At the top-of-descent point, the thrust levers come back to idle, and the aircraft vacates FL330.

Maintain Aircraft on the Descent Path

Recall that the FMC plans a descent by choosing a top-of-descent point such that if the thrust levers are reduced to an idle setting, the airplane will glide down to the assigned crossing restriction. The line that connects the top-of-descent point and the bottom-of-descent point is called the descent path. Looking at the diagram in Figure 3.25, you can see that staying on the planned descent path is rather important. Following any other path will result in overshooting or undershooting the crossing restriction.

Your primary concern when flying the descent is to maintain the airplane on the planned descent path. When VNAV is engaged, remaining on the descent path is the autoflight system's top priority. VNAV will automatically correct any tendency for the airplane to drift above or below the planned descent path. Your job is to monitor the position of the airplane with respect to the path. The Descent page shown in Figure 3.26 displays at line 4L the vertical deviation from the planned descent path. The Descent page in Figure 3.26 shows that you are 30 feet above the planned descent path.

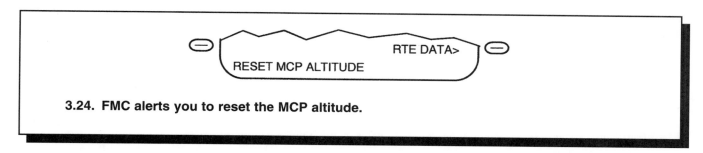

3.24. FMC alerts you to reset the MCP altitude.

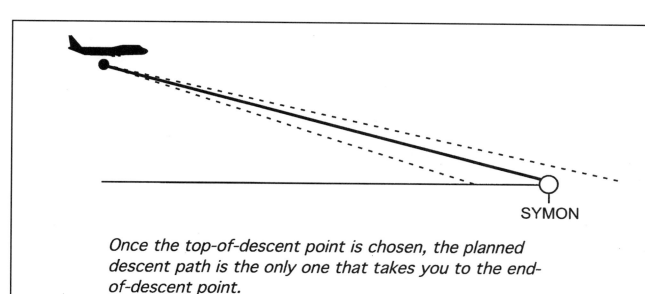

Once the top-of-descent point is chosen, the planned descent path is the only one that takes you to the end-of-descent point.

3.25. Planned descent path; drifting above and below planned descent path.

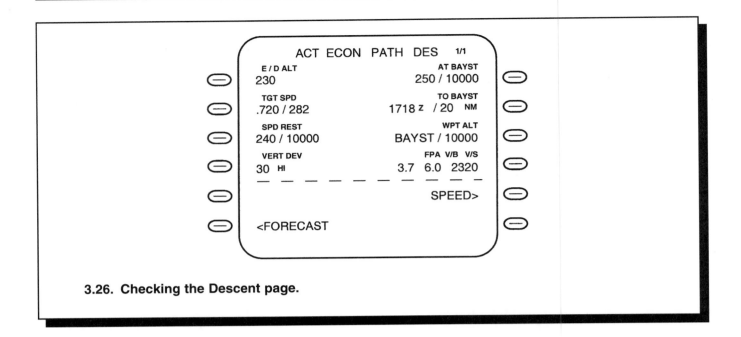

```
                    ACT ECON PATH DES    1/1
          E / D ALT                    AT BAYST
          230                          250 / 10000

          TGT SPD                      TO BAYST
          .720 / 282              1718 Z / 20  NM

          SPD REST                     WPT ALT
          240 / 10000             BAYST / 10000

          VERT DEV                     FPA V/B V/S
          30 HI                        3.7 6.0 2320
          — — — — — — — — — — —
                                       SPEED>

          <FORECAST
```

3.26. Checking the Descent page.

Control Airspeed

You now understand that VNAV does a good job of maintaining the airplane on the planned descent path. Controlling the airspeed of the airplane as it makes its way down the descent path is another story. This job is ultimately the responsibility of the flight crew.

Recall that the top-of-descent point chosen by the flight management computer is based on the cost index that you entered on the Perf Init page. Entering a high cost index results in a top-of-descent point that lies closer to the crossing restriction, a steeper glide, and a faster descent speed. Entering a low cost index results in a top-of-descent point that lies father away from the crossing restriction, a shallower glide, and a slower descent speed. It would seem that airspeed control during the descent is already factored in to the FMC's calculations. The speed of the airplane during the descent is really determined by the steepness of the descent path that the FMC has built.

UNEXPECTED TAILWINDS

The top portion of Figure 3.27 illustrates one situation in which the speed of the airplane during the descent can differ radically from that which was planned. Imagine the case in which the tailwinds you encountered are different from those that the FMC used when planning the descent. Traveling at the planned descent airspeed, an unexpected tailwind would cause you to cover more nautical miles during the descent and threaten your chances of making your crossing restriction. Since remaining on the planned descent path is a

top priority, VNAV will automatically lower the nose of the airplane and descend more steeply to maintain the descent path. This correction results in an increase in airspeed. Since the thrust levers are already positioned to idle, VNAV has no way of correcting this situation. The watchful flight crew must recognize this situation and intervene by using the airplane's speed brakes. Not only does this make for an uncomfortable ride, but you must also take care not to exceed the critical speed of V_{MO} during the descent. The real solution to this problem was to start the descent earlier, but it's too late for that now. The airplane's speed brakes are a common solution to the problem of getting rid of excess energy and returning to the planned descent path.

UNEXPECTED HEADWINDS

The bottom portion of Figure 3.27 illustrates another situation in which the speed of the airplane during the descent can differ radically from that which was planned. Imagine the case in which the headwinds you encountered are different from those that the FMC used when planning the descent. An unexpected headwind will cause the airplane to cover fewer nautical miles during the descent and reach the target altitude prior to reaching the waypoint. In order to maintain the planned descent path, VNAV raises the nose of the airplane to maintain the descent path. Naturally, this action results in a decrease in airspeed below the planned descent airspeed. Unlike the problem of speed control in unexpected tailwinds, VNAV is able to take action against the problem of a decaying airspeed in a descent. Once the airspeed reaches 15 knots below the planned descent air-

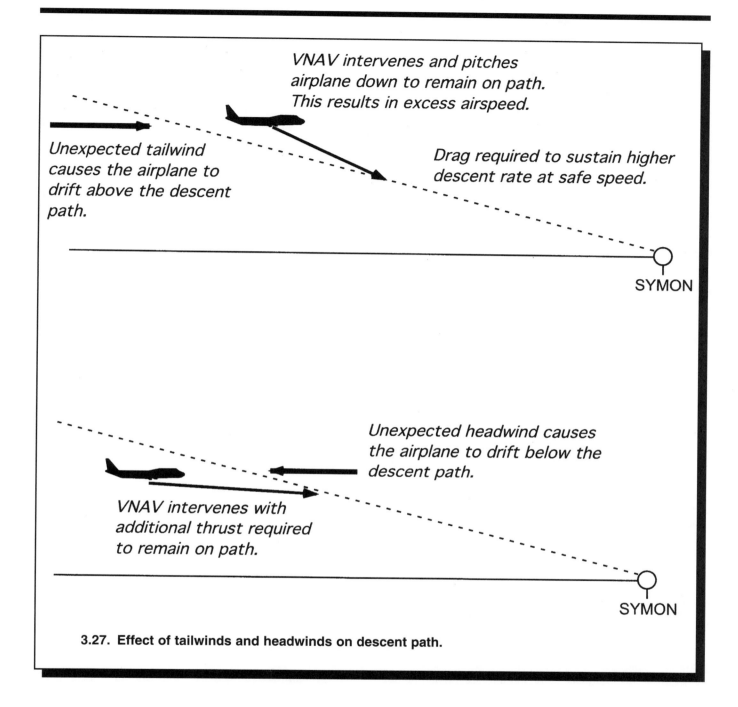

Unexpected tailwind causes the airplane to drift above the descent path.

VNAV intervenes and pitches airplane down to remain on path. This results in excess airspeed.

Drag required to sustain higher descent rate at safe speed.

SYMON

Unexpected headwind causes the airplane to drift below the descent path.

VNAV intervenes with additional thrust required to remain on path.

SYMON

3.27. Effect of tailwinds and headwinds on descent path.

speed, VNAV brings the thrust levers forward and uses a combination of pitch and power to maintain the airplane on the planned descent path. Nevertheless, the watchful flight crew must carefully monitor this unexpected situation.

AVOIDING GETTING CAUGHT BY UNEXPECTED WINDS

You can take certain measures when you suspect that the winds might be significantly different from those pre-dicted. This is often the case when descending out of the jet stream.

The page access prompt at line 6L on the Descent page (see Figure 3.21) calls up another page called the **Descent Forecasts page,** shown in Figure 3.28.

The Descent Forecasts page allows the crew to enter additional information about winds along the descent route. Lines 3R, 4R, and 5R allow the crew to type in wind direction and velocity for any three altitudes along the descent.

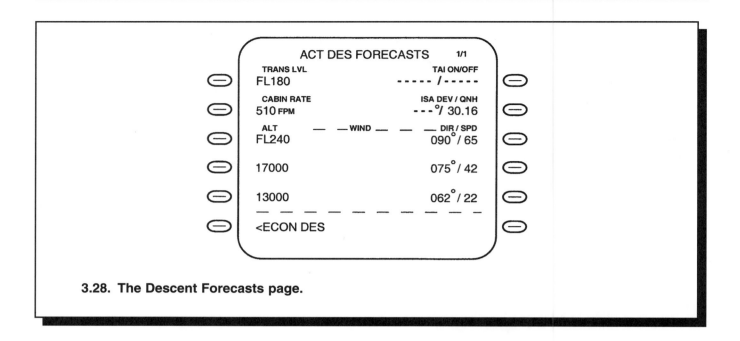

3.28. The Descent Forecasts page.

The altitudes chosen can be any altitudes for which the crew is able to obtain wind information. If entered prior to the top-of-descent, the FMC will refine its calculations for the top-of-descent point.

Prior to reaching the cleared altitude of FL240, you are told to continue your descent and cross SYMON at 12,000 feet and 280 knots. You can now dial the altitude window down to 12000 feet on the MCP.

Upon reaching SYMON intersection, you begin your arrival into the Los Angeles area.

Arrival

After you have reached your descent crossing restriction, you are then left with problem of flying the remaining portion of your arrival procedure. It is usually the case that the remaining waypoints in the arrival procedure are part of the FMC route. If you remain in LNAV and VNAV, flying those waypoints will be business as usual. The aircraft will sequence on to the SMO VOR, the initial approach fix for the VOR or GPS runway 25R approach.

Approach

The KLAX VOR or GPS runway 25R approach is an example of a new kind of approach that allows operators to make use of new navigation technologies such as flight management computers and global positioning system (GPS) receivers. This kind of equipment is loosely referred to as **area navigation** equipment. In some respects, flying an approach using area navigation equipment is no more diffi-

cult than flying along the enroute portion of your flight route. Using area navigation equipment, the approach is nothing more than another sequence of waypoints that have altitudes and speeds associated with them. A variety of rules and requirements apply when conducting an approach using area navigation equipment, and you must be sure that you meet these requirements before conducting this kind of approach.

At this time, there are two types of approaches designed specifically for area navigation equipment. **Overlay approaches** are conventional radio navigation approaches that have area navigation approaches juxtaposed on top of them. Overlay approaches are easy to recognize since they mention the name of two kinds of navigation equipment in their title: one conventional radio navigation technology (e.g., VOR) and one area navigation technology (e.g., FMC or GPS). In order to execute an overlay approach using the area navigation equipment named in the title of the approach, you must also have on board the conventional radio navigation equipment named in the title of the approach.

A **standalone approach** allows an appropriately equipped airplane to fly the approach using area navigation equipment as the sole means of navigation. Furthermore, the area navigation equipment is required to provide an accuracy that is equal to or better than a published **required navigation performance** (RNP) for that approach. The required navigation performance for any airspace or procedure prescribes the maximum error or inaccuracy in nautical miles that the onboard area navigation equipment can exhibit at any time. The accuracy of your onboard area navigation equipment at any given time is called the **actual navigation performance** (ANP).

Area navigation equipment and approaches are relatively new and still very much in development. There is considerable interest in replacing the words FMS and GPS in the titles of area navigation approaches with the title RNAV so that any area navigation technology can be used to fly the approach as long as the required navigation performance criteria are met. The rules for required equipment on board are also being constantly revised. For the present time, airline carriers consult with the FAA on an individual basis for permissions and rules to conduct area navigation approaches.

For the VOR or GPS runway 25R approach, you can actively monitor the VOR signal as your primary means of navigation information. However, you can use LNAV and VNAV to fly the approach all the way to the missed-approach point. If at any time the track along which LNAV and VNAV are guiding the airplane disagrees with the VOR course, you must intervene and continue the approach using the conventional means of radio navigation.

Configuring for the Approach

Regardless of the type of approach flown, the flight crew is left with the job of slowing and configuring the airplane for the final approach segment. This process involves gradual speed reductions and the extension of leading and trailing edge devices on a speed schedule. The **Approach Ref page,** shown in Figure 3.29, helps the crew manage this important task and shows many items of interest to the crew during an approach.

The most useful feature of the Approach Ref page is that it shows the flap reference speeds calculated by the flight management computer. The VREF speeds are shown at lines 1R, 2R, and 3R for three flap positions: 15, 30, and 40 degrees. These speeds initially appear in small font until they are accepted by the flight crew. To accept the speeds, the line button beside each speed must be pushed twice. This causes the speeds to change to large font and also appear on each pilot's electronic attitude director indicator (EADI). Figure 3.29 shows that the first two of the V-speeds have been accepted by the flight crew.

The Approach Ref page can be accessed by pressing the INIT REF button on the front of the CDU while in flight.

THE RADIO ALTIMETER

Another important component of the modern airline cockpit used during an approach is the **radio altimeter.** Unlike the altimeter with which you are already familiar, the radio altimeter does not display corrected pressure altitude as a measure of altitude above mean sea level (MSL). The radio altimeter measures absolute altitude or height above ground level (AGL). The radio altimeter measures absolute altitude by transmitting FM radio signals at the ground and then measuring changes to the signal when they are reflected.

Prior to commencing an approach, it is customary to set the radio altimeter to the decision height for a precision approach or to the minimum descent height for a nonprecision approach. The minimum descent altitude (height), or MDA (H), for the LAX VOR or GPS runway 25R approach is 540′ (438′). Since the radio altimeter measures altitude in AGL, you can dial in 440 feet.

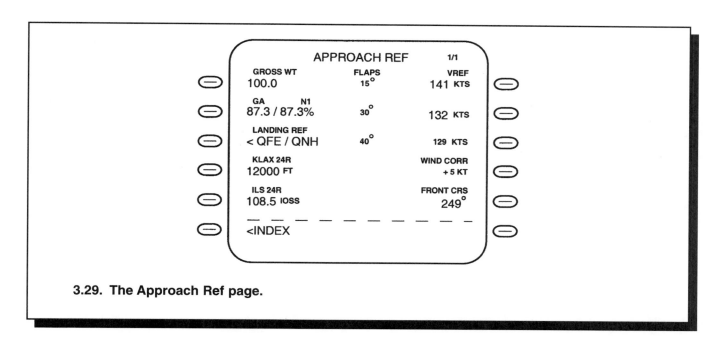

3.29. The Approach Ref page.

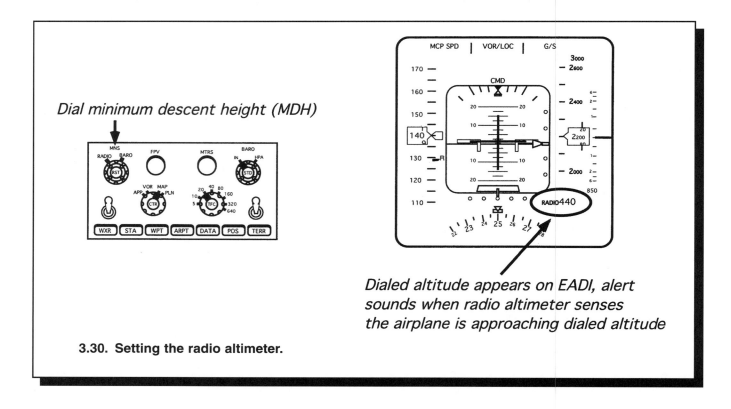

3.30. Setting the radio altimeter.

Radio altitudes can be dialed using the electronic flight instrument control panel (EFCP) shown in Figure 3.30. The dialed radio altitude then appears on the electronic attitude director indicator (EADI). The radio altimeter provides a series of alerts to the flight crew when the airplane approaches the dialed altitude. Different among most fleets, these alerts typically occur in the form of color and symbol changes on the EADI, as well as aural alerts.

Chapter Summary

In this chapter you learned how to use the airplane's autoflight system to follow the flight route that you built prior to departure. You learned how to use two powerful guidance functions offered by the autoflight system: lateral navigation (LNAV) and vertical navigation (VNAV). LNAV and VNAV generate roll, pitch, and power commands that guide the airplane along the planned route. You learned two different ways in which the crew can use these guidance commands. Guidance commands can be sent to a display called a flight director that presents roll and pitch commands to the flight crew, who can then manipulate the control yoke to follow the commands. Alternatively, the crew can choose to engage an autopilot and have the roll and pitch guidance carried out automatically. When the autothrottle is turned on, the power commands are automatically carried out. When the autothrottle is turned off, the pilot flying is responsible for manipulating the thrust levers. In either mode of operation, LNAV and VNAV require the close supervision of the flight crew to ensure that the programmed route agrees with what the aircraft is actually doing and that what the aircraft is doing agrees with what the crew has been instructed to do. It was demonstrated how LNAV and VNAV can be used to follow the planned flight route through the climb, cruise, and descent phases of flight. For each phase of flight, you learned how to monitor the activities of the automation as you made your way along the route.

CHAPTER 4

Dealing with En Route Modifications

NOW THAT YOU are comfortable using the flight management computer and the autoflight system to plan and follow a flight route, in this chapter we begin to address an unfortunate reality. As a pilot you know that there are a lot of airplanes in the sky and that sometimes you don't get to fly your route exactly as you had planned. This fact of life presents you with the problem of dealing with modifications to your flight route made by air traffic control. We begin with some common en route modifications and show you simple techniques that you can use to deal with them.

All of the enroute modifications discussed in this chapter can be accomplished using the pages of the CDU. After modifying the route stored in the FMC, the flight crew will be able to execute the changes and continue following the modified route using the powerful LNAV and VNAV functions.

Direct To

The most common en route modification is one that flight crews often request. Looking at your planned flight route shown in Figure 4.1, you see there are various turns along your way down to Avenal. Negotiating these turns requires time and fuel. It would be a real time and fuel saver if you could simply proceed directly to Avenal.

This "direct to" request is a common one made by flight crews, and it is often granted by ATC. Let's assume that you

have passed Porte intersection and are on your way to Pesca intersection when you are instructed to proceed directly to Avenal. You are now left with the problem of modifying your route to eliminate the waypoints between Porte and Avenal and fly directly from your present position to Avenal.

The FMC provides a special CDU page for complying with the direct-to clearance. Begin by pressing the DIR INTC button on the CDU to access the **Direct To page** shown in Figure 4.2.

The Direct Intercept page shows the same list of waypoints shown on the Route Legs page. The prompt at line 6L allows you to enter the name of a waypoint to which you would like to proceed directly. To comply with your clearance, you need to enter AVE into line 6L. Doing this modifies your route as shown in Figure 4.3.

After Avenal is entered into line 6L, notice that Avenal moves up to line 1L and becomes the active waypoint. A new direct course of 115 degrees has been planned to Avenal. All waypoints before Avenal have been eliminated as shown in Figure 4.3.

You can review your modification by looking at the EHSI in Figure 4.4 and see that the FMC has constructed a tentative path from your present position to AVE, indicated by a dashed line.

Your last step is to make the modification official by pressing the execute button on the front of the CDU. You are now on your way to Avenal, and the EHSI in Figure 4.5 shows your new route.

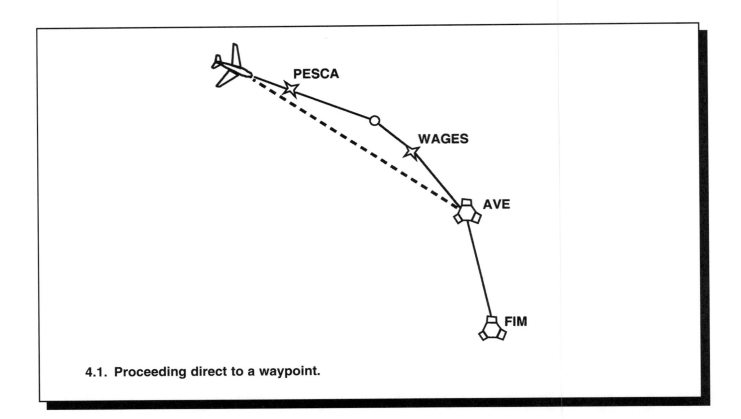

4.1. Proceeding direct to a waypoint.

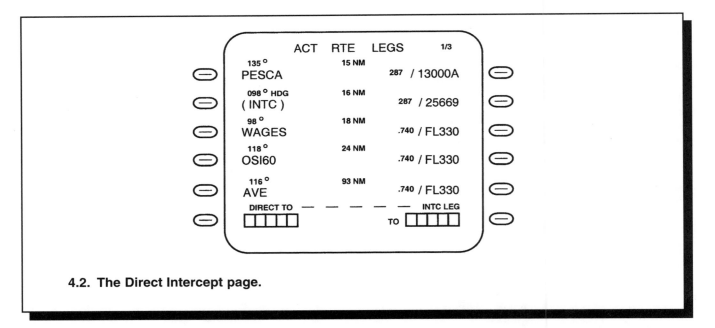

4.2. The Direct Intercept page.

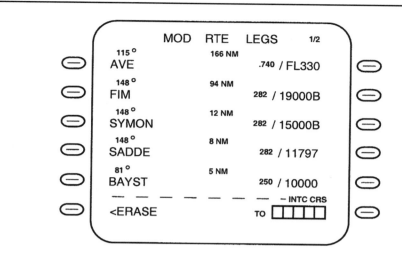

4.3. The Direct Intercept page with Avenal entered.

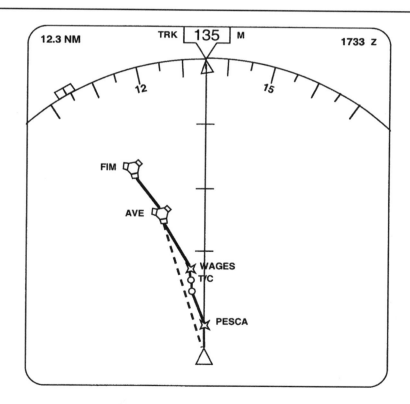

4.4. The EHSI showing the modified route.

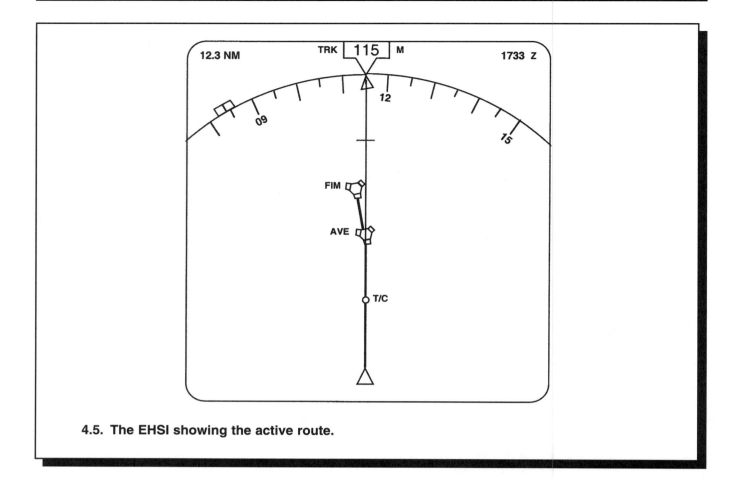

4.5. The EHSI showing the active route.

Speed Change in Cruise

Another popular enroute modification is a speed change during cruise. ATC sometimes makes this request late in your cruise phase for the purpose of adjusting the time of your arrival in the terminal area. Speed changes in cruise phase are rather simple to make. Along your way to Los Angeles, suppose you are instructed to reduce your cruise speed to .7 Mach. Figure 4.6 illustrates how speed changes can be made using the Cruise page.

Simply type the assigned cruise speed into the scratch pad and press the 2L line select button. Once the speed has been entered, press the execute button on the front of the CDU, and your modification will become final. Note that the title of the Cruise page has changed. It no longer says ACT ECON CRZ. This is because you have overridden the FMC's computed economy cruise speed and entered your own speed.

What if ATC calls back and removes the speed restriction? The Cruise page provides a simple way of switching back to the FMC-computed economy speed. Simply press the line select button beside the ECON prompt at line 5L, and then press the execute button. The aircraft will revert to the original economy speed, and the Cruise page will appear once again as it did in Figure 4.6.

Speed Intervention

Newer-generation airplanes offer another way of making temporary changes to the speeds planned by the flight management computer. Rather than going "heads-down" and reprogramming the FMC, a feature called **speed intervention** allows the crew to change the speed targets stored in the FMC using the more "heads-up" mode control panel.

To use the speed intervention feature, first press the SPD INTV button on the front of the mode control panel. Pushing the SPD INTV button causes the **speed window** on the MCP to open and display the current FMC cruise speed from the Cruise page as shown at the top of Figure 4.7.

To change the FMC cruise speed, simply dial the assigned speed into the speed window. The new speed is

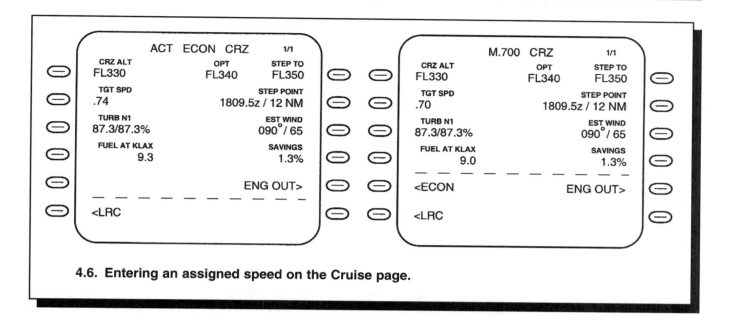

4.6. Entering an assigned speed on the Cruise page.

reflected not only in the speed window but also on the Cruise page of the CDU as shown at the bottom of Figure 4.7.

To revert to the original speed, simply press the SPD INTV button again. This closes the speed window on the MCP and changes the FMC target speed back to the original cruise speed.

New Cruise Altitude

As you make your way along your route and burn fuel, your aircraft becomes lighter and you are able to take advantage of the cost savings associated with flying at higher altitudes. This is often the case on longer flights. Suppose you have decided that climbing to a higher altitude would be beneficial. You submit this request to ATC, who then approves your climb. You can complete this modification using the Cruise page. Simply enter the new cruise altitude at line 1L, and press the execute button to activate your modification. The Cruise page will automatically switch to the Cruise Climb page shown in Figure 4.8.

The most interesting item on this page is line 2R, which provides you with an estimate of the time and distance to the point at which you will reach your new cruise altitude.

Your final step is to dial the new altitude into the altitude window on the mode control panel (MCP). Recall that the aircraft will never exceed the altitude entered into the altitude window on the MCP.

After completing these steps, VNAV will instruct the aircraft to climb. This climb is accomplished in the same manner as your original climb. VNAV commands the autothrottle to maintain an economy climb thrust setting and commands the autopilot to manipulate pitch to maintain the climb speed shown at line 2L on the Cruise Climb page.

Altitude Intervention

Newer-generation airplanes offer another way of making temporary changes to the altitudes stored in the flight management computer. Rather than going heads-down and reprogramming the FMC, a feature called **altitude intervention** allows the crew to change the target altitudes stored in the FMC using the more heads-up mode control panel. The altitude intervention feature works in essentially the same manner as the speed intervention feature. Altitude intervention is illustrated in Figure 4.9.

To use the altitude intervention feature, first dial the new cruising altitude of 37000 into the altitude window on the MCP. Next, press the ALT INTV button on the MCP. Pushing the ALT INTV button causes the dialed altitude to appear on the Cruise page.

Delete Crossing Restriction

Another common in-flight route modification is the deletion of a crossing restriction. Suppose prior to starting your descent into the Los Angeles area, you are instructed to disregard the 12,000-foot and 280-knot crossing restriction at Symon intersection. Your new clearance instructs you to cross Bayst intersection at 10,000 feet and 250 knots. You can comply with this clearance using the Route Legs page.

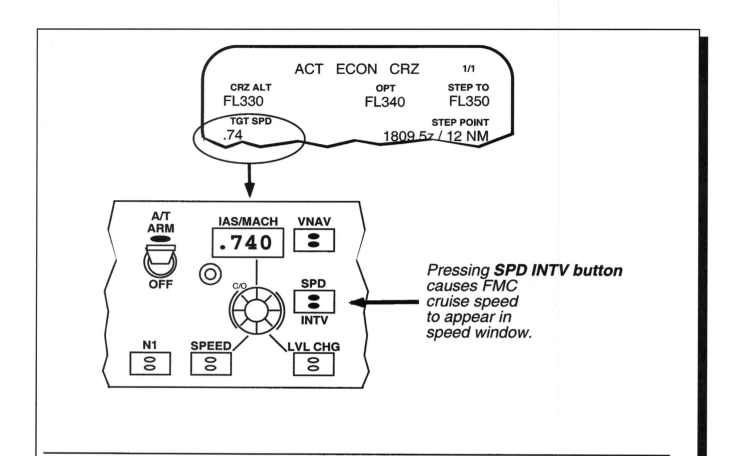

ACT ECON CRZ   1/1

CRZ ALT   **OPT**   **STEP TO**
FL330   FL340   FL350

TGT SPD   **STEP POINT**
.74   1809.5z / 12 NM

*Pressing **SPD INTV button** causes FMC cruise speed to appear in speed window.*

Dialing assigned speed into speed window causes dialed speed to appear on the Cruise Page.

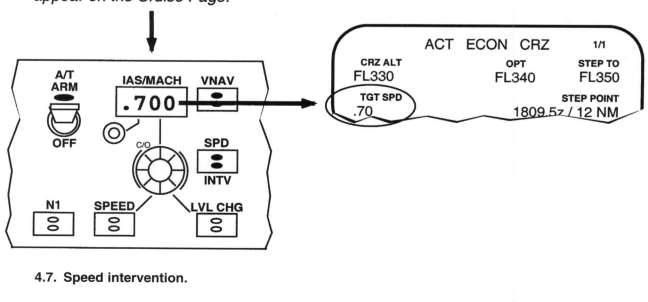

ACT ECON CRZ   1/1

CRZ ALT   **OPT**   **STEP TO**
FL330   FL340   FL350

TGT SPD   **STEP POINT**
.70   1809.5z / 12 NM

4.7. Speed intervention.

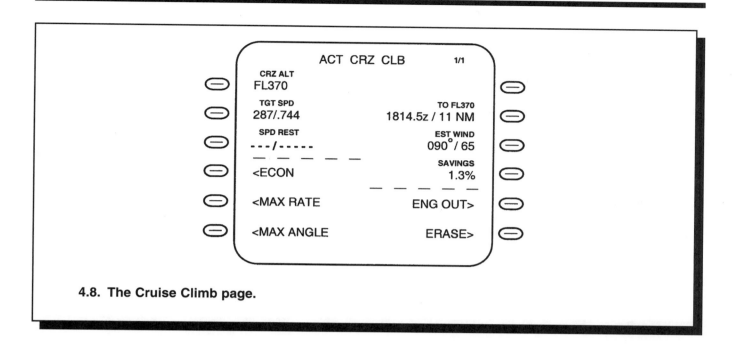

4.8. The Cruise Climb page.

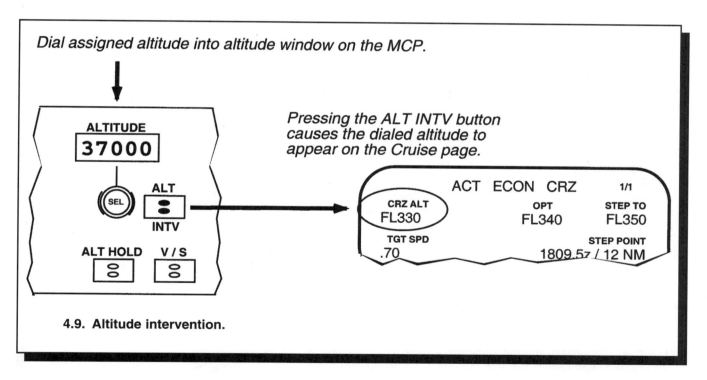

4.9. Altitude intervention.

Simply press the DEL key that appears on the front of the CDU. This causes DELETE to appear in the scratch pad as shown at the left of Figure 4.10.

Pressing the 5R line select button causes DELETE to be applied to the right side of the Symon waypoint line. This removes the crossing restriction and causes the FMC to recompute the descent path, making Bayst at 10,000 feet the new bottom-of-descent point. Note that the altitude that now appears beside the Symon waypoint appears in small font, indicating that this altitude is predicted by the FMC rather than a required crossing restriction.

	ACT RTE LEGS 1/3
116 WAGES	11 NM .740 / 33000
116° OSI60	24 NM .740 / 33000
116° AVE	93 NM .740 / 33000
148° FIM	94 NM 282 / 19000B
148° SYMON	12 NM 280 / 12000
— — — — — — — — — RTE DATA>	
DELETE	

	ACT RTE LEGS 1/3
116 WAGES	11 NM .740 / 33000
116° OSI60	24 NM .740 / 33000
116° AVE	93 NM .740 / 33000
148° FIM	94 NM 282 / 19000B
148° SYMON	12 NM 282 / 13143
— — — — — — — — — RTE DATA>	

4.10. Deleting a crossing restriction.

Altitude Intervention (Again)

The altitude intervention feature offers an alternative way of deleting crossing restrictions. This feature is designed to allow the crew to keep their heads up while making this modification to the programmed route. You can edit the lines that appear on the Route Legs page by dialing the altitude window below the altitude required by the next crossing restriction. Pressing the ALT INTV button on the MCP causes the next altitude restriction to be deleted. For example, to delete the crossing restriction of 12,000 feet at Symon intersection, the MCP altitude must be dialed down below 12,000 feet and the ALT INTV then pressed as shown in Figure 4.11.

Following these steps causes the Route Legs page to be changed in the same manner as shown in Figure 4.10.

Holding Pattern

One of the more unpopular route modifications is the hold clearance. Fortunately, the FMC provides a painless way of setting up, entering, and exiting a holding pattern.

Programming the Holding Pattern

Suppose you are inbound to San Francisco via the Big Sur Two Arrival, and you are instructed to hold west of Skunk intersection on Victor 27, 12,000 feet, left-hand turns, 15 NM legs, and to expect further clearance at 2015Z.

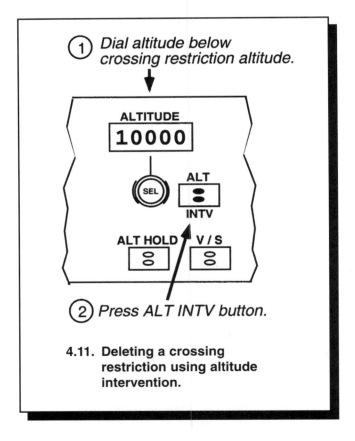

① Dial altitude below crossing restriction altitude.

ALTITUDE
10000

② Press ALT INTV button.

4.11. Deleting a crossing restriction using altitude intervention.

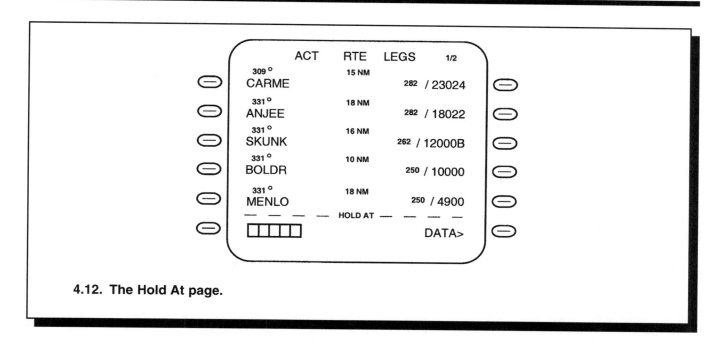

4.12. The Hold At page.

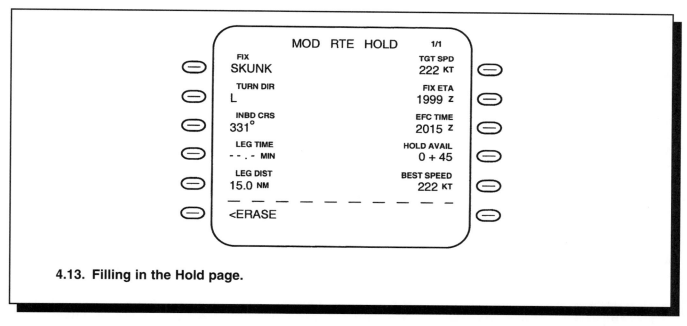

4.13. Filling in the Hold page.

Holds are programmed using the **Hold At page,** which is accessed by pressing the HOLD button on the front of the CDU. The Hold At page, shown in Figure 4.12, displays the same list of waypoints shown on the Route Legs page but also contains a prompt at 6L that allows you to enter the name of a waypoint at which you would like to hold.

You can enter Skunk here, either by typing it, or by line selecting it down from above. When a waypoint name is entered, you are automatically switched to the **Hold page** shown in Figure 4.13.

The Hold page contains a number of box prompts that ask you to enter the details of your hold procedure. Line 1L echoes the waypoint at which you will build your holding pattern. Check line 1L, and be sure that it is the one you want.

Line 2L asks you to enter the turn directions for your hold. The FMC defaults to right-hand turns. If no entry is made, the FMC will assume right-hand turns. This is certainly not what you want, so you enter L to indicate left-hand turns.

Line 3L asks you to enter the inbound course to the holding pattern. If no entry is made, the FMC will assume you want the inbound course to be the same course that you fly to this waypoint. You have been asked to hold on Victor 27, and you are currently following Victor 27 to Skunk. Hence, you can simply leave line 3L as is, and the FMC will use your current course to the holding pattern.

Line 4L allows you to enter the length of the legs in the holding pattern in minutes. If no entry is made, 1-minute legs are assumed by the FMC at or below 14,000 feet, and 1.5-minute legs if above 14,000.

Line 5L allows you to enter the length of the legs in the holding pattern in nautical miles. An entry made here overrides any entry made at line 4L. You have been instructed to fly 15 DME legs, so you enter that here.

Finally, you must enter a time at which you expect to depart the holding pattern. ATC has given you an expect-further-clearance time of 2015Z. This can be entered at line 3R. Entering an expect-further-clearance time allows the FMC to calculate how much fuel will be consumed in the hold and calculate the fuel remaining and ETA to your final destination.

Entering the Holding Pattern

Once you have entered all of the information relevant to the holding pattern, you can enter the hold by pressing the execute button, which became illuminated once you made your entries. Upon pressing the execute button, the title of the Hold page becomes ACT RTE HOLD, indicating that the holding pattern is now active and the aircraft will now proceed to the hold fix and commence the holding pattern. The Hold page along with the EHSI showing a graphical depiction of the programmed hold is shown in Figure 4.14.

During your hold, the Hold page provides you with several critical pieces of information.

Line 4R displays the FMC's calculation for the amount of time that the aircraft can remain in the holding pattern and then make it to its final destination with adequate fuel reserves on board. It is important to monitor this line and make sure that ATC does not ask you to hold longer than you are safely able to do so.

Line 5R shows you what the FMC has calculated to be the most economical speed to use during the hold. This best speed is automatically used by the FMC and is also displayed at line 1R. If, for some reason, the crew decides to use a different speed, it can be entered at line 1R. Entering a speed other than the best speed will reduce the amount of time that the aircraft is able to remain in the holding pattern. The reduced time will be reflected at line 4R.

Exiting the Holding Pattern

When ATC instructs you to exit the hold, two simple steps are required. You first push line select button 6R to select the Exit Hold function. Doing this causes the execute button to illuminate. To activate your hold exit, you must press the execute button. After executing your modification, the aircraft will continue along the holding pattern until the hold fix is reached. Upon reaching the hold fix, the aircraft will then resume following the lateral portion of the FMC-programmed flight route.

Diverting to an Alternate Airport

An even less popular in-flight route modification is a diversion to an alternate airport. The FMC provides the flight crew with several important information resources that help keep the crew informed about what airports are nearby. The Alternate Destinations page shown in Figure 4.15 accepts entries from the flight crew about potential alternate airports.

Any time a diversion to an alternate airport is considered, the crew can enter the identifiers of up to five airports on the **Alternate Destinations page.** The Alternate Destinations page will continually update the distance, estimated time enroute, and the predicted fuel remaining for a diversion to each airport.

Selecting any airport on the Alternate Destinations page calls up a page dedicated to that airport as shown in Figure 4.16.

This page provides detailed information about the aircraft's position with respect to that airport. The VIA entry on the top line indicates that the distance, ETA, and fuel remaining predictions are based on a direct route from the aircraft's present position to the airport. Since most diversions occur after a missed approach at another destination airport where the weather was below minimums, line 5L allows the flight crew to select a MISSED APP option. Making this selection causes the FMC's predictions to be based on a route that takes the airplane from its present position, through the missed approach, and then direct to the alternate airport.

Should the crew be caught by surprise enroute with no alternate airport identifiers entered, a second page called the **Nearest Airports page** continually displays the five airports that are closest to the present position of the aircraft. The Nearest Airports page can be accessed by pressing the page

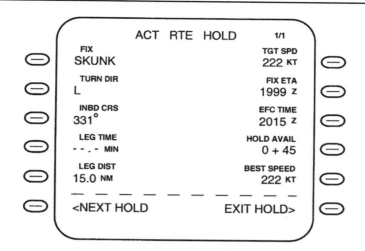

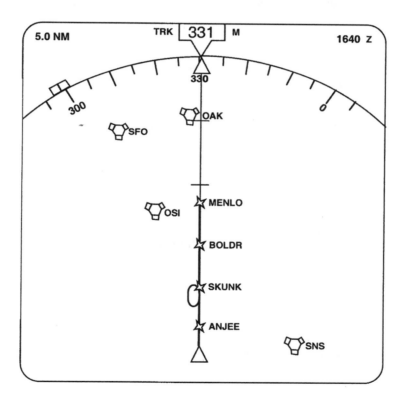

4.14. The Active Hold page.

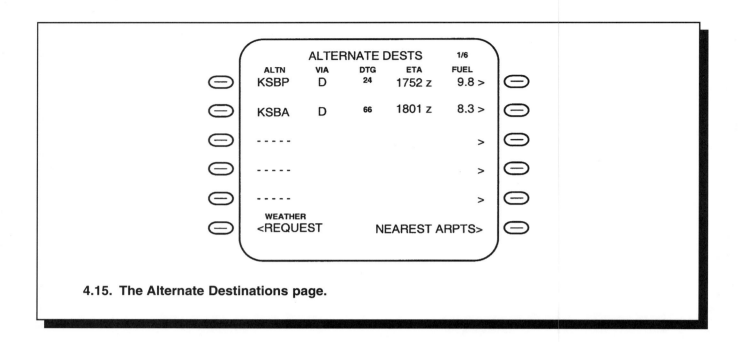

4.15. The Alternate Destinations page.

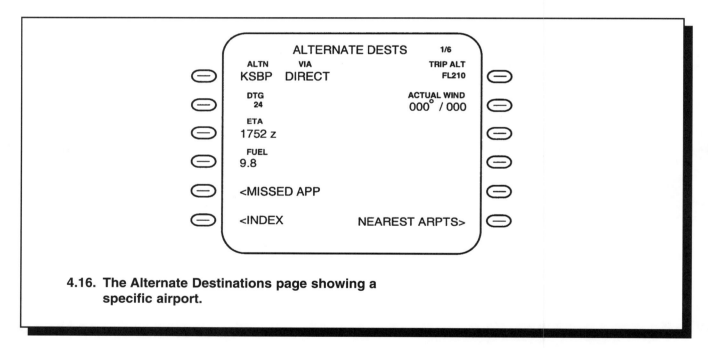

4.16. The Alternate Destinations page showing a specific airport.

```
                    NEAREST APTS          1/6
            ALTN    VIA   DTG    ETA      FUEL
            KSBP    D     24    1752 z    9.8 >

            KPRB    D     26    1752 z    9.8 >

            KSMX    D     54    1758 z    8.8 >

            KSBA    D     66    1801 z    8.3 >

            KSNS    D     102   1808 z    7.3 >

                                    PREVIOUS>
```

4.17. The Nearest Airports page.

access prompt at line 6R on the Alternate Destinations page. The Nearest Airports page is shown in Figure 4.17.

Chapter Summary

In this chapter you learned how to make simple modifications to the route that you programmed into the flight management computer prior to departure. These modifications amounted to simple changes to the series of waypoints that make up the FMC route. You learned how to skip waypoints in your route and proceed direct to an assigned waypoint, change your cruising altitude or speed, program and execute holding patterns, delete crossing restrictions, and consider diversions to alternate airports.

CHAPTER 5

Flying off of the Planned Route

THERE ARE MANY situations in which the highly automated LNAV and VNAV guidance functions are perhaps not the best choice. In this chapter we describe several of these situations and introduce a collection of simpler guidance functions offered by the airplane's autoflight system that allow you to fly the airplane in a much more straightforward way.

Complying with Simple ATC Directives

When the job of the air traffic controller gets difficult due to converging traffic or significant weather, controllers sometimes decide that the best flight plan is to have no flight plan at all. In these situations ATC often issues simple directives that instruct the crew to fly a particular heading or airspeed or to climb or descend to an assigned altitude. What is needed in these situations is not the sophisticated navigation and guidance support offered by LNAV and VNAV but rather a fast and simple way for the crew to aim the airplane at assigned heading, altitude, and speed targets.

Takeoff and Approach

The same need for simple control of the airplane occurs during takeoff and approach. Even in these modern times, these critical phases of flight make use of old-fashioned stick and rudder skills and ground-based radio navigation aids. What is needed in these situations is simple guidance support that helps the crew achieve a target pitch attitude, speed, or thrust; intercept a localizer; or follow a glide slope.

A Collection of Simpler Guidance Functions

Aside from the highly automated LNAV and VNAV functions, the autoflight system makes available a collection of simpler guidance functions. These functions allow the flight crew to put aside the master flight plan that is stored in the flight management computer and pursue much simpler targets such as assigned headings, airspeeds, altitudes, radials, localizers, and glide slopes.

Simple Guidance Functions for Complying with Simple ATC Directives

Five guidance functions allow the crew to more directly control the aircraft in the first type of situation we discussed: when ATC issues simple and direct orders to fly an assigned heading, altitude, airspeed, or vertical speed.

Heading Select

Heading Select is perhaps the simplest of all functions and is illustrated in Figure 5.1. Heading Select allows the crew to dial a target heading and then command the aircraft to steer to that heading.

Once the Heading Select function is engaged, the aircraft will continue to follow the specified heading until the

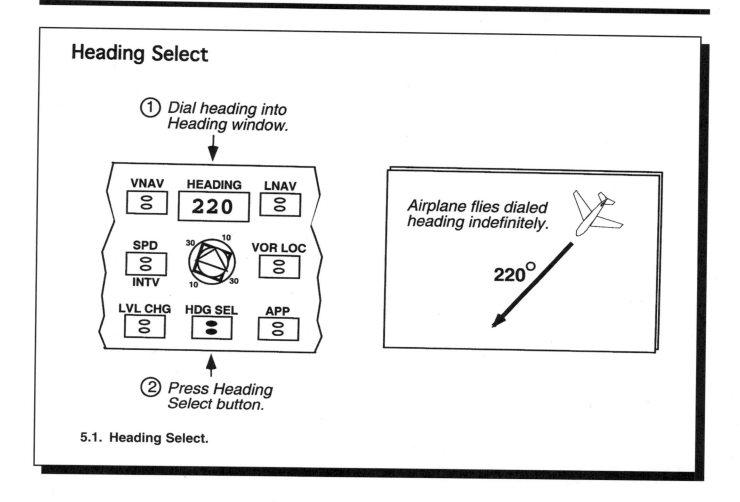

5.1. Heading Select.

crew selects a different function or another function causes Heading Select to disengage.

Altitude Hold

Altitude Hold allows the flight crew to maintain the aircraft's present altitude with the push of a button. Once Altitude Hold is engaged, the aircraft will maintain the present altitude until the crew engages another guidance function or some condition causes Altitude Hold to disengage. Altitude Hold is illustrated in Figure 5.2.

Speed

Speed, shown in Figure 5.3, allows the crew to easily maintain a designated speed. Once Speed is engaged, the aircraft will hold the specified speed until a different function is engaged.

Level Change

Level Change, illustrated in Figure 5.4, provides the crew with a fast way of climbing or descending to a new altitude. Once Level Change is engaged, the aircraft will initiate a climb or descent until it reaches the vicinity of the target altitude. Once in the vicinity of the target altitude, Level Change will initiate a capture maneuver and then switch to Altitude Hold.

During the climb or descent to the target altitude, Level Change also provides speed control. If the crew does not specify a new climb or descent speed, Level Change will maintain the same speed the aircraft was flying before Level Change was engaged. The crew can change this speed at any time by dialing a new speed into the Speed window located on the MCP. Once the aircraft reaches the desired altitude, Speed function is automatically engaged.

Altitude Hold

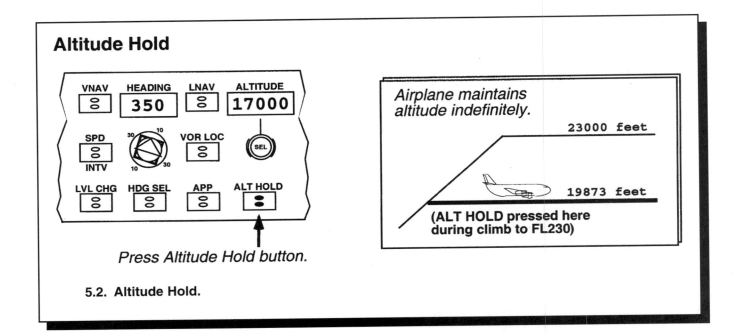

Press Altitude Hold button.

Airplane maintains altitude indefinitely.

23000 feet

19873 feet

(ALT HOLD pressed here during climb to FL230)

5.2. Altitude Hold.

Speed

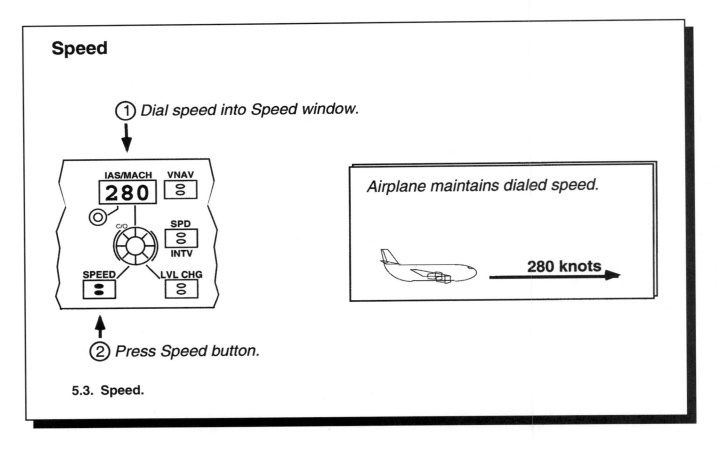

① Dial speed into Speed window.

② Press Speed button.

Airplane maintains dialed speed.

280 knots

5.3. Speed.

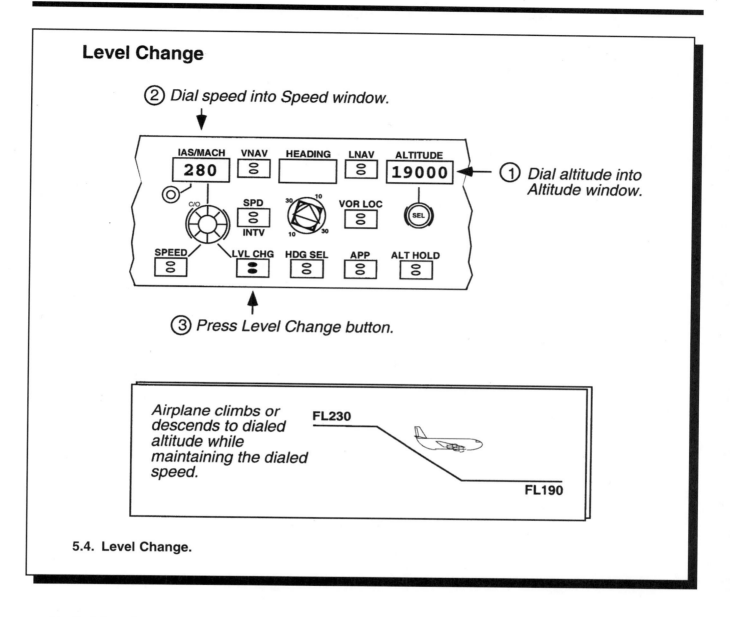

Level Change

② *Dial speed into Speed window.*

① *Dial altitude into Altitude window.*

③ *Press Level Change button.*

Airplane climbs or descends to dialed altitude while maintaining the dialed speed.

FL230

FL190

5.4. Level Change.

Vertical Speed

Vertical Speed, shown in Figure 5.5, allows the crew to climb or descend at a constant vertical speed.

Simple Guidance Functions for Takeoff and Approach

Three guidance functions provide the crew with guidance support during the second type of situation we discussed: during the critical phases of takeoff and approach.

Takeoff/Go-Around

The **Takeoff/Go-Around** function provides guidance commands for pitch, roll, and power during the takeoff roll and during early climb. Takeoff/Go-Around function is illustrated in Figure 5.6.

Takeoff/Go-Around function is engaged by dialing the takeoff safety speed into the speed window of the MCP and pressing the Takeoff/Go-Around button located on the front of the thrust levers.

Once Takeoff/Go-Around function is engaged, the airplane will attempt to establish the takeoff thrust that was computed by the FMC and is shown on the N1 Limit page and by the cursors appearing on the N1 gauges. Not always perfect, Takeoff/Go-Around function allows the crew an opportunity to check and refine the thrust setting made by the autothrottle once the aircraft has reached a critical speed. At that point, the crew can use the N1 gauge to make sure that the needles indicating the actual thrust setting line up with the cursors.

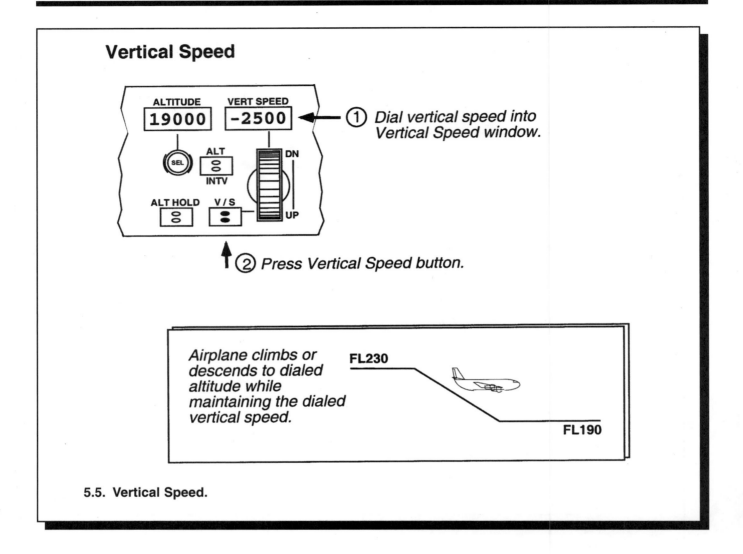

5.5. Vertical Speed.

Once off the ground, the flight director command bars will provide pitch commands that result in the initial climb speed that was planned by the FMC (V_2 plus 15 knots). Takeoff/Go-Around function is used until the aircraft reaches a safe maneuvering altitude when a different guidance function such as VNAV can be engaged.

Prior to engaging Takeoff/Go-Around function, you must first dial the assigned altitude into the Altitude window on the mode control panel. The aircraft will never climb above the altitude that is dialed into the Altitude window during a climb and never descend below the dialed altitude during a descent regardless of what guidance function is engaged.

VOR/LOC

The **VOR/LOC** function provides a handy way of capturing a VOR radial or a localizer. Using VOR/LOC function to capture a localizer or radial is illustrated in Figure 5.7.

Note that using the VOR/LOC function requires the use of two guidance functions in succession. To use VOR/LOC, you must first establish the aircraft on an acceptable intercept heading for the desired radial or localizer. Heading Select is the popular choice for accomplishing this. Once you engage Heading Select, you can dial the radial or localizer and press the VOR/LOC button. When you press the VOR/LOC button, the VOR/LOC function does not

Takeoff/Go-Around

Dial takeoff safety speed (V_2)
into speed window

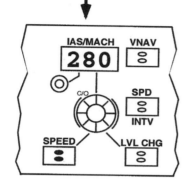

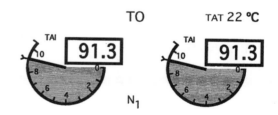

Press TOGA buttons

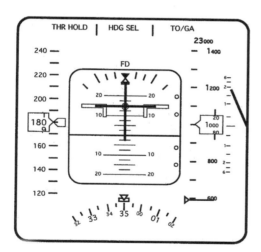

Flight director commands level pitch
and a speed of V_2 + 15 knots

TO   TAT 22 °C

91.3 91.3

N_1

Engine indicators command takeoff thrust

5.6. Takeoff/Go-Around.

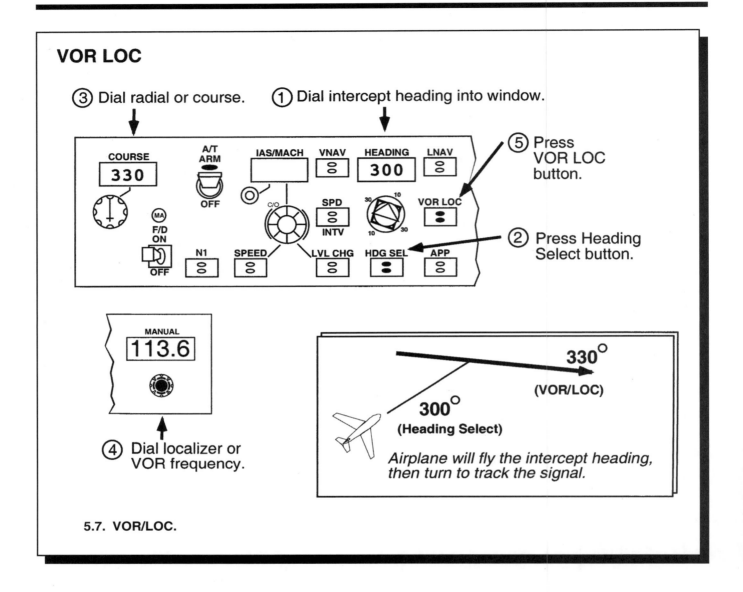

5.7. VOR/LOC.

immediately engage. Prior to reaching the dialed radial, the VOR/LOC function is **armed.** When a guidance function is armed, it is set to become **engaged** once its conditions for engagement are met. Once the dialed radial is reached, Heading Select disengages and VOR/LOC changes from armed to engaged and is now in control of the lateral track of the airplane.

Approach

Similar but more powerful than the VOR/LOC function, the **Approach** function allows the airplane to capture and track both a localizer and a glide slope, providing both lateral and vertical guidance throughout an ILS approach. The use of Approach function is illustrated in Figure 5.8.

Once the aircraft reaches the localizer that has been dialed, the aircraft will turn in the direction of the localizer and maintain a level altitude until the glide slope is also captured. Once both the localizer and glide slope have been captured, the aircraft will begin to track both signals down to the runway threshold.

Two Ways to Use the Simple Guidance Functions

When the guidance functions just described are engaged by the flight crew, the autoflight system generates the roll, pitch, and power commands necessary to guide the aircraft to the targets that the crew has dialed. As is the case for complex functions such as LNAV and VNAV, the crew has the same two options for making use of the guidance commands generated by the simpler guidance functions.

Approach

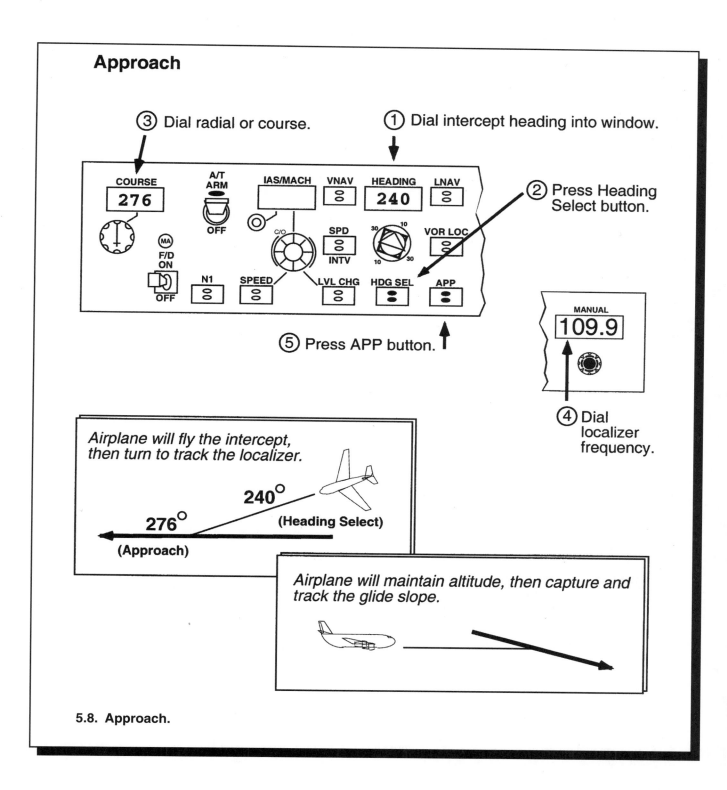

③ Dial radial or course.

① Dial intercept heading into window.

② Press Heading Select button.

COURSE
276

A/T ARM · OFF

IAS/MACH

VNAV

HEADING
240

LNAV

MA
F/D ON · OFF

C/O

SPD / INTV

VOR LOC

N1

SPEED

LVL CHG

HDG SEL

APP

⑤ Press APP button.

MANUAL
109.9

④ Dial localizer frequency.

Airplane will fly the intercept, then turn to track the localizer.

240° (Heading Select)

276° (Approach)

Airplane will maintain altitude, then capture and track the glide slope.

5.8. Approach.

When the flight directors are turned on, the command bars show the pilot flying how to manipulate the control yoke to steer to the specified target. When turned on, the autopilot automatically steers the aircraft. Similarly, the thrust commands are shown on the engine indicators. When the autothrottle is turned on, the thrust levers are automatically manipulated in response to the thrust commands.

Keeping Track of Which Guidance Functions Are Engaged

Probably the most confusing part of using guidance functions is keeping track of which ones are currently engaged. Imagine the situation in which the flight crew thinks one function is engaged when in reality some other function is engaged. Many flight crews have been surprised when they expected an aircraft to turn to intercept a radial or localizer while the aircraft continued to fly straight ahead.

What makes keeping track of guidance functions so problematic? When you push a button on the mode control panel, the function engages. What could be difficult about that? After reading this section, you will realize that the pilot's interface to the autoflight system is a little more complicated than "you push it, you get it." We describe a new cockpit display that helps the flight crew stay on top of what functions are controlling the aircraft. As you learn more about this new display, you will understand the details of how guidance functions do their job.

Let's first point out ways in which the problem of keeping track of which functions are engaged can be more complicated than it may first appear.

Guidance Functions Sometimes Turn Themselves On and Off

Some guidance functions automatically turn themselves off when their job is finished. For example, recall that Level Change switches to Altitude Hold once the aircraft has reached the desired altitude. Some functions automatically turn themselves on when their conditions for engagement have been met. For example, VOR/LOC is automatically engaged once the aircraft reaches the radial or localizer that the crew has set to capture. Guidance functions that turn themselves on and off require that the crew pay close attention as the aircraft progresses through each maneuver.

Vertical Guidance Functions Are Complicated

Every pilot knows that controlling the vertical trajectory of an aircraft means coordinating both pitch and thrust. For example, to accomplish a constant-speed climb, Level Change functions must coordinate both pitch and thrust. It turns out that every vertical guidance function is a combination of two separate functions, one that manipulates pitch, and one that manipulates thrust. To truly understand what your aircraft is doing when performing vertical guidance, you will have to understand these pitch and power functions and learn how to track them as they do their job.

Checking the Status of the Autopilot and Flight Directors

Recall that all of the guidance functions can be used in two different ways. The crew can choose to have the guidance commands followed automatically by the autopilot or have them presented to the pilot flying on the flight director. It is important for the crew to remain aware of who or what is following the guidance commands being generated by the autoflight system.

The Flight Mode Annunciator (FMA)

How can you keep track of what guidance functions are currently in use? A display called the **flight mode annunciator** (FMA) tells the story. It is the only place the crew can and should look to get the scoop on what guidance functions are in charge. Figure 5.9 shows a detailed view of the flight mode annunciator.

As you can see, the **flight mode annunciator** is somewhat complicated. Some of the annunciations such as LNAV, HDG SEL, and VOR/LOC look familiar, while others do not. This is because the flight mode annunciator does not display the names of guidance functions directly. Rather, the FMA shows the names of a set of underlying functions, called **modes,** that make up each guidance function.

Let's work our way through this new display by discussing the modes that underlie each of the guidance functions we have discussed throughout the book.

Annunciations for the Lateral Guidance Functions

Three of the guidance functions we have discussed are used to control the lateral trajectory of the aircraft. These guidance functions are LNAV, Heading Select, and VOR/LOC. These guidance functions are simple in that they use a single axis of flight, roll, to control the lateral trajectory of the aircraft. Consequently, there is only one mode that underlies each of these functions. These modes are referred to as **roll modes.** The center of the FMA is devoted to displaying roll modes. There are two types of roll mode annunciations.

The **roll engaged mode** annunciation appears at the top center of the FMA and reflects the roll mode that is currently

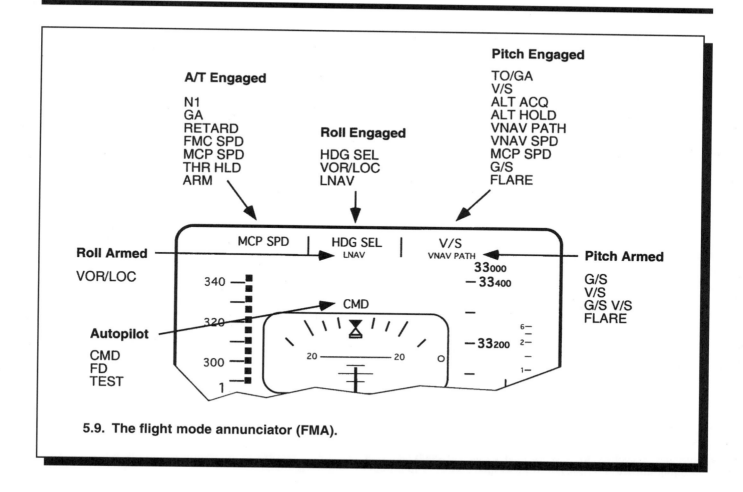

A/T Engaged

N1
GA
RETARD
FMC SPD
MCP SPD
THR HLD
ARM

Roll Engaged

HDG SEL
VOR/LOC
LNAV

Pitch Engaged

TO/GA
V/S
ALT ACQ
ALT HOLD
VNAV PATH
VNAV SPD
MCP SPD
G/S
FLARE

Roll Armed

VOR/LOC

Autopilot

CMD
FD
TEST

Pitch Armed

G/S
V/S
G/S V/S
FLARE

MCP SPD | HDG SEL | V/S
LNAV | VNAV PATH

340
320
300
1

CMD

33₀₀₀
33₄₀₀

33₂₀₀

5.9. The flight mode annunciator (FMA).

engaged. Whenever you are following the FMC route using LNAV, the roll engaged mode reads LNAV. When you are tracking a heading using Heading Select mode, the roll engaged mode reads HDG SEL. When you are tracking a VOR radial or a localizer using the VOR/LOC mode, the roll engaged mode reads VOR/LOC.

The **roll armed mode** annunciation appears just below the roll engaged annunciation in a smaller font. An armed mode is one that has been preengaged such that it will automatically take over once its conditions for engagement have been met. In our discussion of the VOR/LOC mode, you learned that you can arm the VOR/LOC mode. That is, you can engage Heading Select and get the aircraft headed toward a localizer or radial and then set VOR/LOC mode to capture the localizer or radial once you get there. Upon reaching the intercept point, VOR/LOC will change from the roll armed mode to the roll engaged mode. When used to intercept a VOR or a localizer, the roll armed mode annunciation will read VOR/LOC.

Annunciations for the Vertical Guidance Functions

The vertical guidance functions we have discussed are VNAV, Level Change, Vertical Speed, Takeoff/Go-Around, and Approach. Since every vertical guidance function must make use of a coordination of pitch and thrust to do its work, the name of each vertical guidance function is really a nickname for a combination of a pitch mode and an autothrottle mode. A **pitch mode** accepts a target from either the FMC (appearing on one of the CDU pages) or the autopilot (dialed into the mode control panel). A pitch mode uses the airplane's elevators to achieve a target speed, a target vertical speed, or a trajectory or path. An **autothrottle mode** uses the airplane's thrust levers to achieve a target thrust or a target speed. An autothrottle mode also accepts a target either from the FMC or the MCP. Pitch and autothrottle modes cannot be engaged directly by the flight crew. Pitch and autothrottle modes exist so that they can be combined to make interesting guidance functions such as VNAV and Level Change.

We can now describe in detail the five vertical guidance functions. The descriptions provide you with three very important things to know about how the vertical guidance functions work. If you take the time to understand each of these three things for each of the five vertical guidance functions, you will have the knowledge that will put you in total command of your aircraft.

First, the descriptions of each guidance function tell you what targets the autoflight system is trying to achieve when each function is being used. It is rather difficult to judge how well the autoflight system is doing unless you are crystal clear on what the automation is supposed to be doing.

Second, the descriptions tell you where the altitude, speed, and thrust targets come from when each vertical guidance function is used. Again, imagine a situation in which you are not satisfied with a target the autoflight system is trying to achieve. It would certainly help to know whether the target is coming from one of the pages of the CDU (you have some typing to do) or from one of the windows on the mode control panel (you have some dialing to do).

Third, the descriptions tell you how each vertical guidance function manipulates pitch and power to accomplish its work. This information will help you understand how vertical guidance functions fly an airplane in the same terms that you understand how to fly an airplane.

For each of the five vertical guidance functions, your attention will be directed to three items on the flight mode annunciator. The **autothrottle engaged mode** appears at the top left of the flight mode annunciator and reflects the autothrottle mode that is currently engaged. The **pitch engaged mode** appears at the top right of the FMA and reflects the current pitch mode. Finally, the **pitch armed mode** appears just below the pitch engaged mode and reflects a pitch mode that has been set to take over when its engagement conditions become satisfied.

As you read through the descriptions of the guidance functions, you will also notice that the combinations of pitch and autothrottle modes that make up each of the five vertical guidance functions sometimes changes depending on the phase of flight or maneuver being accomplished.

VNAV

VNAV works differently during climb, cruise, and descent.

During climb, VNAV is a combination of the **VNAV Speed** pitch mode and the **N1** autothrottle mode. VNAV Speed mode commands pitch to control to the target climb speed that appears at line 2L of the Climb page. N1 mode commands the thrust levers to maintain the target economy climb thrust setting that appears on the N1 Limit page.

During cruise, VNAV is a combination of the **VNAV Path** pitch mode and the **FMC Speed** autothrottle mode. VNAV Path mode commands pitch to maintain the cruise altitude that appears at line 1L on the Cruise page. FMC Speed mode commands thrust to maintain the target economy cruise speed that appears at line 2L on the Cruise page.

During descent, VNAV is a combination of the VNAV Path pitch mode and the **Arm** autothrottle mode. VNAV Path mode commands pitch to maintain the planned descent path. In Arm mode, the throttle levers are left in the idle position until another autothrottle mode is engaged or the pilot flying repositions them.

LEVEL CHANGE

Level Change also works differently in a climb and in a descent.

In a climb, Level Change is a combination of the **MCP Speed** pitch mode and the N1 autothrottle mode. MCP Speed mode commands pitch to control to the target climb speed that appears in the Speed window on the mode control panel. N1 mode commands thrust to maintain a target economy climb thrust setting that appears on the N1 Limit page.

During descent, Level Change is a combination of the MCP Speed mode and the Arm autothrottle mode. Again, MCP Speed mode commands pitch to control to the target climb speed that appears in the Speed window on the mode control panel, while the thrust levers remain at an idle setting.

When Level Change reaches the dialed altitude, it transfers control to the combination of **Altitude Hold** pitch mode and the **Speed** autothrottle mode. Altitude Hold mode commands pitch to maintain the altitude that appears in the Altitude window on the MCP. Speed mode commands the thrust to maintain the speed that appears in the Speed window on the MCP.

VERTICAL SPEED

The Vertical Speed guidance function is actually a combination of the **Vertical Speed** pitch mode and the Speed autothrottle mode. Vertical speed mode commands pitch to control to the vertical speed target that appears in the Vertical Speed window on the MCP. Speed mode commands the thrust to maintain the speed that appears in the Speed window on the MCP.

TAKEOFF

Takeoff/Go-Around is the most complex of all guidance functions. The Takeoff/Go-Around function is a combination of the **Takeoff/Go Around** (TO/GA) pitch mode and a series of autothrottle modes. When the TO/GA button is

HOW IT WORKS — MODE ANNUNCIATIONS

GUIDANCE FUNCTION	HOW IT WORKS	Roll	Pitch	Thrust
Heading Select	Roll used to maintain heading dialed into heading window.	HDG SEL		
LNAV	Roll used to track airplane between waypoints that appear on the Route Legs page.	LNAV		
VOR/LOC	Roll used to track localizer or course dialed into course window.	VOR/LOC		
Speed	Thrust used to maintain speed dialed into speed window.			MCP SPD
Altitude Hold	Pitch used to maintain present altitude.		ALT HOLD	
VNAV (climb)	Thrust set to climb thrust shown on Climb page. Pitch used to maintain climb speed shown on Climb page.		VNAV SPD	N1
VNAV (cruise)	Thrust used to maintain cruise speed shown on Cruise page. Pitch used to maintain cruising altitude shown on Cruise page.		VNAV PTH	FMC SPD
VNAV (descent)	Thrust moved to idle. Pitch used to maintain airplane on planned descent path.		VNAV SPD	RETARD then ARM
Level Change (climb)	Thrust advanced to climb thrust setting shown on N1 Page. Pitch used to maintain speed appearing in speed window.		MCP SPD	N1
Level Change (descent)	Thrust moved to idle. Pitch used to maintain speed dialed into speed window.		MCP SPD	RETARD then ARM
Approach	Roll used to track dialed localizer. Thrust used to maintain speed dialed into speed window. Pitch used to maintain airplane on glide slope.	VOR/LOC	G/S	MCP SPD
Vertical Speed	Thrust used to maintain speed dialed into speed window. Pitch used to maintain vertical speed dialed into vertical speed window.		V/S	MCP SPD

5.10. Summary of guidance function mode annunciations.

pressed, the autothrottle mode becomes N1. N1 mode during takeoff commands the takeoff thrust that appears on the N1 Limit page. The autothrottle mode remains N1 until the aircraft reaches a critical speed that varies with aircraft type. At this critical speed, the autothrottle mode becomes **Thrust Hold.** Thrust Hold mode leaves the thrust levers at the last position they were placed. When in Thrust Hold mode, the crew can manually reposition the thrust levers. When the airplane reaches an altitude of approximately 800 feet, the autothrottle mode changes to Arm mode. Arm mode indicates that no autothrottle mode is currently engaged and the autothrottle is awaiting the engagement of another vertical guidance function by the crew.

Takeoff/Go Around commands pitch to maintain a speed of V2 plus 15 knots.

APPROACH

Approach function is a combination of the **Glide Slope** pitch mode, the **VOR/LOC** roll mode, and the MCP Speed mode. Glide Slope mode commands pitch to maintain the aircraft on the glide slope signal, while VOR/LOC mode tracks the localizer. MCP Speed mode commands thrust to maintain the approach speed that appears in the Speed window on the MCP. It is customary for flight crews to turn off the autothrottle when flying an approach and to manually manipulate the thrust levers using the airspeed indicator as the primary speed reference.

SUMMARY OF THE GUIDANCE FUNCTIONS

Figure 5.10 summarizes the guidance functions we have discussed in this chapter. For each guidance function, Figure 5.10 lists the name of the function, where the guidance function gets its targets (MCP or FMC), and the roll, pitch, and autothrottle mode annunciations for each function.

Annunciations for the Autopilot and Flight Directors

The FMA provides the crew with some other items of interest. Throughout the book we have made the distinction between having the autopilot turned on or off. Recall that when the autopilot is turned on, it has the authority to assume control of the ailerons and elevators and accomplish the flight route automatically. When the autopilot is turned off and the flight directors are turned on, the guidance commands are presented on the flight director where they must then be followed by the pilot flying.

Since the status of the autopilot and the flight director is such important information, the flight mode annunciator displays it to the crew at all times. The status of the flight director and autopilot are displayed on top of the attitude indicator. If the autopilot is turned on, CMD is annunciated. When the autopilot is off and the flight directors are on, FD is annunciated.

Another Flight Mode Annunciator Feature

Besides showing which functions are currently engaged, the FMA also shows which functions have been recently engaged. For ten seconds after any function has been engaged, a rectangle will appear around the name of the associated mode on the flight mode annunciator. This handy feature allows the crew to glance at the FMA and see "what's new." The rectangle stands out against the other mode names and helps the crew quickly locate the annunciation for a guidance function that has just been engaged.

Chapter Summary

In this chapter you learned about a new set of guidance functions available to the flight crew. These guidance functions allow the crew to issue simple heading, altitude, speed, and vertical speed targets directly to the autoflight system. You learned that these guidance functions allow you to fly the aircraft in a simpler way. These guidance functions are useful when ATC instructs you to do something that is significantly different from your FMC-programmed route or when the crew wishes to assume closer control of the aircraft for any reason. You also learned the details of another important flight deck display that shows the crew which guidance functions are in use at any time. In learning about the flight mode annunciator (FMA), you also learned that guidance functions are really just nicknames for combinations of roll, pitch, and thrust modes.

CHAPTER 6

Rejoining the Planned Route

IN THIS CHAPTER we return to the topic of departing the flight route and consider the one remaining possibility: What if you depart the FMC route but then have a chance to rejoin it later? This situation is more common than you may think. In this chapter we discuss a variety of common ATC directives that ask you to make temporary deviations from the FMC route and then to return to it. The skills you will use for these maneuvers are a blend of those you learned in previous chapters. During these maneuvers you will depart the route, disengage LNAV and/or VNAV in favor of simpler guidance functions, and later rejoin the route using LNAV and VNAV.

Intercept Leg To

A first example of a "leave the route and come back later" maneuver requires the flight crew to intercept a course to a waypoint that is already a leg in your planned route. A hypothetical midwest flight illustrates this modification. Suppose you are at cruising altitude and are instructed to fly a heading of 230 and intercept J80 to Capital as diagrammed in Figure 6.1.

Your first step is to immediately comply with the heading clearance. The heading clearance takes you off of the FMC route, and ATC expects a response immediately. Your only practical choice is to use the Heading Select function. As soon as you dial the heading and press the Heading Select button, the aircraft turns and you depart the FMC route.

Your second step is to decide whether you can rejoin the path at a later time. Looking at the Route Legs page and the EHSI, you can see that J80 and CAP are already a part of the FMC route. In other words, you have been asked to resume your original FMC route once you intercept the jet route. ATC has in effect given you a shortcut.

The FMC provides a simple way of performing this modification using the same Direct Intercept page you used to handle the direct-to clearance. You begin by pushing the DIR INT button on the CDU. This brings up the Direct Intercept page shown in Figure 6.2.

The prompt at line 6R allows you to enter the name of the waypoint at which you wish to intercept a course. You have been instructed to intercept a course to CAP. You enter CAP at 6L by line-selecting it down from line 3L. This results in the page shown in Figure 6.3.

Once you enter CAP as the waypoint that you would like to fly toward, the Direct Intercept page prompts you to enter a course that you wish to follow to CAP at line 6R. This entry is optional. If no entry is made, the FMC will assume that you want to follow the original course to the waypoint. In this case, that was a course of 269 degrees. If you look at the CAP waypoint at line 1L, you can see that the 267 degrees course is also reflected there. You can enter 269 into line 6R and then press the execute button to get the Route Legs page shown in Figure 6.4.

Your final step is to make a plan for recapturing the FMC path and engaging LNAV and VNAV once again. The solution is to monitor your progress as you make your way toward the intercept point. Upon reaching the intercept point, simply engage LNAV, which will capture the jet route, turn toward CAP, and proceed on course.

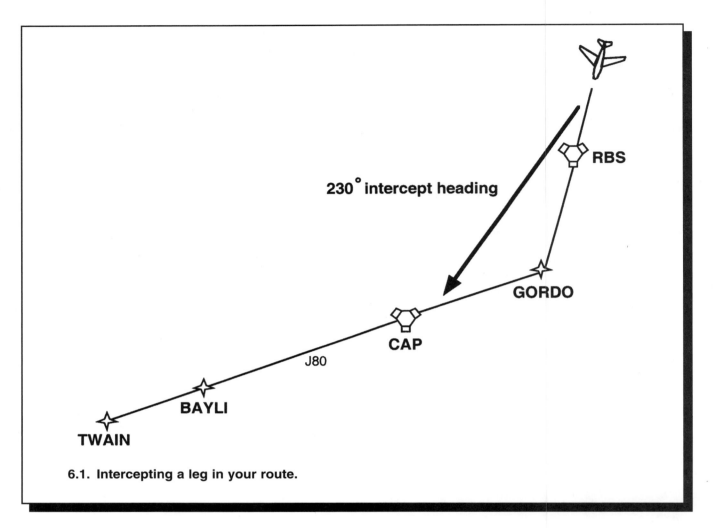

6.1. Intercepting a leg in your route.

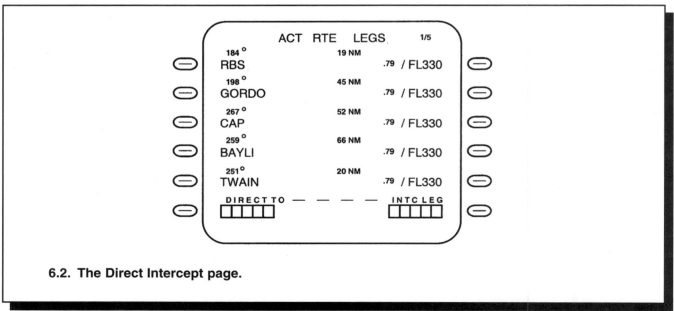

6.2. The Direct Intercept page.

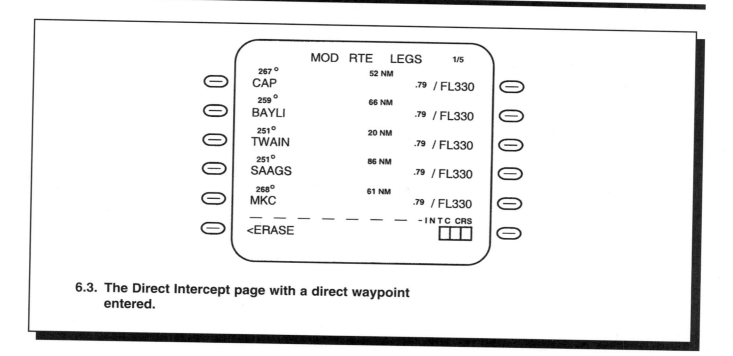

6.3. The Direct Intercept page with a direct waypoint entered.

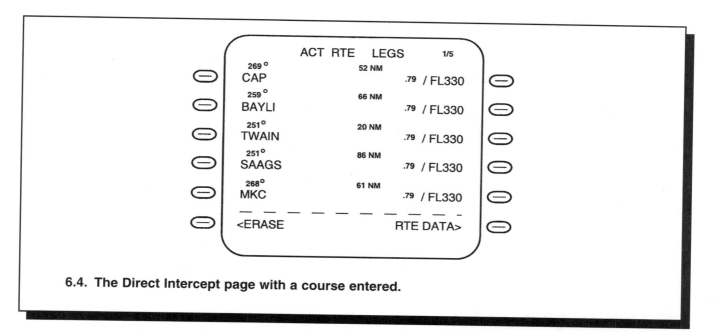

6.4. The Direct Intercept page with a course entered.

Intercept Radial

A common variation on the intercept course maneuver just described is one that requires you to intercept a radial. Radial intercepts are essentially the same as course intercepts except that ATC has asked you to follow a different course to the waypoint. For the intercept course example,

you were allowed to follow the FMC-planned course of 267 degrees to CAP. When you chose CAP as the intercept leg to waypoint, you left the INTC CRS prompt blank. Suppose ATC asks you to fly a heading of 230 degrees and intercept the 080-degree radial from the Capital VOR. This modification is diagrammed in Figure 6.5.

To comply with this request, all you need to do is fill in the INTC CRS prompt after you designate CAP as the

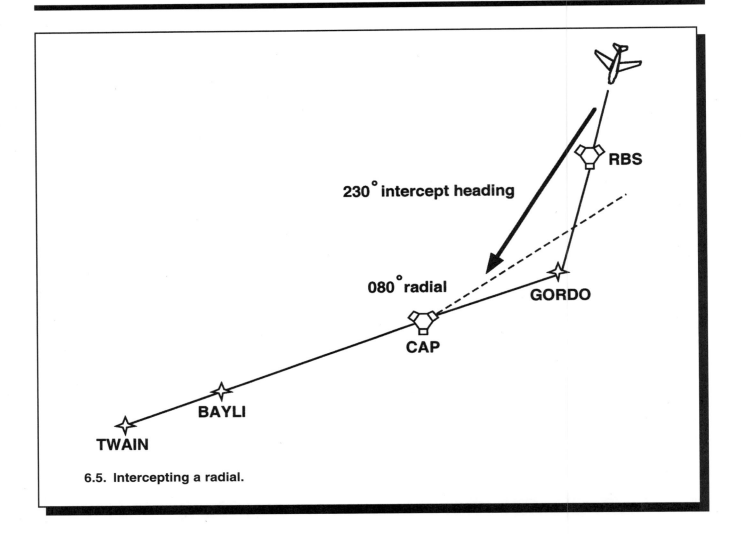

230° intercept heading

080° radial

RBS

GORDO

CAP

BAYLI

TWAIN

6.5. Intercepting a radial.

intercept leg to waypoint. Do you simply enter 080 here? No! Since you are flying inbound to CAP, you need to enter the reciprocal of the radial. Entering 260 into the prompt at 6R will set you up to capture a course that is roughly equivalent to the 080 radial from CAP as shown in Figure 6.6.

Intermediate Level-Off during Climb

A common ATC directive you will often get during a climb is the intermediate level-off. ATC has a lot of airplanes coming in and out of the terminal area and sometimes needs to make adjustments to ensure adequate separation. Your initial departure clearance was to climb to FL230. Prior to departure you dialed 23000 into the Altitude window on the mode control panel. On the Climb page, you see your planned cruise altitude of FL330. You anticipated being cleared up to your planned cruising altitude of FL330 some-

time after departure. You are now approaching FL230 and haven't heard from ATC. What do you do?

The answer to this dilemma is simple. Recall that the airplane will never climb above the altitude that is dialed into the Altitude window on the mode control panel. So what will happen once the aircraft reaches FL230? VNAV will disengage itself and transfer control to the Altitude Hold mode. The aircraft will then stay there until you command it to do something different.

Soon you approach FL230 and the aircraft levels off. After a few minutes, you are then cleared up to FL330. As it turns out, all you really need to do is to dial 33000 into the Altitude window on the MCP and then push VNAV again. Recall that during climb, VNAV does not take seriously the notion of a climb path. That is, there is no pathway-in-the-sky that the aircraft tries to follow as there is during a VNAV descent. If at any time the climb progress of the aircraft is suspended and then resumed, the FMC simply recalculates a new top-of-climb point. If you look down at your EHSI,

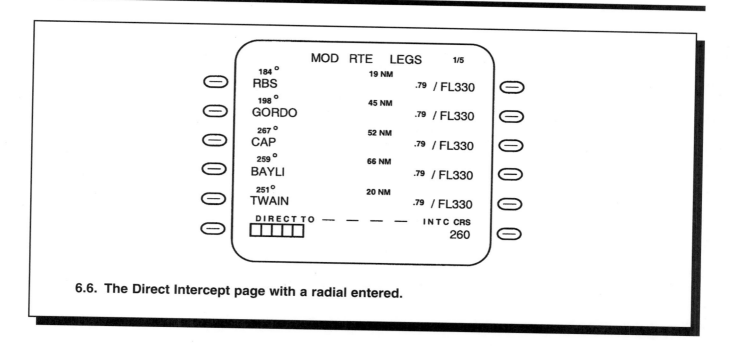

6.6. The Direct Intercept page with a radial entered.

you will soon see a new top-of-climb point. This top-of-climb point is slightly farther downstream than the original the FMC had calculated before your level-off. If you flip over to the Progress page, you can see the details of your new top-of-climb point displayed at line 5L.

After pushing VNAV again, the aircraft will immediately resume its climb to FL330, and you are back in business.

Early Descent

The trickiest kinds of "leave the path and then rejoin it" maneuvers are those that require you to depart the FMC path during your descent. Unfortunately, they are also the most common, so you will need to understand them quite well. The first maneuver requires that you start your descent early. Suppose that you are 40 NM short of the FMC-planned top-of-descent point, and you are instructed to descend and maintain FL240. You have been asked to start down early. As far as you know, you will still be required to cross Symon at 12,000 feet. You have been asked to start your descent early but to still end up at the same descent restriction. In other words, you have been asked to perform a shallower descent. This situation is diagrammed in Figure 6.7.

Because early descents are so common, the FMC offers a packaged solution on the Descent page. As soon as the line button beside the Capture prompt (line 5R) is pressed, the aircraft begins an immediate descent at a rate of 1,000 feet per minute. This shallow trajectory initially takes the aircraft below the original descent path. During the descent the air-

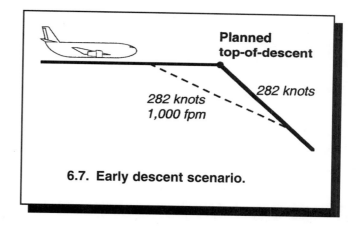

6.7. Early descent scenario.

craft will maintain the original target descent speed that is shown at line 2L on the Descent page.

The aircraft will continue to descend along the shallow trajectory until it crosses the original descent path, which the FMC has not forgotten. Upon reaching the original descent path, the aircraft will intercept the path and resume following it, reaching the crossing restrictions as originally planned.

The flight mode annunciations for the descent capture maneuver can be somewhat puzzling. If you are in LNAV and VNAV prior to using the descent capture feature, the flight mode annunciator will continue to read LNAV and VNAV. This may seem odd since the aircraft has departed the programmed vertical path. The answer to the puzzle is simple. Flying below the originally planned vertical profile

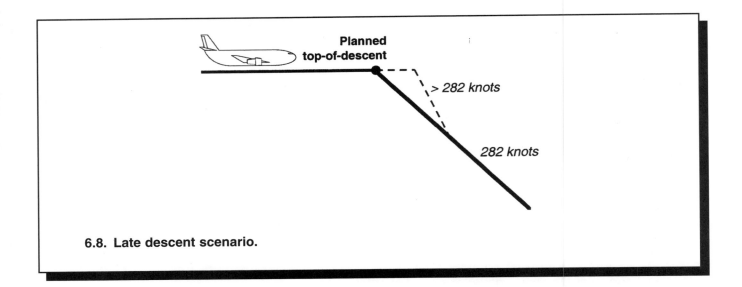

6.8. Late descent scenario.

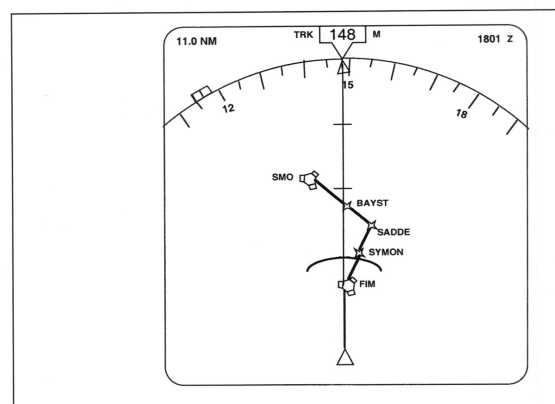

6.9. The green arc showing the end-of-descent point on the EHSI.

is all part of VNAV's plan in performing the descent capture maneuver. The position-tracking components we talked about earlier keep VNAV informed at all times as to the vertical position of the aircraft during the maneuver—all the way up to the point at which VNAV guides the aircraft back onto the original vertical trajectory.

Late Descent

A related maneuver is the late descent. Suppose you are a few miles short of the FMC-planned top-of-descent point and you still haven't heard from ATC giving you clearance to start your descent. You query ATC, who tells you to expect lower in 2 minutes due to crossing traffic. You look down at your EHSI and see that after 1 minute, you will be past the FMC top-of-descent point. You are going to end up in the situation diagrammed in Figure 6.8. You think of having to "slam dunk" the airplane once ATC finally comes through with the clearance. What do you do?

The first thing you want to do in this situation is slow down. Slowing down will lessen the distance by which you overrun the top-of-descent point while you are waiting for your clearance. To slow down, you can simply engage Speed mode using the MCP. You dial in a slower speed, and the aircraft slows immediately. Engaging the Speed mode also kicks you out of VNAV and into Altitude Hold. The good news is that the aircraft is doing just what you want it to: slow to the selected speed and maintain your assigned cruising altitude.

After a minute, ATC calls back and tells you to start your descent. Now the fun begins. You need to get the air-

plane back on the original descent path because you still have to cross Symon at 12,000 feet. To recapture the path, engage the Vertical Speed mode. Dial in a vertical speed that allows you to reach 12,000 feet sometime prior to Symon intersection. How do you know how much vertical speed is enough? The EHSI provides a handy feature that allows you to quickly make this determination. A handy feature of the EHSI called the **green arc** graphically shows you the point at which your aircraft will reach the altitude that is dialed into the Altitude window on the MCP. The green arc shown on the EHSI in Figure 6.9 indicates that you will reach 12,000 feet just slightly before Symon intersection.

Now that you know you are going to make your crossing restriction, you could simply remain in Vertical Speed until you get in the vicinity of 12,000 feet. But that strategy is inefficient and causes too much work. It is much easier to recapture the original descent path and let VNAV handle the rest. Without being careless with your airspeed, dial in a higher vertical speed that will allow you to capture the path prior to reaching Symon. The more aggressive vertical speed will get you down to the descent path quicker. Once the original descent path is reached, you can reengage VNAV and recapture the path. You will then be following the original descent path as if you had never left it.

Chapter Summary

In this chapter you learned some new maneuvers that allow you to part ways with the FMC-programmed route and then rejoin it later. You learned several common situations in which you will be asked to perform these maneuvers.

CHAPTER 7

Human Factors of Cockpit Automation

WHENEVER YOU BRING up the topic of cockpit automation, a popular impression among nonpilots is that cockpit automation eliminates the need for human pilots. An old joke says that the cockpit of the future will contain two members: a pilot and a dog. The pilot is there to feed the dog. The dog is there to bite the pilot in case he or she tries to touch anything. While this old saw is worth a few laughs, 14 CFR 91.3 reminds us:

The pilot in command of an aircraft is directly responsible for, and is the final authority as to, the operation of that aircraft.

Cockpit automation does not relieve you from your duties as a pilot. Rather, automation changes your job to what might best be described as manager-pilot. Sometimes you perform the familiar duties of planning a flight route and steering the airplane along the route yourself. Sometimes you delegate parts of these duties to the automation. When you do delegate responsibilities to the automation, your job changes to that of manager. Throughout the book we have discussed many of the human factors issues associated with using cockpit automation. In this chapter we discuss these issues in more detail.

Staying in the Loop

Easily the most talked-about issue relating to the use of cockpit automation is what is often long referred to as **staying in the loop** or **situation awareness.** The problem of staying in the loop can be simply stated. When a human operator transfers control of a process to an automated system, there is a tendency for the operator's attention to drift onto other matters. Pilots who operate automation-equipped aircraft frequently talk about the problem of remaining aware of what is going on while the automation has control of the aircraft. A Boeing 767 captain once said, "I know I'm not in the loop, but I'm not exactly out of the loop. It's more like I'm flying alongside the loop."

Human factors experts have studied the problem of staying in the loop since assembly-line automation was introduced to the manufacturing industry many years ago. Experts have formulated many theories about why the phenomenon occurs. Some theories argue that it is human nature to move on to other matters once your worries about doing a good job have been satisfied. These theories relate situation awareness to the notion of trust. If the human operator trusts that the automation will do a good job, there is little reward for time spent "looking over the shoulder" of the automation. Other theories suggest that boredom is the culprit. Watching an automation device perform its job flawlessly bores us into a hypnotic-like state in which the events that transpire no longer meaningfully register in our brains.

We can spend countless hours entertaining ourselves with creative theories about why our ability to stay in the loop is challenged when automation is at work, but that misses the point. The important point is that automation does indeed appear to challenge our ability to remain in close contact with what an automated system is doing at any given time. Our only goal is to understand how we can combat the tendency to lose touch with what is going on.

Staying in the loop when using cockpit automation requires that you adopt the idea that you are a manager. Like any good manager, you have a number of management responsibilities on your plate at all times. Throughout this book we have discussed techniques for keeping track of what responsibilities you have during each phase of flight and which responsibilities you have delegated to the automation.

What Guidance Functions Are Currently Engaged?

A first responsibility of the flight crew that makes intelligent use of flight deck automation is to remain at all times aware of what guidance functions are engaged. Your instructors will remind you time and time again that the flight mode annunciator (FMA) is the ultimate source of information about who is in charge of what. The flight mode annunciator tells you at all times what guidance functions are engaged, and your knowledge of those functions tells you what the airplane will ultimately do. Why do instructors have to yell at pilots time and time again about the FMA? Because pilots seem to acquire a popular habit of using their memory to tell them what guidance functions are engaged. For example, if you engage Altitude Hold on the mode control panel, you remember doing that and assume that Altitude Hold is engaged. Pilots acquire another habit of relying solely on their perception of what the aircraft is doing to tell them what is going on. One pilot pointed out that when using Level Change to perform a climb, if "the houses are getting smaller," you know that everything is going according to plan.

Although there is nothing wrong with paying attention to the buttons you press and the behavior of the airplane, there are two basic reasons why the FMA must remain a principal information resource for keeping yourself informed about what guidance functions are engaged. First, the complexity of cockpit automation makes the behavior of these systems difficult to predict. Guidance functions have many details, special circumstances, and quirks that can cause them to work differently from what you expect. Second, when unexpected events do occur, cockpit automation does not always provide simple, high-visibility feedback that the crew can easily recognize. An unexpected guidance function disengagement is displayed to the crew using a few small symbols on the flight mode annunciator. If the crew hopes to catch an event like this, they had better be looking for it. Consider the case of the Eastern Airlines L-1011 that crashed near the Florida Everglades. While attending to a possible malfunction in the cockpit, the crew inadvertently disengaged the autopilot. The aircraft entered a very slow spiraling descent that went unnoticed and crashed into the Everglades.

What Targets Is the Automation Trying to Achieve?

A second responsibility of the flight crew that makes intelligent use of cockpit automation is to remain aware of what targets each engaged guidance function is aiming to achieve and the progress that the automation is making in trying to achieve them. For every guidance function discussed in this book, we have tried to point out the places that

the crew can go to get information about what targets are set and how the aircraft is progressing toward those targets. The informed crew monitors this information to ensure that the aircraft is executing the intended plan. The second part of target checking is to ensure that the targets themselves are correct. When the simpler guidance functions are being used, the targets are entered in the windows of the mode control panel for all to see. When LNAV or VNAV are being used, however, the targets are somewhat hidden among the pages of the CDU.

It is also important for the crew to verify the calculations made by the FMC. Do your own descent calculations, and compare them with the FMC-calculated top-of-descent. Will you land with the appropriate amount of fuel? Do the ETAs agree with what you had planned?

Sharing Your Intentions, Goals, and Information

It is important not only to keep track of what the automation plans to do next but also to keep all other crew members informed of your intentions and the actions you take with the automation. It is often easy to forget that there are two pilots in every automation-equipped flight deck. It is important to avoid situations in which one crew member decides on a plan and enters it into the CDU, while the other crew member remains in the dark. Some companies enforce a procedure that states that whenever a target is set by one crew member, the other crew member must review and acknowledge the action.

In short, if you know the answers to "What's it doing now?" and "What's it going to do next?" you will less often find yourself having to ask "Why did it do that?" Your brain should be 50 NM ahead of the airplane, not behind it.

Knowing How and When to Use Cockpit Automation

Another human factor of cockpit automation use concerns understanding the capabilities and limitations of the automation as well as the advantages and disadvantages of using it in any situation. The classic example that illustrates this point is choosing guidance functions to comply with clearances in a busy terminal area. Remember that when you need to make route modifications, LNAV and VNAV are generally heads-down functions, whereas the simpler guidance functions are heads-up functions. If you need to be paying attention out the window, think twice about trying to program the FMC. Similarly, if the FMC has you stumped during a maneuver, think about not using it. Don't allow your attention to be drawn inside the cockpit for long periods of time. Fly the airplane first, and worry about solving your FMC mystery when you are down on the ground.

Being Aware of Common Automation Pitfalls

Aside from the procedures that you follow when using cockpit automation, the intelligent use of the automation requires that you be aware of a number of pitfalls that can arise when human and machine work together. When the first flight management computers came online in the early 1980s, human factors experts Earl Wiener and Ren Curry were instrumental in identifying many of the potential traps that can occur in the modern automated flight deck. The problems they pointed have manifested themselves in the form of mishaps. We discuss several of them here.

Blunders Made Easy

The power of the flight management computer allows the flight crew to command maneuvers with the push of a button or a few keystrokes. As Wiener points out, this allows the crew to make large blunders with small actions. Consider the crash of the American Airlines 757 en route to Cali, Colombia, in December 1995. Although no definite conclusions have been drawn, there is reason to believe that the crew typed in what they thought was the identifier for one waypoint when in fact they had entered the identifier for a different waypoint. The route from the aircraft's present position to the erroneous waypoint took the aircraft into mountainous terrain. Wiener notes that automation lowers the requirements for making big errors. With cockpit automation, disaster can sometimes be just an errant keystroke away. Accidents like the one in Cali emphasize the importance of using all available sources of information in the cockpit: the flight instruments, the EHSI, the many pages of the CDU, ATC, and the opinions of the other crew members on board.

Automation Can Mask Problems

Automated systems are sometimes able to compensate for problems that arise, avoiding the need to command the crew's attention. In some cases this saves the crew the trouble of having to deal with the problem. In other cases it can result in near disaster. Wiener presents the case of a China Airlines 747 heading for Los Angeles that developed a gradual power loss in its number 4 engine while cruising at FL410. As the engine thrust gradually deteriorated, the yaw damper corrected the yaw tendency by adding increasing amounts of rudder correction. An automatic correction that is part of the yaw damper's normal job, the crew never noticed the reduced engine output. Eventually the engine output fell below what could be corrected by the yaw damper, and the aircraft rolled to right and entered an almost vertical nose dive. The crew was fortunate to regain control of the aircraft at 9,500 feet and saved the day. One can argue that the engine output was at all times reflected on the engine indicators and that the crew had not been monitoring them. While this may be true, it is also true that the yaw damper removed an important cue about the failing engine: the feel of an aircraft that was abnormally yawing to the right.

Automation Overtrust

The powerful capabilities of cockpit automation can naturally provide us with a sense of trust in its abilities to perform the duties that we assign to it. If we couldn't trust an automated system, why would we ever use it? There are some cases in which the flight crew's trust of the automation can be put to test. Consider the case of a Texas International DC-9, departing Denver. The stick shaker went off as the aircraft reached a critical speed on the takeoff roll. The crew aborted the takeoff and overran the runway. The stick shaker was a false alarm. The crew trusted the errant warning system, and the takeoff resulted in a mishap. If you can't trust a warning system, who can you trust?

Loss of Manual Flying Skills

Cockpit automation systems reduce the need for human pilots to manually perform many traditional piloting duties. After a time these manual flying skills naturally begin to atrophy. Wiener queried 200 Boeing 757 pilots regarding their feelings about cockpit automation and skill degradation. Fifty percent of the pilots expressed concern about losing their manual flying skills due to their use of the automation. Ninety percent of the pilots reported that they manually operated the aircraft during a portion of the flight in order to keep their skills sharp.

Chapter Summary

In this chapter we identified several ways in which using cockpit automation can lead to undesirable circumstances. These negative aspects of cockpit automation seem to be naturally occurring phenomena when humans share responsibilities with machines when performing critical tasks. Rather than attempt to eliminate these problems, human factors experts believe that the best way to confront automation problems is to raise our level of awareness and remain on the lookout for them at all times when using cockpit automation.

CHAPTER 8

Putting It All Together

THROUGHOUT THE BOOK we have introduced you to the features of the modern airline cockpit, one by one, taking time out to explain how things work and why they work the way they do. In this chapter we put to use what you have learned by walking you through a transcript of an actual flight from SFO to LAX.

The first aim of this chapter is to show you how everything you have learned can be put to use during an everyday flight. The second aim is to help point out what you now understand and what you might need to review. When you can read through this chapter and understand everything that happens, you can feel confident that you have mastered the important concepts that this book has attempted to convey. If any of the events that transpire during the flight still seem puzzling, you can go back to the appropriate sections of the book for some review.

Preflight

After doing a walk-around of the aircraft, you start the APU and work through your checklist. You then call clearance delivery for your IFR clearance. Clearance delivery responds:

"Cleared to the Los Angeles airport via the Porte Three departure, Avenal transition, as filed. Climb and maintain flight level two three zero, expect flight level three three zero, one zero minutes after departure. Departure frequency is one three two point zero five. Squawk two four zero four."

You can now start building your route in the FMC (Figure 8.1). Starting off on the Ident page, you check to make sure the navigation databases are current. After doing this, you hit the 6R line button and move on to the Pos Init page. You enter KSFO into line 2L. The FMC responds by calling up the lat/long coordinates for SFO. You flip over to the second page of the Pos Init page and remember that this airplane has GPS. You line select the position the GPS unit reports and plug it into line 5R on the Pos Init page. Again you hit the 6R line button, which advances you to the next page in the preflight sequence. You type in SFOLAX1 for the company route. You press the Departures button on the front of the CDU, which moves you over to the KSFO Departures page. You select the Porte Three departure, Avenal transition as you have been instructed in your departure clearance. You again follow the 6R line button prompt and have a quick look at the Route page to see how your route is shaping up. Another 6R page prompt and you arrive at the Perf Init page. You enter the zero fuel weight, fuel reserves, cost index, your cruising altitude of FL330, and the predicted winds at FL330. Finally, moving over to the Takeoff Ref page you enter the outside air temperature. You check the bottom of the Takeoff Ref page and see the PREFLIGHT COMPLETE annunciation.

You briefly flip back through the pages of the CDU that you have just filled out to make sure you entered everything correctly.

Taxi

The aircraft is now ready to push. You disconnect ground power, call for a pushback clearance, and get cleared to push. As the tug pushes you out into the alley, you ask the first officer to start the engines. After both engines are started, you call for the After Start checklist. You now contact ground control and ask for a taxi clearance. *Taxi to runway 1L via the outer. Hold short of runway 1L."* You push the thrust levers forward slightly, and the aircraft begins to roll forward. At the end of the alley, you turn onto the Outer taxiway. You slowly make your way down the Outer and turn left toward runway 1L and apply the brakes.

```
┌─────────────────────────────────┐          ┌─────────────────────────────────┐
│          IDENT          1/1      │          │         POS INIT        1/2      │
│   MODEL          ENG RATING      │          │                    LAST POS      │
│   737-600            22K         │          │              N037°37.5 W122°21.8 │
│   NAV DATA          ACTIVE       │          │  REF AIRPORT                     │
│   SMC6268661   SEP29OCT27/01     │          │  KSFO        N037°37.1 W122°22.3 │
│                                  │          │   GATE                           │
│                                  │          │   - - - -                        │
│   OP PROGRAM                     │          │                    SET IRS POS   │
│   549849-001 (U10.0)             │          │              N037°37.2 W122°22.4 │
│                                  │          │   GMT - DY / MON                 │
│ _ _ _ _ _ _ _ _ _ _ _ _ _ _      │          │   1712.3 ᶻ                       │
│ <INDEX             POS INIT>     │          │  <INDEX              ROUTE>      │
└─────────────────────────────────┘          └─────────────────────────────────┘

┌─────────────────────────────────┐          ┌─────────────────────────────────┐
│        MOD   RTE        1/2      │          │      KSFO DEPARTURES    1/1      │
│   ORIGIN            DEST         │          │  SIDS               RUNWAYS      │
│   KSFO             KLAX          │          │  PORTE3 <SEL>      <SEL> 01L     │
│   CO ROUTE         FLT NO        │          │  TRANS                           │
│   SFOLAX1          - - - -       │          │  AVE    <SEL>                    │
│   RUNWAY                         │          │                                  │
│   1L                             │          │                                  │
│   VIA              TO            │          │                                  │
│   PORTE3           WAGES         │          │                                  │
│                                  │          │                                  │
│   J1               AVE           │          │                                  │
│ _ _ _ _ _ _ _ _ _ _ _ _ _ _      │          │ _ _ _ _ _ _ _ _ _ _ _ _ _ _      │
│                    PERF INIT>    │          │ <INDEX              ROUTE>       │
└─────────────────────────────────┘          └─────────────────────────────────┘

┌─────────────────────────────────┐          ┌─────────────────────────────────┐
│         PERF INIT       1/1      │          │       TAKEOFF REF       1/2      │
│   GW / CRZ CG      TRIP/CRZ ALT  │          │  OAT             VSPDS     V1    │
│   107.2 / 23.6%   19000 / FL330  │          │  19  °C          131 >  131 KT  │
│   PLAN / FUEL      CRZ WIND      │          │  SEL TEMP                 VR    │
│   16.6 / 16.6      075°/ 24      │          │  - - - °C        132 >  132 KT  │
│   ZFW              ISA DEV       │          │  TO N1                    V2    │
│   90.6             - - - °C      │          │  87.3/87.3%      139 >  - - - KT│
│   RESERVES         T/C OAT       │          │  FLAPS           GW    / TOW    │
│   6.0              - - - °C      │          │  5           107.2 /  107.2     │
│   COST INDEX       TRANS ALT     │          │ _ _ _ PRE-FLIGHT COMPLETE _ _ _ │
│   20               18000         │          │                                  │
│ <INDEX             TAKEOFF>      │          │ <INDEX                           │
└─────────────────────────────────┘          └─────────────────────────────────┘
```

8.1. CDU preflight pages.

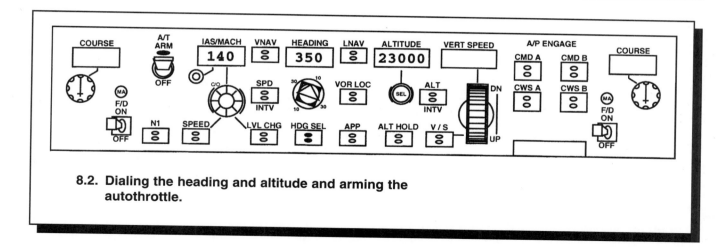

8.2. Dialing the heading and altitude and arming the autothrottle.

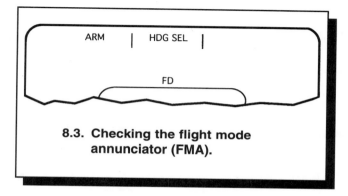

8.3. Checking the flight mode annunciator (FMA).

At the runway threshold, you remember that your departure clearance gave you an initial altitude of FL230. The first officer dials 23000 into the Altitude window on the mode control panel along with the takeoff safety speed of 140 knots. You acknowledge this with a point of the finger. The Porte Three departure procedure requires that you follow a heading of 350 degrees until reaching 4 DME from the San Francisco VOR. You double-check the Route Legs page and see that the 4 DME waypoint is indeed the active waypoint. You decide to use Heading Select to fly this initial portion of the procedure and ask your first officer to dial the 350 heading into the Heading window and press the Heading Select button (Figure 8.2).

You remember to verify that the flight directors are turned on and that the autothrottle is armed. You see that the switches are thrown on the MCP (Figure 8.2) and that the FMA is annunciating FD and ARM for the autothrottle mode (Figure 8.3).

You call for the Before Takeoff checklist and quickly run through it.

Takeoff

Soon you get the call. *"Climb and maintain flight level 230, winds two niner zero at six, cleared for takeoff runway one left."* You push the thrust levers forward about halfway and check your engine indicators. You appear to have two good engines. You press a takeoff/go-around button (TOGA) on the thrust levers. The autothrottle aims for the takeoff thrust calculated by the FMC. The engines spool up, and the aircraft is moving at about 80 knots. You call out "takeoff thrust" to the first officer. The first officer adjusts the thrust levers slightly and announces that your target takeoff thrust is set. You keep your hand on the thrust levers ready to pull them back to idle in case something doesn't look right. The first officer calls out V1 speed. You remove your hand from the thrust levers as you reach the point of no turning back. At your planned rotation speed, V_R, you pull back on the yoke and gently lift the airplane off the ground.

On your EADI, your attitude indicator and vertical speed indicators show a positive rate of climb. You call for the landing gear to be raised. The flight director command bars tell you what amount of pitch will give you V_2 plus 15 knots. The flight director command bars are also instructing you to maintain a level roll attitude (Figure 8.4).

Climb

Passing through 800 feet you call for LNAV and VNAV. The first officer presses the two buttons on the MCP (Figure 8.5).

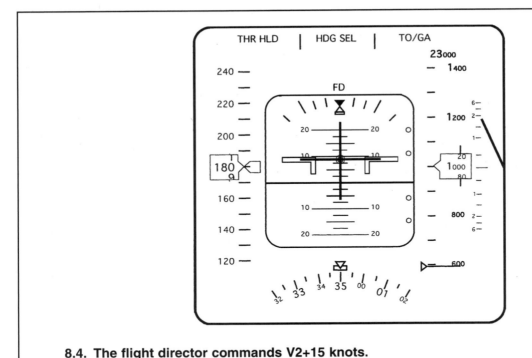

8.4. The flight director commands V2+15 knots.

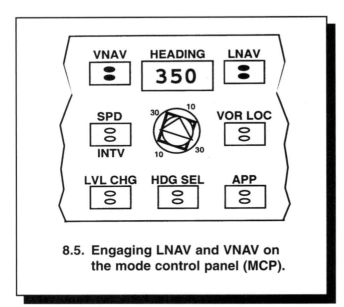

8.5. Engaging LNAV and VNAV on the mode control panel (MCP).

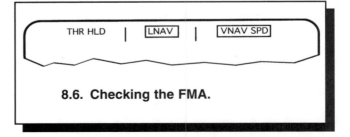

8.6. Checking the FMA.

You glance down at the flight mode annunciator and see that LNAV is annunciated for the roll-engaged mode and VNAV Speed is shown for the pitch-engaged mode. Rectangles appear around both annunciations. The autothrottle mode still reads THR HLD (Figure 8.6).

Climbing out of 1,000 feet, you hear the autothrottle reduce the thrust. A quick glance at the FMA reveals that the autothrottle is now in N1 mode (Figure 8.7). This means that the autothrottle is commanding the climb thrust setting calculated by the FMC.

You think about flipping over to the N1 Limit page to see the target climb thrust, but you are too busy. You remember someone once saying that the FMC provides more information than most pilots have time to look at. You call for the After Takeoff checklist and keep flying.

Down on the CDU, the Route Legs page is showing. You see that the active waypoint is the waypoint defined by a distance of 4 DME from the SFO VOR (Figure 8.8).

Soon your first officer announces that you are approaching the 4 DME waypoint and are about to start a left turn to join the 135-degree course to Porte. Back on the

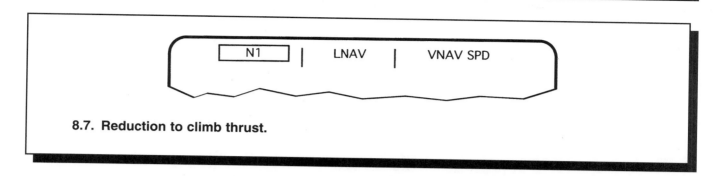

8.7. Reduction to climb thrust.

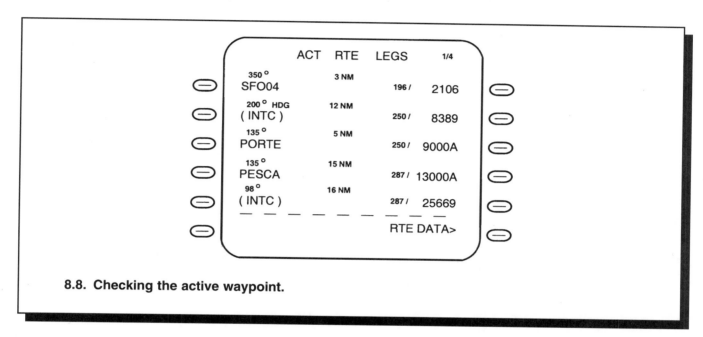

8.8. Checking the active waypoint.

flight director, the command bars begin to command a climbing turn to the left (Figure 8.9).

Back on the Route Legs page you notice that the DME waypoint has gone by. The active waypoint is now the intercept point on the 135-degree radial off of the Point Reyes VOR. The heading to this waypoint is 200 degrees and the one that the flight directors are commanding now (Figure 8.10).

You work the yoke and keep the attitude indicator lined up with the flight director. You are following the FMC's guidance commands closely even though there is a little chop climbing out.

Passing though 8,000 feet, your first officer flips over to the Climb page to check the economy climb speed (Figure 8.11). You see that the FMC is planning to keep your speed at 240 knots until reaching 10,000 feet. ATC calls: *"Resume normal speed."* You decide to let the FMC speed the airplane up passing through 10,000 feet, which should be in about 30 seconds.

You reach up to the MCP and press the CMD button and let go of the yoke. You see the flight director move, commanding slight adjustments in the pitch and roll attitude of the aircraft. The autopilot is now following the flight director automatically (Figure 8.12).

The CMD annunciation on the FMA indicates that the autopilot has indeed engaged (Figure 8.13).

In a moment the aircraft initiates a smooth turn to capture the PYE 135 radial. Not a second too soon or late, the airplane uses a cozy 15 degrees of bank. Just before the intercept point, the aircraft starts to roll out. A perfectly planned and executed turn, you roll out onto the radial in style.

You get a call from Bay Departure telling you to contact Oakland Center. Your first officer dials in the frequency and makes the call. Oakland Center responds by clearing you up to your planned cruising altitude: *"Climb and maintain FL330."* Your first officer reaches up to the Altitude window on the MCP and dials in 33000 (Figure 8.14). You call out

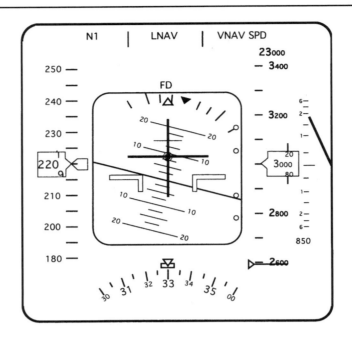

8.9. Flight director commands a climbing left turn.

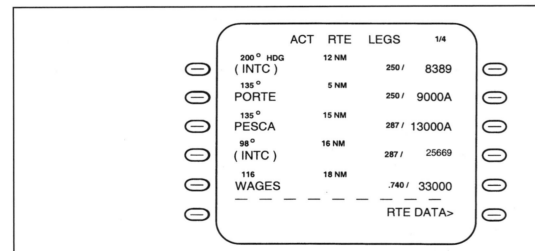

8.10. The Route Legs page advances to the next active waypoint.

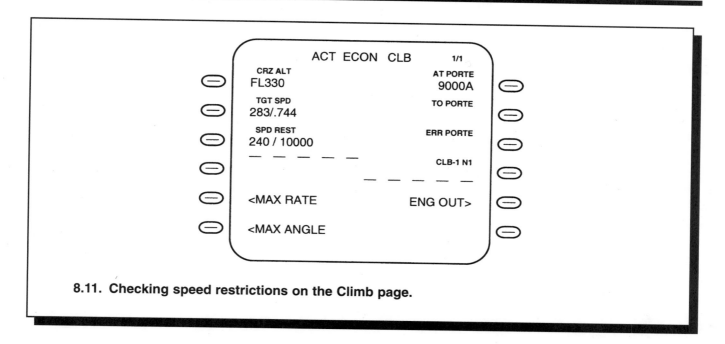

8.11. Checking speed restrictions on the Climb page.

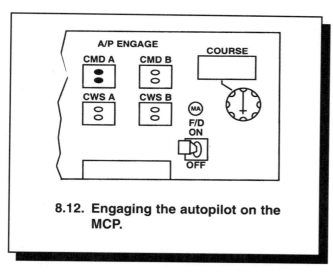

8.12. Engaging the autopilot on the MCP.

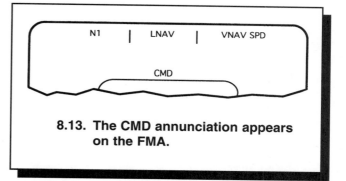

8.13. The CMD annunciation appears on the FMA.

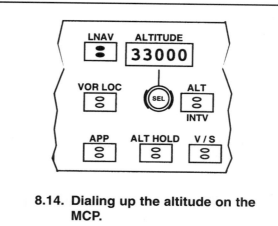

8.14. Dialing up the altitude on the MCP.

33000 and point to the Altitude window to let the first officer know that you are in the loop.

Established on course, you are now on your way to Porte intersection along your planned route to Los Angeles International. You reach down to the CDU and push the Progress button. The Progress page shows you your ETA and fuel remaining at each waypoint along your route. You see that you are now 71 NM short of the point at which the FMC predicts that you will reach your assigned cruising altitude of FL330 (Figure 8.15).

Passing Porte intersection, you look down to the EHSI and see the symbol indicating the top-of-climb point (Figure 8.16).

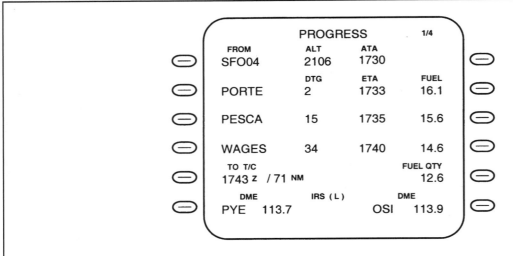

8.15. Checking the top-of-climb point on the Progress

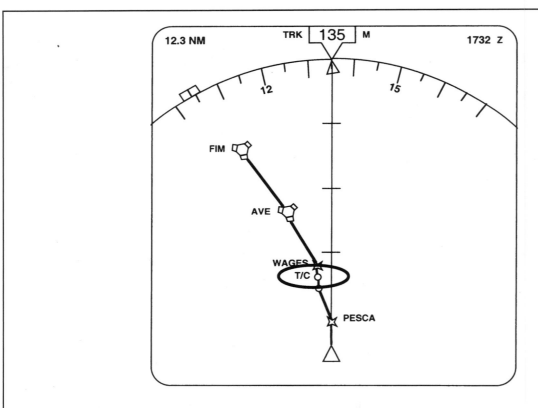

8.16. Checking the top-of-climb point on the EHSI.

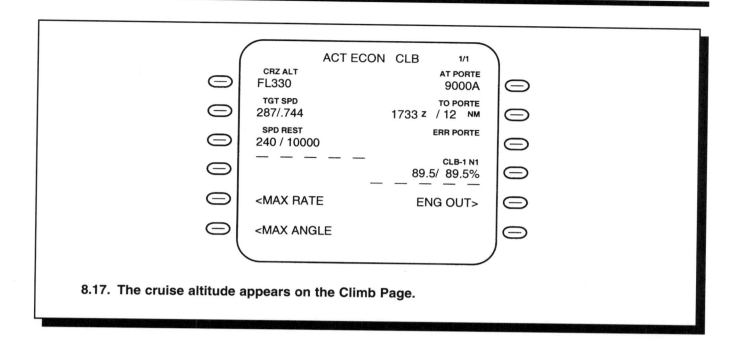

8.17. The cruise altitude appears on the Climb Page.

You reach down to the CDU and call up the Climb page. You see your assigned cruising altitude of FL330 appearing at line 1L (Figure 8.17).

The aircraft continues to climb. As you approach your assigned cruising altitude of FL330, the aircraft eases back the thrust and levels off.

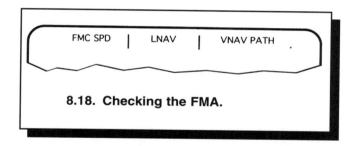

8.18. Checking the FMA.

Cruise

You look down at the flight mode annunciator and see that both the pitch and autothrottle mode are now different. The FMA reads VNAV Path for the pitch-engaged mode and FMC Speed for the autothrottle-engaged mode (Figure 8.18).

You flip over to the Cruise page and check your economy cruise speed (Figure 8.19).

You look at the EHSI and watch Avenal get closer and closer to the aircraft symbol at the bottom of the display. After a while ATC calls with a request: *"Reduce speed to .72 Mach."* You flip back to the Econ Cruise page and enter .72 into line 2L. The title of the page becomes M.720 CRZ (Figure 8.20).

You press the execute button, and the aircraft begins to slow to .72 Mach.

As you approach Avenal, LA Approach gives you the Sadde Six arrival procedure: *"Cleared to the Los Angeles airport via the Sadde Six arrival."* On the CDU, your first officer calls up the KLAX Arrivals page. This brings up a menu of arrival procedures for LAX. The first officer selects the Sadde Six arrival with the Avenal transition (Figure 8.21).

Looking at the list of approaches, you suspect that you will be given the ILS runway 24L approach today but hold off on making any entries for now.

You flip over to the Route Legs page and see that all of the waypoints that make up the Sadde Six arrival procedure have been inserted into your programmed route (Figure 8.22).

You remember from your approach chart that you need to cross Symon at 12,000 feet. Down on your EHSI you see the symbol marking the top-of-descent point (Figure 8.23).

You push the DES button on the CDU. On the Descent page you see your crossing restriction at Symon reflected at line 1 right. At line 2 left you see your economy descent speed. You can see that the FMC plans to meet the crossing restriction and that the descent speed looks reasonable (Figure 8.24).

A few miles short of the FMC's planned top-of-descent point, ATC calls: *"Descend pilot's discretion flight level two four zero, speed your discretion."* The first officer reaches up to the MCP, dials 24000 into the Altitude window, and calls

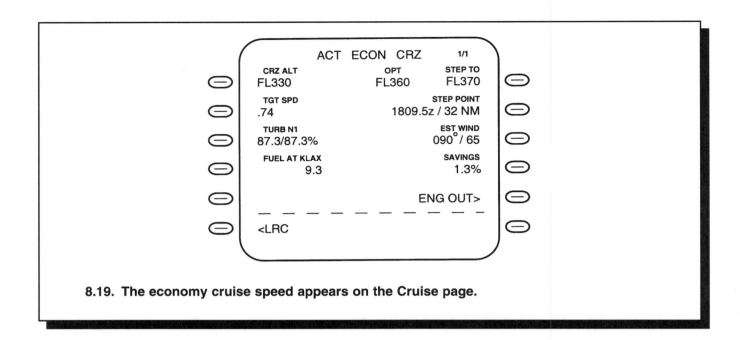

8.19. The economy cruise speed appears on the Cruise page.

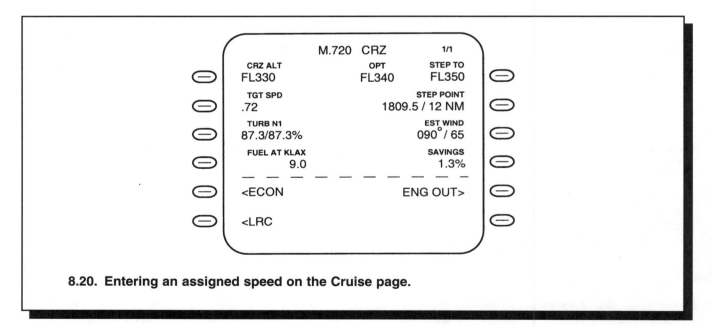

8.20. Entering an assigned speed on the Cruise page.

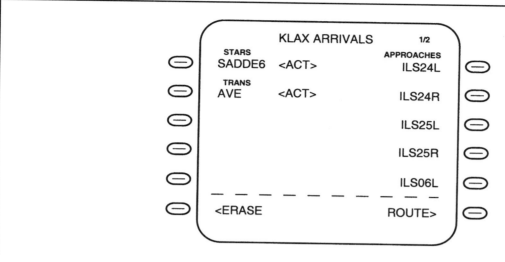

8.21. Selecting an arrival procedure on the Arrivals page.

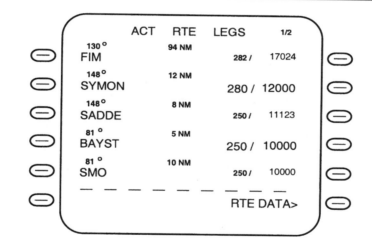

8.22. The waypoints in the arrival procedure appear on the Route Legs page.

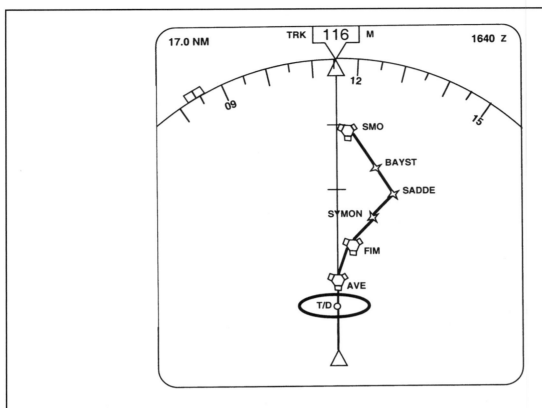

8.23. Checking the top-of-descent point on the EHSI.

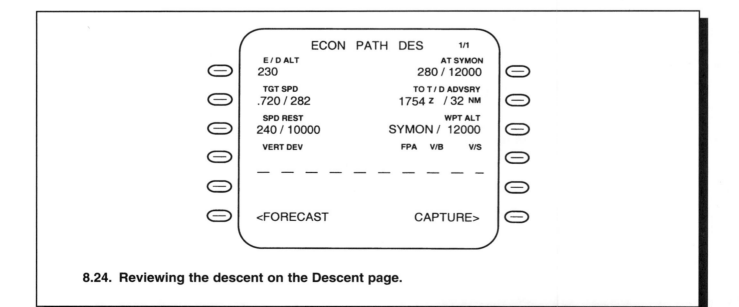

8.24. Reviewing the descent on the Descent page.

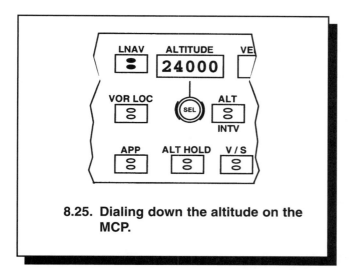

8.25. Dialing down the altitude on the MCP.

out FL240 (Figure 8.25). You acknowledge this entry made by your FO. The aircraft remains at FL330.

Descent

As you reach the top-of-descent point, the thrust levers come back to idle and the aircraft vacates FL330. You glance down at the FMA and see VNAV PATH still annunciated for pitch and ARM annunciated for the autothrottle mode. The thrust levers have been pulled back to idle. You notice some occasional changes in pitch as you make your way down.

You continue down toward FL240 but still no word from ATC about a lower altitude. You put in a call to LA Center requesting clearance to continue your descent. LA Center responds with: *"Unable due to crossing traffic.*

Expect lower in 1 minute." As you approach FL240, the airplane initiates a capture maneuver and levels off. On the FMA, ALT HOLD is now annunciated for the pitch mode and MCP SPD for the autothrottle mode. You start to worry about making the 12,000 feet restriction at Symon. Realizing the Speed function is now engaged, you ask your first officer to dial down your speed to 210 knots. If you're going to overshoot the planned top-of-descent point, you want to overshoot it as little as possible. After a minute, ATC calls: *"Descend and maintain 12,000, cross Symon at 12,000 and 280 knots."* A classic late-descent scenario, ATC has kept you up at altitude and now still wants you to make Symon at 12,000 feet. The first officer quickly dials 12000 into the Altitude window, presses the Level Change button (Figure 8.26), and announces what he has done.

The aircraft starts down to 12,000 feet and you both wonder whether you have already gathered too much energy to make your crossing restriction. Looking down at the EHSI you see that the green arc now appears after Symon (Figure 8.27).

You briefly discuss your options with your first officer. You check your vertical speed and airspeed indicators and decide to take closer control of your descent rate. You call for Vertical Speed, and the first officer dials –3500 feet per minute and presses the V/S button on the MCP (Figure 8.28).

The airplane now begins to descend more quickly as the airspeed moves closer to the "barber pole." You and the FO both notice this and keep a close eye on the airspeed. You pull the lever to extend the airplane's speed brakes. After a few moments you check the EHSI again. The green arc moves closer and closer to Symon intersection. After a minute your first officer points out that the green arc has moved well within the safe side of Symon intersection (Figure 8.29). You now know that you can make your crossing

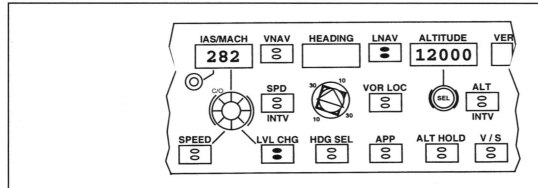

8.26. Engaging Level Change.

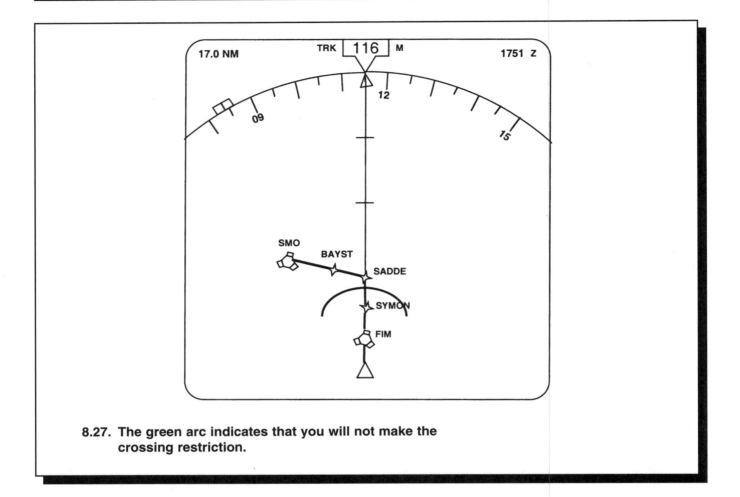

8.27. The green arc indicates that you will not make the crossing restriction.

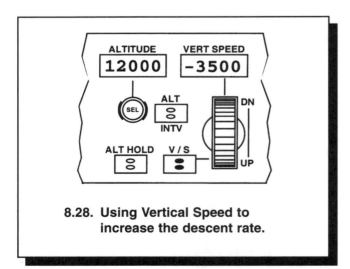

8.28. Using Vertical Speed to increase the descent rate.

restriction. You retract the speed brakes, reengage Level Change, dial a slower airspeed, and allow the aircraft to descend at a more relaxed pace.

Arrival

As you approach Symon intersection SoCal Approach issues the following clearance: *"Proceed direct SMO. Descend and maintain 10,000. Depart SMO heading 070. Expect ILS runway two four left approach."* You look down at the FMA and see that LNAV is still the roll-engaged mode. The first officer pushes the DIR INTC button on the CDU and pulls up the Direct Intercept page (Figure 8.30).

The FO line selects the SMO waypoint down to line 6L. SMO then advances to the top of the page, making it the active waypoint (Figure 8.31).

The FO presses the execute button, and the aircraft turns east to the Santa Monica VOR. Very busy and approaching a crowded terminal area, your first officer

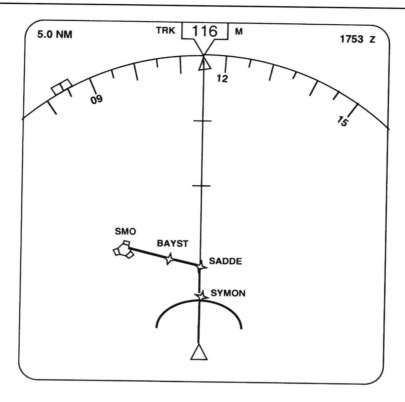

8.29. The green arc indicates that you will make the crossing restriction.

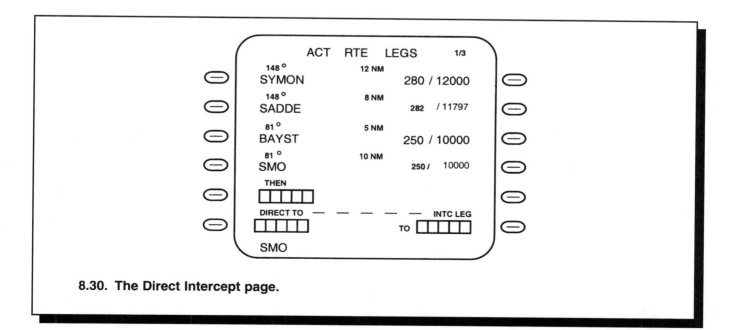

8.30. The Direct Intercept page.

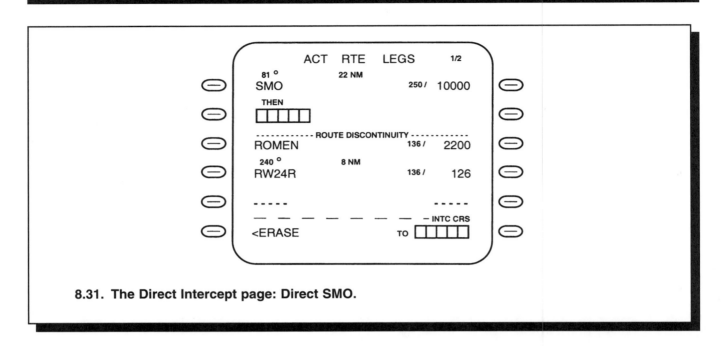

8.31. The Direct Intercept page: Direct SMO.

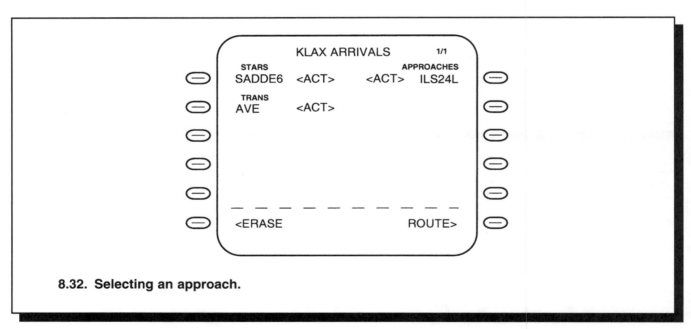

8.32. Selecting an approach.

quickly flips over to the Arrivals page and selects the ILS 24L approach (Figure 8.32).

However useful the FMC may be, you both agree that this is the last time you will go heads-down to make entries into the FMC. You press the autopilot disconnect switch on the control yoke and decide to follow the flight director manually from here on. The first officer dials in the frequency for the ILS runway 24L approach on the navigation radio panel (Figure 8.33).

SoCal Approach calls again: *"Reduce speed to 210 knots."* Looking at the FMA, you see that you are still in Level Change. MCP SPD is annunciated for pitch and ARM for the autothrottle mode (Figure 8.34).

The first officer reaches up to the MCP and dials 210 into the Speed window (Figure 8.35). You call for 1 degree of flaps to be extended.

The flight director commands you to pitch up slightly as the autothrottle reduces the power. ATC calls again:

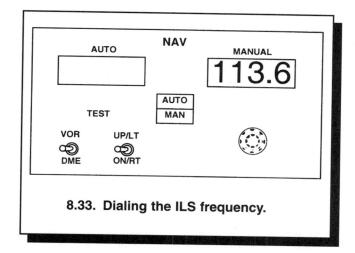

8.33. Dialing the ILS frequency.

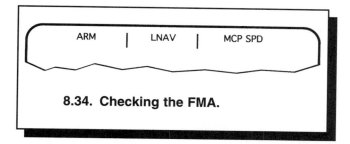

8.34. Checking the FMA.

"Descend and maintain 7,000." The first officer dials 7000 into the Altitude window. The FMA is still indicating Level Change (Figure 8.36).

SoCal Approach calls again: *"Descend and maintain 5,000. Reduce speed to 200 knots."* The first officer dials 200 into the Speed window and 5000 into the Altitude window (Figure 8.37). You acknowledge this input to the MCP.

You look down at the Route Legs page and see the route discontinuity after SMO, followed by the waypoints for the ILS runway 24L approach that you have selected (Figure 8.38).

You realize that LNAV will disconnect at SMO and that you will need to find other means of navigating to the final approach course. Before the aircraft reaches the Santa Monica VOR, you dial 070 into the Heading window in anticipation of using Heading Select once you reach SMO (Figure 8.39).

Approach

As the aircraft reaches SMO, you call for Heading Select. The first officer presses the Heading button, and the flight director commands a left turn and then rolls out on a heading of 070 degrees. You look down at the FMA and see that HDG SEL is now annunciated for the roll-engaged mode (Figure 8.40).

You quickly review your situation in your head. The flight director is commanding a heading of 070 degrees and you are steering to it. The autothrottle is controlling to the speed that appears in the speed window on the MCP.

SoCal Approach calls with another altitude clearance: *"Descend and maintain 4,000."* The first officer dials 4000 into the Altitude window (Figure 8.41), and you continue the descent maintaining the dialed airspeed. You are still in Heading Select and Level Change.

You are now flying parallel to runway 24L and heading away from the airport. SoCal Approach calls: *"Fly heading 160, vectors final approach course, descend and maintain 2,200."* Your first officer dials 160 into the heading window and 2200 into the altitude window (Figure 8.42). You turn and continue the descent.

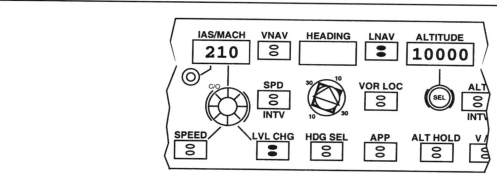

8.35. Dialing the assigned speed: 210 knots.

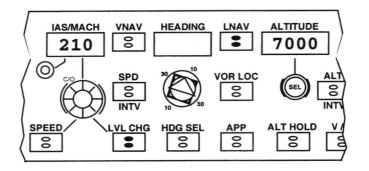

8.36. Dialing the assigned altitude: 7000 feet.

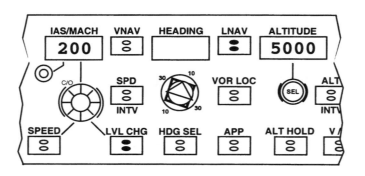

8.37. Dialing the assigned altitude (5000 feet) and the assigned speed (180 knots).

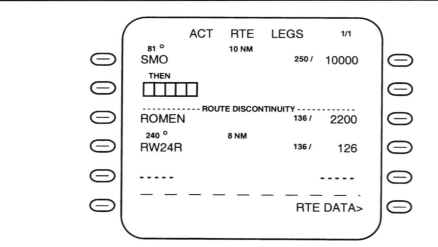

8.38. Route discontinuity on the Route Legs page.

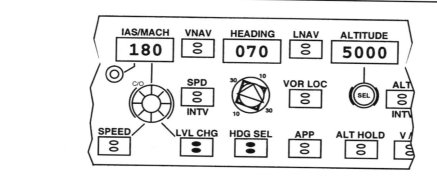

8.39. Dialing the assigned heading: 070.

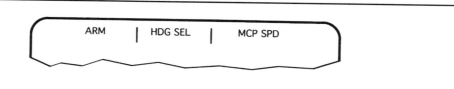

8.40. Checking the FMA.

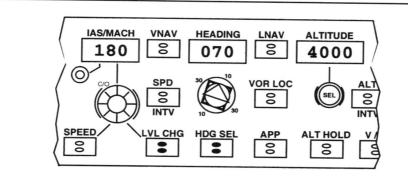

8.41. Dialing the assigned altitude: 4000 feet.

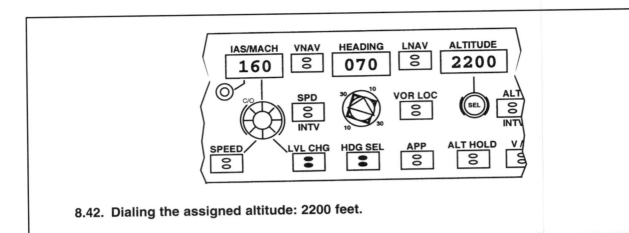

8.42. Dialing the assigned altitude: 2200 feet.

You call for the speed to be dialed down to 180 knots and for 5 degrees of flaps. A minute later you receive your approach clearance: *"Fly heading 210, maintain 2,200 until established, cleared ILS runway two four left approach."* Contact the tower on 133.9. The first officer dials 210 into the heading window, and the flight director commands the turn. A quick glance at the FMA shows that the airplane is engaged in Altitude Hold and Heading Select as you level off at 2,200 feet.

You are now established on an intercept heading for the localizer. You call for the Approach function to be armed. The first officer pushes the Approach button on the MCP. Your FMA annunciates HDG SEL as the roll-engaged mode and VOR/LOC as the roll-armed mode. The pitch-engaged mode is still ALT HOLD while the pitch-armed mode is G/S (Figure 8.43).

You contact LA Tower and get: *"Winds two eight zero at six, cleared to land runway two four right."* As you approach the localizer, your localizer needle comes alive on your EADI. The flight director then commands a turn toward the runway and establishes you on the localizer. The FMA now reads VOR/LOC for the roll-engaged mode. The pitch-engaged mode is still ALT HOLD while the pitch-armed mode is G/S (Figure 8.44).

The aircraft is now locked onto the localizer. As your speed decreases, you call for the gear to be extended, 15 degrees of flaps, and the landing checklist. The airplane approaches the glide slope from below, maintaining level flight. You disconnect the autothrottle and nudge the power forward as the gear and flaps slow the airplane. You call for 25 degrees of flaps. Soon the Approach function captures the glide slope. The pitch-engaged mode now reads G/S on the FMA (Figure 8.45). You call for landing flaps and the final items on the landing checklist.

The familiar localizer and glide slope indicators appear on your attitude indicator together with your flight director

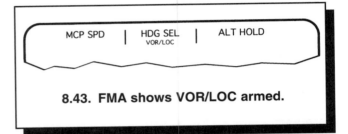

8.43. FMA shows VOR/LOC armed.

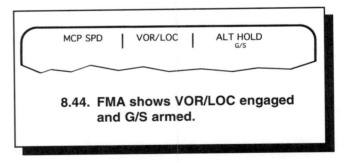

8.44. FMA shows VOR/LOC engaged and G/S armed.

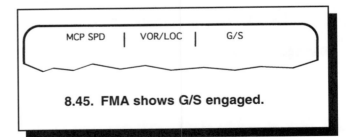

8.45. FMA shows G/S engaged.

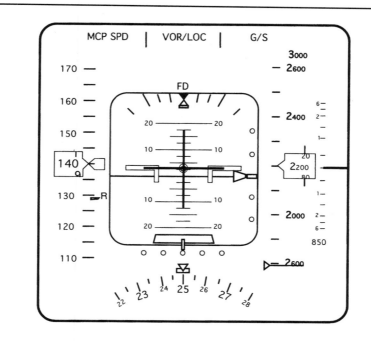

8.46. Localizer and glide slope needles on the EADI.

(Figure 8.46), and all of a sudden you are doing something quite familiar: shooting an ILS approach.

After the flare and the wheels hit the ground, you see the ground spoilers come up. You reach over for the reverse thrust handles and put two engines in reverse. Your autobrakes are hard at work, and together with the ground spoilers and thrust reversers, your speed comes down quickly. You fall below the critical speed of 60 knots, and you have the aircraft under control. You exit the runway and head for the gate.

Chapter Summary

In this chapter you reviewed what you have learned in the context of a real flight from San Francisco to Los Angeles.

CHAPTER 9

Cockpit Automation in Other Airplanes

THROUGHOUT THIS BOOK we have described the kind of automation that one might find in the cockpit of the next-generation Boeing 737. This chapter gives you a quick tour of the cockpits of two other airplanes. Although made by different manufacturers, you will see that all cockpit automation systems are essentially the same. Having invested the time to learn your way around one modern airline cockpit, transitions to other airplanes should be a straightforward exercise.

Boeing 747-400

A look at the Boeing 747-400 illustrates the similarity between the cockpits of other modern Boeing aircraft. Spending the time to note the differences will also allow you to practice what you have learned using the PC-based 747-400 simulator made by Aerowinx (www.aerowinx.com).

Planning the Route

The flight-planning sequence used in the Boeing 747-400 is highly similar to that of the next-generation Boeing 737 we have discussed throughout the book. The control display unit (CDU) found in the 747-400 is shown in Figure 9.1.

The CDU pages used to build a flight route are shown in Figure 9.2.

Flying the Route

Once you are airborne, guiding the airplane along the route you have created can be accomplished using the 747-400's LNAV and VNAV functions. The 747-400's guidance functions are engaged using the mode control panel shown in Figure 9.3.

Monitoring your progress along your route is accomplished using a **navigation display,** shown in Figure 9.4, that provides the "big picture."

Familiar CDU pages provide the crew with the details of what the airplane is doing now and what it plans to do next. Figure 9.5 shows the Route Legs and Progress pages. These pages are accessed using the same LEGS and PROG buttons located on the front of the CDU.

The Climb, Cruise, and Descent pages are shown in Figure 9.6. Rather than having a separate button for each page, these pages are accessed by pressing the **VNAV button** that appears on the front of the CDU.

Modifying the Route

The 747-400 offers the same CDU pages that allow you to proceed direct to a waypoint, intercept a course to a waypoint, and program holds (Figure 9.7).

Flying off the Route

The 747-400 also offers a collection of simple guidance functions that allow the crew to comply with simple head-

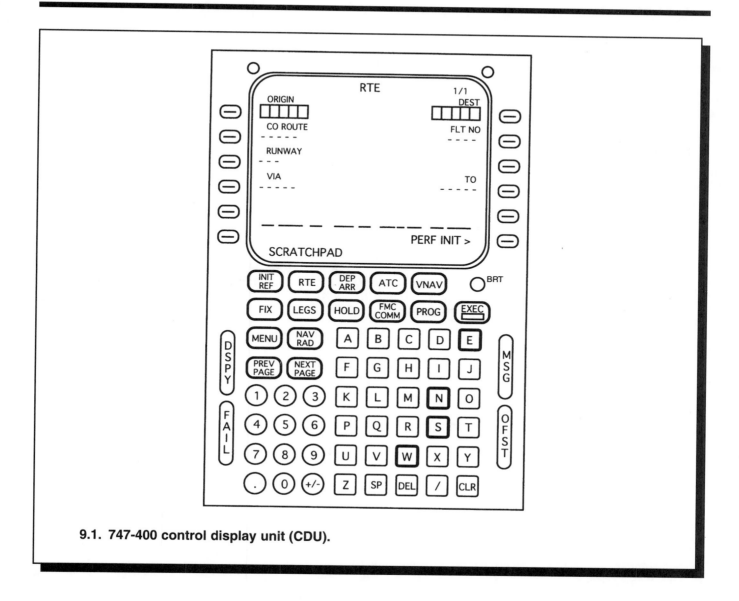

9.1. 747-400 control display unit (CDU).

ing, altitude, and speed clearances. Looking at the MCP in Figure 9.3, you can see that the names of some of the guidance functions are slightly different.

Reading the flight mode annunciator on the 747-400 is probably the only thing that will require significant effort to master. The 747-400 flight mode annunciator appears at the top of the primary flight display and is shown in Figure 9.8.

Different combinations of roll, pitch, and autothrottle modes indicate the guidance functions. Figure 9.9 shows the roll, pitch, and thrust mode annunciations for the guidance functions we have discussed.

Rejoining the Route

Early descents are accomplished in the same manner in the 747-400. As you can see on the Descent page shown in Figure 9.6, the prompt for the function used to carry out an early descent has been renamed DES NOW. Upon activating the DES NOW option, the 747-400 initiates a 1,200-foot-per-minute descent and then recaptures the VNAV path from below.

The 747-400 introduced one vertical guidance function that simplified the process of performing intermediate

IDENT

MODEL
747-400

ENGINES
PW4056

NAV DATA
BE49701001

ACTIVE
JAN02JAN30/01

JAN30FEB27/01

OP PROGRAM
PS14657 SC211

DRAG/FF
+0.0/+0.0

CO DATA
747PW1

< INDEX   POS INIT >

POS INIT   1/2

LAST POS
N037°37.5 W122°21.8

REF AIRPORT
KSFO

N037°37.1 W122°22.3

GATE
72

N037°37.2 W122°22.4

UTC(MAN)
0923z

SET IRS POS
N037°37.2 W122°22.4

< INDEX   ROUTE >

KSFO DEPARTURES   1/1
RTE 1

SIDS
PORTE9

RUNWAYS
01L

EUGEN5

01R

RTE 1   1/2

ORIGIN
KSFO

DEST
KLAX

RUNWAY
01R

FLT NO
1719

CO ROUTE
SFOLAX1

< RTE 2   PERF INIT >

PERF INIT

GR WT
851.5

CRZ ALT
FL330

FUEL
370.8 CALC

ZFW
480.7

BALLAST
-- . --

RESERVES
30.0

CRZ CG
20.0%

COST INDEX
20

STEP SIZE
ICAO

< INDEX   THRUST LIM >

TAKEOFF REF

FLAP/ACCEL HT
20/1500FT

V1
163KT

E/O ACCEL HT
1500FT

VR
175KT

THR REDUCTION
1500FT   CLB

V2
180KT

WIND/SLOPE
H00/U0.0

TRIM
+7.3

CG
19%>

POS SHIFT
RW01R   000FT

< INDEX   THRUST LIM >

THRUST LIM

SEL
- - -

OAT
15°C

TO EPR
1.52

< TO   <SEL>   <ARM>   CLB>

TO 1
< -20%

CLB 1>

TO 2
< -20%

CLB 2>

< TO B

< INDEX   TAKEOFF >

9.2. 747-400 route-planning pages.

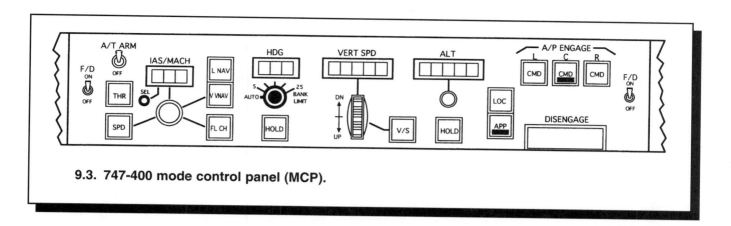

9.3. 747-400 mode control panel (MCP).

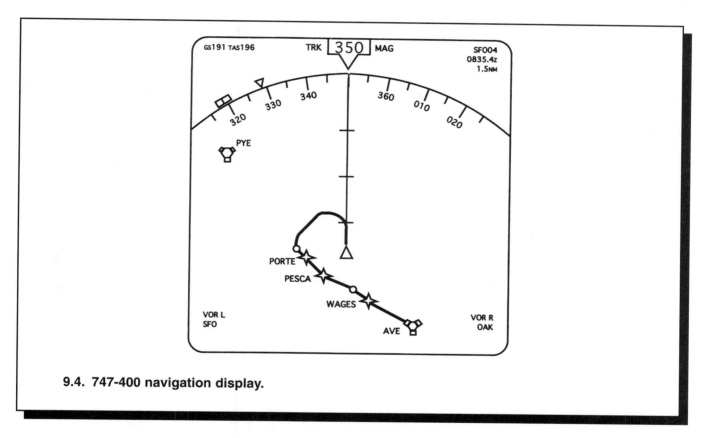

9.4. 747-400 navigation display.

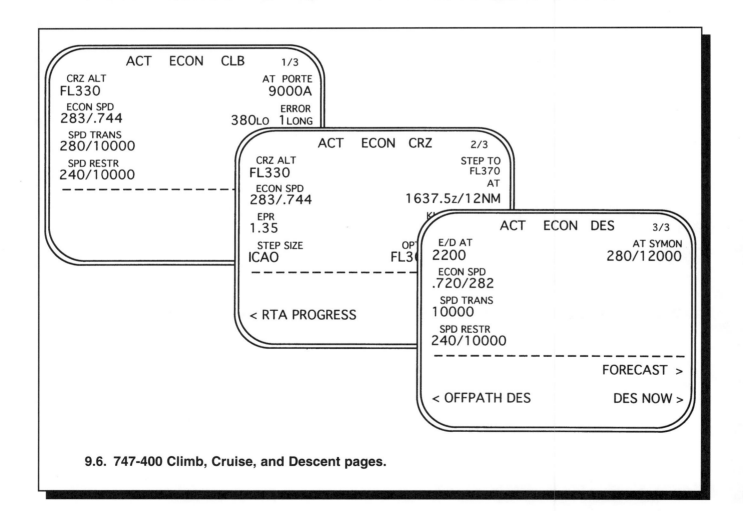

```
        ACT  RTE 1  LEGS      1/4
   350°              3NM
  SFO04                  196/    2106
   200° HDG           12NM
  (INTC)                  250/    8389
   135°               5NM
  PORTE                   250/   9000A
   135°              15NM
  PESCA                   287/ 13000A
   098°              16NM
  (INTC)                  287/   25669
  - - - - - - - - - - - - - - - - - - -
  < RTE 2 LEGS            RTE DATA >
```

```
            PROGRESS          1/4
  LAST        ALT      ATA       FUEL
  SFO04       2106     1615      323.9
  TO          DTG      ETA
  PORTE        2       1619      317.5
  NEXT
  PESCA       15       1624      311.3
  DEST
  KLAX       320       1710      288.5
  ECON  SPD                      TO T/C
  283/.744             1637z / 65NM
  - - - - - - - - - - - - - - - - - - -
  < POS REPORT           POS REF >
```

9.5. 747-400 Route Legs and Progress pages.

```
        ACT   ECON   CLB     1/3
  CRZ ALT            AT PORTE
  FL330                 9000A
  ECON SPD           ERROR
  283/.744       380LO  1LONG
  SPD TRANS
  280/10000
  SPD RESTR
  240/10000
  - - - - - - - - - - - - -
```

```
        ACT   ECON   CRZ      2/3
  CRZ ALT              STEP TO
  FL330                  FL370
  ECON SPD             AT
  283/.744       1637.5z/12NM
  EPR
  1.35
  STEP SIZE            OPT
  ICAO                 FL3
  - - - - - - - - - - - - - - -
  < RTA PROGRESS
```

```
        ACT   ECON   DES      3/3
  E/D AT             AT SYMON
  2200                 280/12000
  ECON SPD
  .720/282
  SPD TRANS
  10000
  SPD RESTR
  240/10000
  - - - - - - - - - - - - - - -
                     FORECAST >
  < OFFPATH DES       DES NOW >
```

9.6. 747-400 Climb, Cruise, and Descent pages.

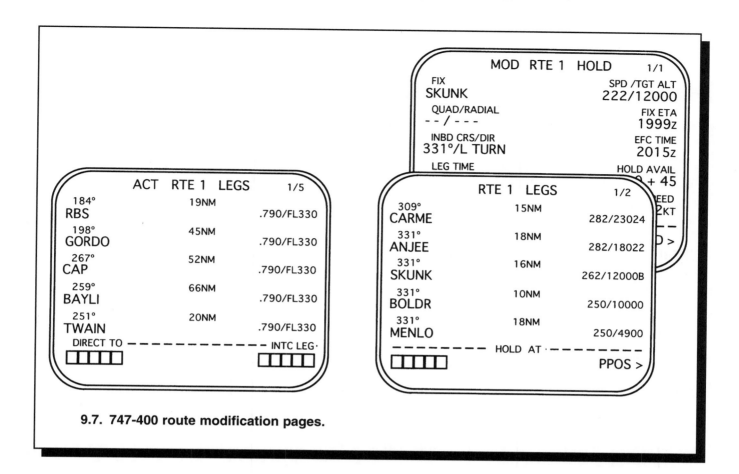

9.7. 747-400 route modification pages.

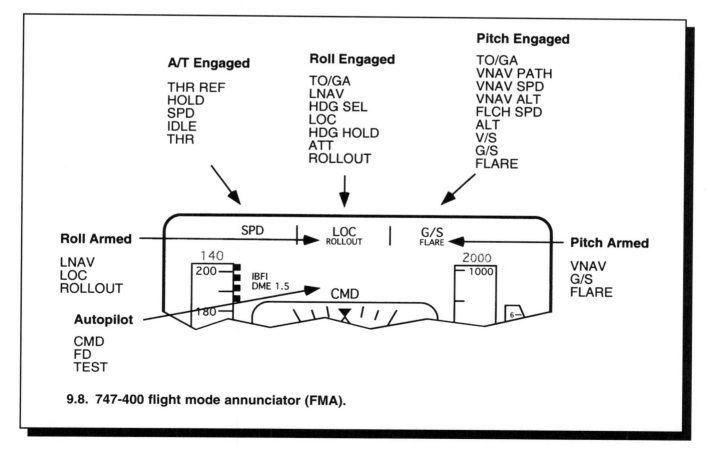

9.8. 747-400 flight mode annunciator (FMA).

GUIDANCE FUNCTION	HOW IT WORKS	MODE ANNUNCIATIONS		
		Roll	Pitch	Thrust
Heading Hold	Roll used to maintain heading dialed into heading window.	HDG HOLD		
LNAV	Roll used to track airplane between waypoints that appear on the Route Legs page.	LNAV		
Loc	Roll used to track dialed localizer.	LOC		
Speed Hold	Thrust used to maintain speed dialed into speed window.			SPD
Altitude Hold	Pitch used to maintain present altitude.		ALT	
VNAV (climb)	Thrust set to climb thrust shown on Climb page. Pitch used to maintain climb speed shown on Climb page.		VNAV SPD	THR REF
VNAV (cruise)	Thrust used to maintain cruise speed shown on Cruise page. Pitch used to maintain cruising altitude shown on Cruise page.		VNAV PTH	THR REF
VNAV (descent)	Thrust moved to idle. Pitch used to maintain airplane on planned descent path.		VNAV SPD	HOLD
Flight Level Change (climb)	Thrust advanced to climb thrust setting on Thrust Limit page. Pitch used to maintain speed appearing in speed window.		FLCH SPD	THR REF
Flight Level Change (descent)	Thrust moved to idle. Pitch used to maintain speed dialed into speed window.		FLCH SPD	HOLD
Approach	Roll used to track dialed localizer. Thrust used to maintain speed dialed into speed window. Pitch used to maintain airplane on glide slope.	LOC	G/S	SPD
Vertical Speed	Thrust used to maintain speed dialed into speed window. Pitch used to maintain vertical speed dialed into vertical speed window.		V/S	SPD

9.9. 747-400 flight mode annunciations.

level-offs during climb and descent. Suppose you have programmed the FMC to climb to a cruising altitude or descend to a crossing restriction altitude but have not yet dialed the altitude on the mode control panel. This situation occurs when you have not yet received a clearance to climb or descend to your desired altitude. In earlier versions of autoflight system software, VNAV disconnects upon reaching the dialed altitude and transfers control to the Altitude Hold function. Resuming your climb or descent to the final altitude requires that you dial the new altitude into the altitude window on the MCP and then reengage VNAV.

A new guidance function called **VNAV ALT** was introduced in the 747-400 to relieve the crew from having to manually switch between guidance functions during the intermediate level-off maneuver. VNAV ALT is illustrated in Figure 9.10. The airplane at the top of Figure 9.10 is operating in VNAV and is about to reach the planned top-of-descent point. If the crew does not dial down the altitude on the MCP, VNAV automatically transfers control to VNAV ALT. Once a clearance is received for a lower altitude and the altitude is dialed into the altitude window, the airplane descends in an effort to

*Airplane remains at altitude and automatically switches to **VNAV ALT** if altitude is not dialed down upon reaching the top-of-descent point.*

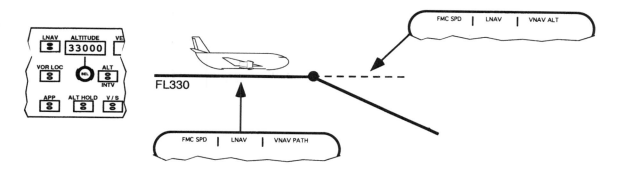

Airplane descends to recapture path when altitude is dialed down. Automatically switches back to VNAV PATH when path is recaptured.

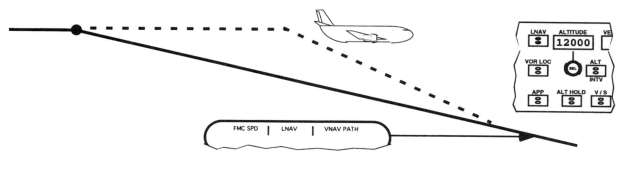

9.10. 747-400 VNAV ALT mode.

recapture the VNAV path. Once the original path is reached, VNAV automatically reengages.

A related feature of the Boeing 747-400 autoflight system, not offered in the 737, is that LNAV and VNAV can be armed. This feature is useful when performing maneuvers in which you are required to depart and then rejoin the planned route. For example, when Heading Hold is used to set up to intercept an airway, the crew can push the LNAV button before, reaching the point of interception of the airway. Although Heading Hold is still engaged, LNAV is now armed and will automatically take over once the intercept point is reached. The same thing is true for VNAV in the 747-400. When using Vertical Speed to dive and capture the planned descent path, the crew can arm VNAV prior to reaching the path. Once the path is reached, VNAV will automatically take over.

Canadair Regional Jet

A look inside the cockpit of the Canadair Regional Jet will allow pilots-in-training to experience the look and feel of the automation found in one of the first jet transport aircraft that they may operate as professional pilots.

Planning the Route

The control display unit (CDU) found in the CRJ is shown in Figure 9.11.

The CDU pages used to build a flight route are shown in Figure 9.12. Although several minor differences exist,

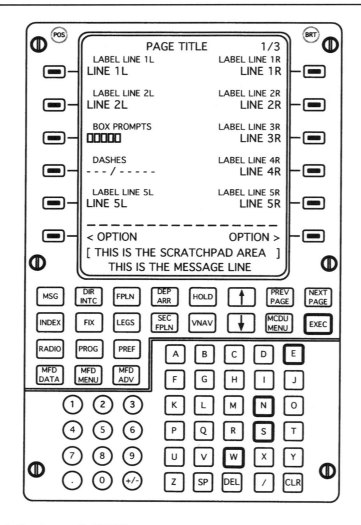

9.11. CRJ control display unit (CDU).

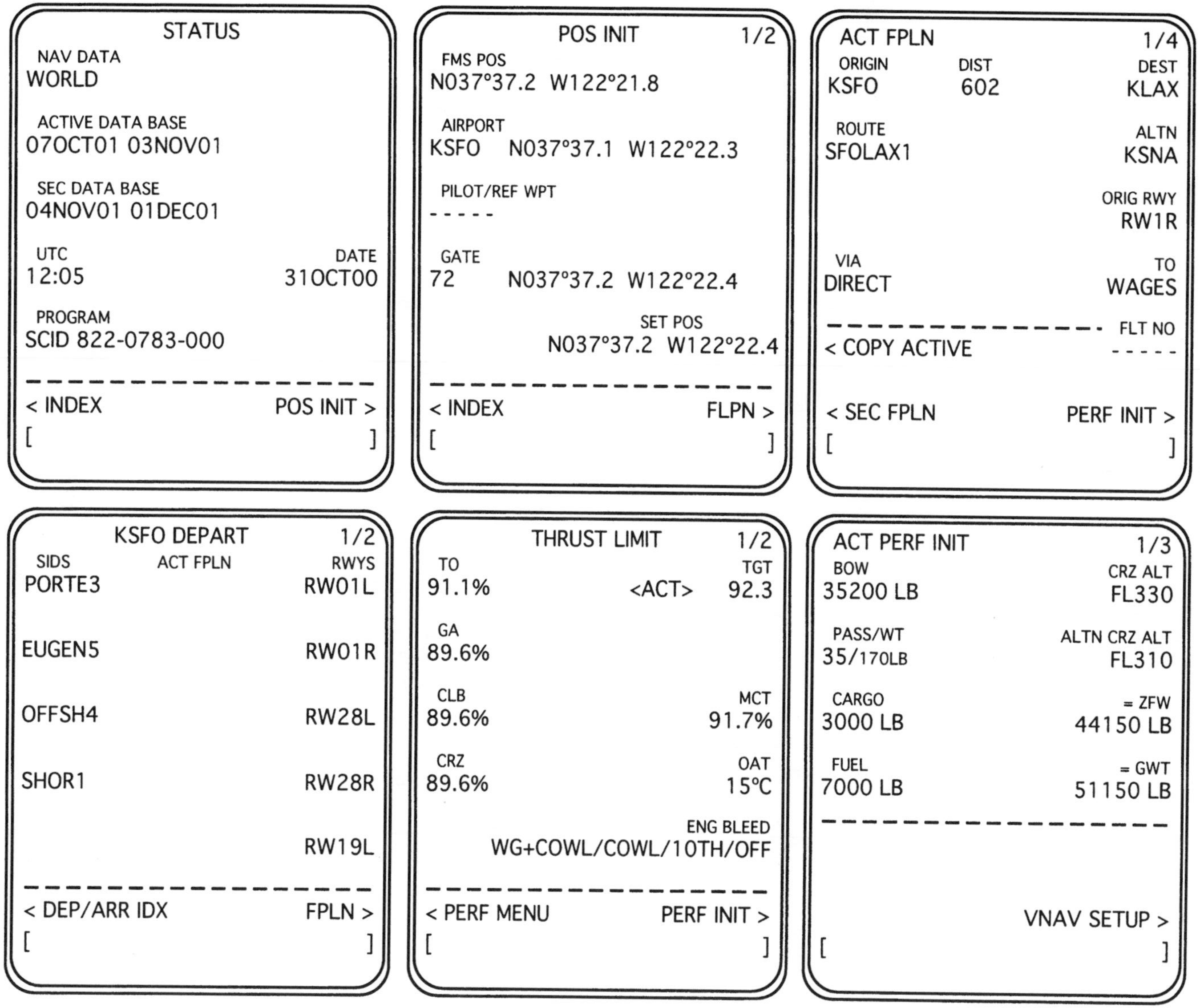

STATUS

NAV DATA
WORLD

ACTIVE DATA BASE
07OCT01 03NOV01

SEC DATA BASE
04NOV01 01DEC01

UTC   DATE
12:05   31OCT00

PROGRAM
SCID 822-0783-000

< INDEX   POS INIT >
[   ]

POS INIT   1/2

FMS POS
N037°37.2 W122°21.8

AIRPORT
KSFO   N037°37.1 W122°22.3

PILOT/REF WPT
- - - - -

GATE
72   N037°37.2 W122°22.4

SET POS
N037°37.2 W122°22.4

< INDEX   FLPN >
[   ]

ACT FPLN   1/4

ORIGIN   DIST   DEST
KSFO   602   KLAX

ROUTE   ALTN
SFOLAX1   KSNA

                    ORIG RWY
                    RW1R

VIA   TO
DIRECT   WAGES

                    FLT NO
< COPY ACTIVE   - - - - -

< SEC FPLN   PERF INIT >
[   ]

KSFO DEPART   1/2

ACT FPLN   RWYS
SIDS
PORTE3   RW01L

EUGEN5   RW01R

OFFSH4   RW28L

                    RW28R
SHOR1

                    RW19L

< DEP/ARR IDX   FPLN >
[   ]

THRUST LIMIT   1/2

                    TGT
         <ACT>   92.3

TO
91.1%

GA   MCT
89.6%   91.7%

CLB
89.6%

CRZ   OAT
89.6%   15°C

                    ENG BLEED
WG+COWL/COWL/10TH/OFF

< PERF MENU   PERF INIT >
[   ]

ACT PERF INIT   1/3

BOW   CRZ ALT
35200 LB   FL330

PASS/WT   ALTN CRZ ALT
35/170LB   FL310

CARGO   = ZFW
3000 LB   44150 LB

FUEL   = GWT
7000 LB   51150 LB

                    VNAV SETUP >
[   ]

9.12. CRJ route-planning pages.

building a flight route with this flight management computer is fundamentally the same.

Flying the Route

Monitoring your progress as you make your way along the planned route is accomplished in part by using a **multifunction display** (MFD) shown in Figure 9.13.

Combining the features of a control display unit and a pictorial navigation display, the MFD allows the crew to configure the display to show text information, a graphical depiction of the route, or a combination of both. For example, the MFD in Figure 9.13 shows information drawn from the Progress page at the top and a graphical navigation display at the bottom. The multifunction display can be set up in different configurations using a set of CDU pages designed for this purpose and shown in Figure 9.14. These pages can be accessed by pressing the MFD MENU button located on the front of the CDU. Using the **MFD Menu pages,** the flight crew can select the features they wish to appear on the MFD.

Familiar CDU pages provide the crew with the details of what the airplane is doing now and what it plans to do next. Figure 9.15 shows the Legs and Progress pages. These pages are accessed using the LEGS and PROG buttons located on the front of the CDU.

One interesting difference about the Legs page in the CRJ is that the active waypoint is shown on the second line rather than the first. The first line of the Legs page shows the previous waypoint (the waypoint that the airplane is coming from).

The Climb, Cruise, and Descent pages are shown in Figure 9.16. These pages are accessed by pressing the VNAV button that appears on the front of the CDU.

Guiding the airplane along the planned route is somewhat easier in a CRJ. This is because the CRJ does not have an autothrottle system. In exchange for having to manually push and pull on the throttle levers, one benefit is that the guidance functions are much simpler.

To guide the airplane along the lateral portion of the FMC route, you can engage the **Navigation** function on the **flight control panel** (FCP) shown in Figure 9.17.

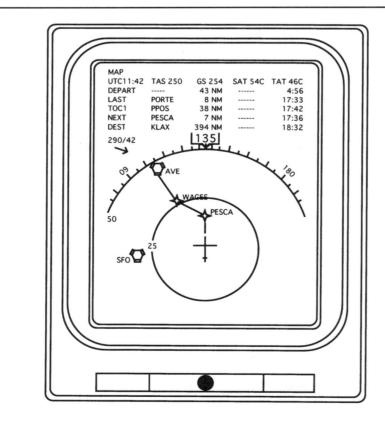

9.13. CRJ multifunction display (MFD).

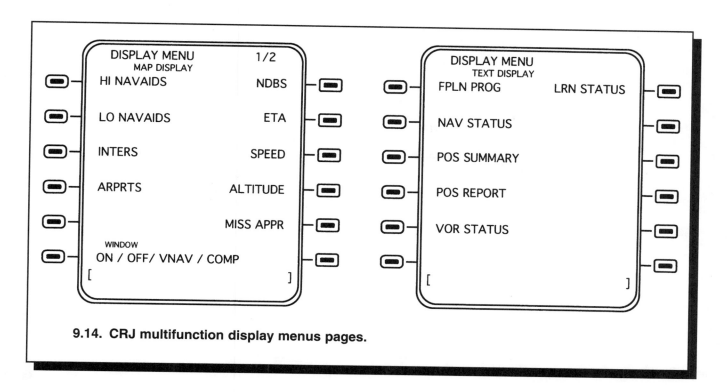

9.14. CRJ multifunction display menus pages.

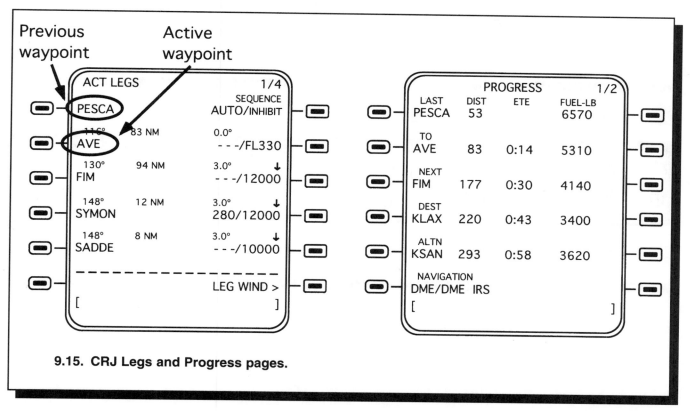

9.15. CRJ Legs and Progress pages.

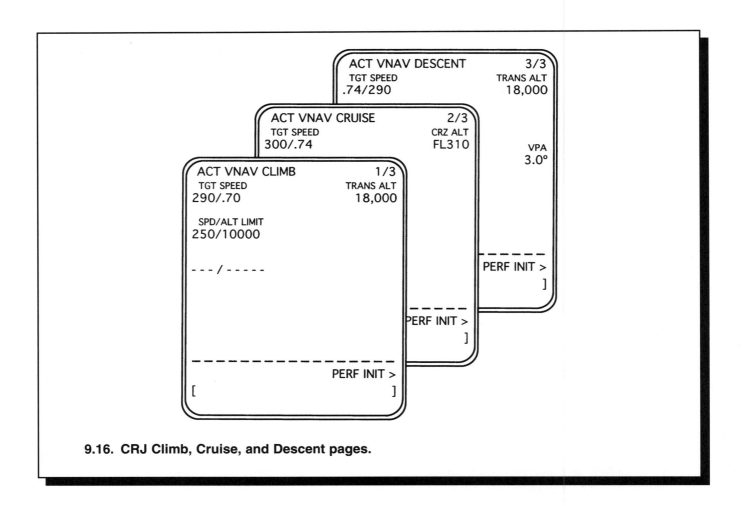

ACT VNAV DESCENT   3/3
TGT SPEED   TRANS ALT
.74/290   18,000

                             VPA
                             3.0°

                      - - - - - -
                      PERF INIT >
                               ]

ACT VNAV CRUISE   2/3
TGT SPEED   CRZ ALT
300/.74   FL310

                      - - - - - -
                      PERF INIT >
                               ]

ACT VNAV CLIMB   1/3
TGT SPEED   TRANS ALT
290/.70   18,000

SPD/ALT LIMIT
250/10000

- - - / - - - - -

- - - - - - - - - - - - - - -
                      PERF INIT >
[   ]

9.16. CRJ Climb, Cruise, and Descent pages.

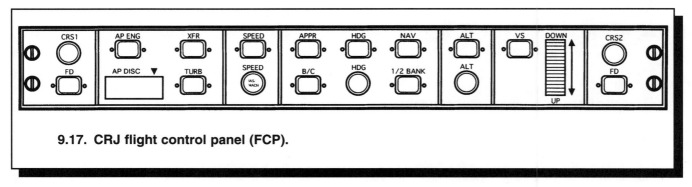

9.17. CRJ flight control panel (FCP).

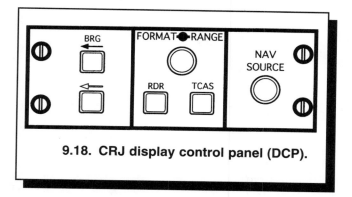

9.18. CRJ display control panel (DCP).

Before you engage the Navigation guidance function, the CRJ makes you tell it whether you wish to navigate to the route stored in the FMC or along VOR radials that you choose to tune and twist yourself. You can make this selection using the **display control panel** (DCP) shown in Figure 9.18.

Rotate the NAV SOURCE knob on the DCP and verify your selection using the annunciator on the primary flight display shown in Figure 9.19.

The FMS annunciation tells the airplane that you wish to navigate to the route stored in the flight management computer.

Since the CRJ does not have an autothrottle, there is no vertical guidance function like the VNAV guidance function offered in Boeing airplanes. To follow the vertical portion of your route, you must adjust the thrust levers yourself and use the simpler vertical guidance functions offered by the CRJ discussed later.

Modifying the Route

The CRJ offers the same CDU pages that allow you to proceed direct to a waypoint, intercept a course to a waypoint, and program holds (Figure 9.20).

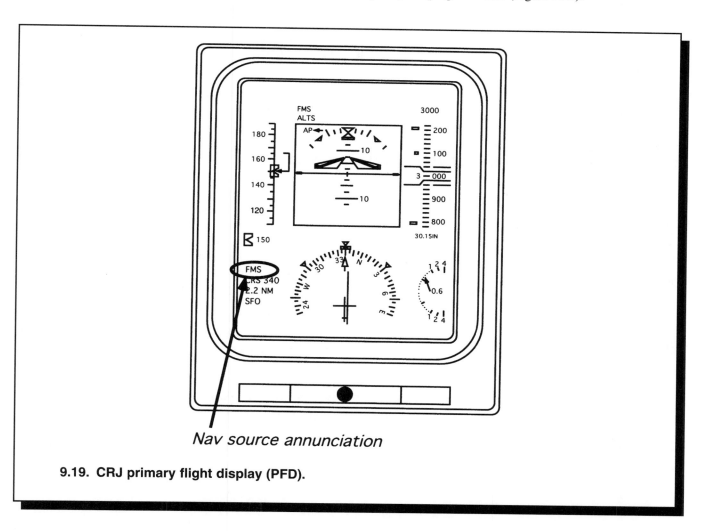

Nav source annunciation

9.19. CRJ primary flight display (PFD).

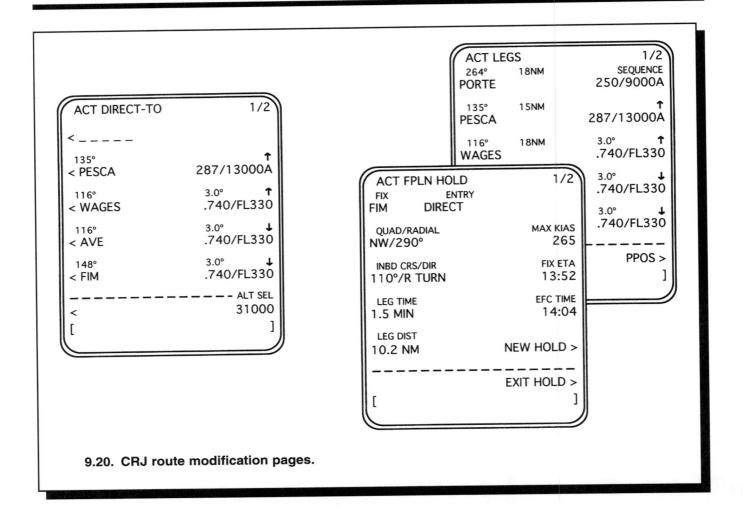

9.20. CRJ route modification pages.

Flying off the Route

The CRJ also offers a collection of simple guidance functions that allow the crew to comply with simple heading, altitude, and speed clearances. These guidance functions are engaged using the buttons on the flight control panel (FCP) shown in Figure 9.17.

The **Heading Select** function can be engaged by dialing the desired heading and pressing the HDG button on the FCP. As shown in Figure 9.21, the dialed heading is reflected by the heading bug that appears on the HSI on the primary flight display.

The Navigation function can also be used to track a localizer or VOR radial. Dial the course using either of the CRS knobs on the FCP and press the NAV button. Before pressing the NAV button, you must go back over to the display control panel (DCP) shown in Figure 9.18 and select the VOR/LOC setting. This tells the system that you want the NAV function to pay attention to radio navigation signals and not the FMC. Having two very difference consequences result from pushing the

same button is known among human factors experts to result in occasional confusion. The CRJ tries to alleviate this problem by making the annunciations for the FMS setting appear in white and the annunciations for the VOR/LOC setting appear in green. Whether the "green data" vs. "white data" distinction is effective in avoiding this kind of error is an open question.

The **Speed** function is analogous to the (Flight) Level Change functions found in Boeing airplanes. To climb or descend at a constant speed, simply dial the desired altitude and speed on the FCP and press the SPD button. Note that the Speed function is not similar to the functions of the same name in the Boeing airplanes. If you have made it this far, you're ready for your first trick question. When in level flight in the CRJ, how do you increase or decrease your speed? The answer: Just push or pull on the thrust levers. There is no autothrottle in the CRJ, so there is no function that controls speed like in the Boeing airplanes. Don't let the names fool you.

The **Vertical Speed** function allows you to climb or descend at a constant rate, just as in Boeing airplanes.

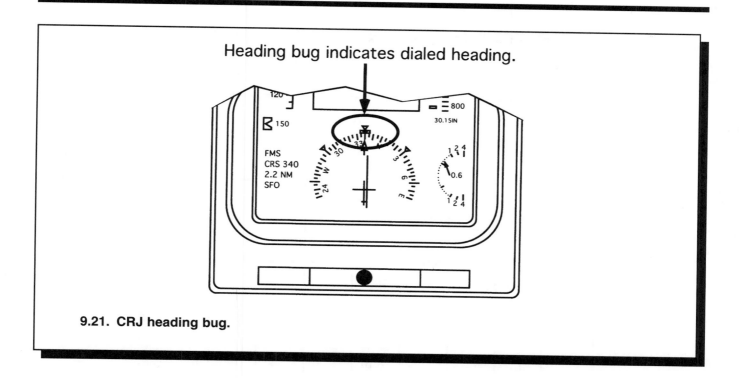

Heading bug indicates dialed heading.

9.21. CRJ heading bug.

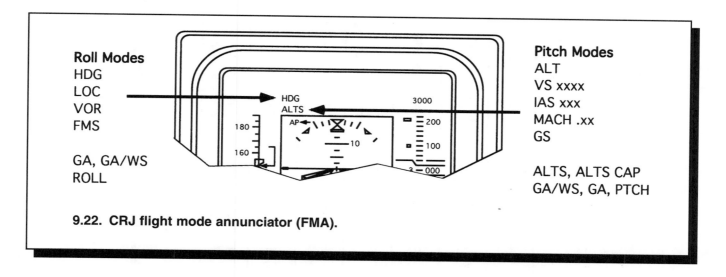

Roll Modes
HDG
LOC
VOR
FMS

GA, GA/WS
ROLL

Pitch Modes
ALT
VS xxxx
IAS xxx
MACH .xx
GS

ALTS, ALTS CAP
GA/WS, GA, PTCH

9.22. CRJ flight mode annunciator (FMA).

How do you keep track of which guidance functions are engaged? A **flight mode annunciator** (FMA) appears at the top of the primary flight display (PFD). A detailed flight mode annunciator is shown in Figure 9.22.

Since there is no autothrottle, there are only two kinds of modes: roll and pitch. Figure 9.23 shows the roll and pitch mode annunciations for the guidance functions we have discussed.

Flying in the Vertical Dimension

Although the CRJ does not have an autothrottle or a VNAV guidance function, it is important to realize that the flight management computer plans the same kind of vertical path created by any other FMC. The multifunction display (MFD) in Figure 9.24 shows the top-of-descent point that has been planned by the FMC.

GUIDANCE FUNCTION	HOW IT WORKS	MODE ANNUNCIATIONS	
		Roll	Pitch
Heading Select	Roll used to maintain heading dialed into heading window.	HDG	
NAV (on white data)	Roll used to track airplane between waypoints that appear on the Legs page.	FMS	
Altitude Hold	Pitch used to maintain present altitude.		ALT
Speed	Pitch used to maintain speed dialed into speed window during a climb or descent. Similar to Level Change in the Boeing 737.		IAS xxx or M .xx
Vertical Speed	Pitch used to maintain vertical speed dialed into vertical speed window during a climb or descent.		V/S
NAV (on green data)	Roll used to track dialed localizer.	VOR or LOC	
Approach	Roll used to track dialed localizer. Pitch used to maintain airplane on glide slope.	LOC	G/S

9.23. CRJ flight mode annunciations.

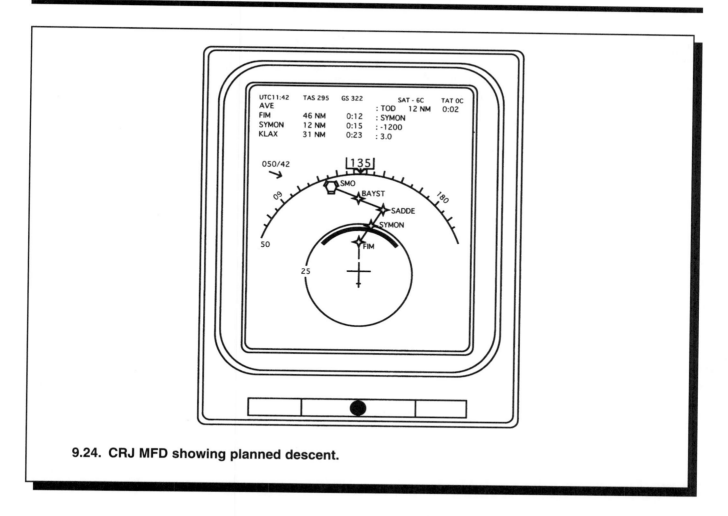

9.24. CRJ MFD showing planned descent.

Without a VNAV guidance function, the flight crew must find other ways to guide the airplane up to the planned cruising altitude and back down again on the planned vertical descent path. A variety of guidance functions supports the flight crew in performing this task.

Climbing up to the assigned cruising altitude can be achieved using the Speed or the Vertical Speed functions. When ATC clears you higher, simply dial a higher altitude into the FCP. Why do other airplanes bother with a VNAV guidance function for climb? The main difference is that the Speed and Vertical Speed functions do not automatically obey the speed and altitude restrictions that apply to your departure procedure. For example, to obey a 250-knot-below-10,000-feet speed restriction, you must manipulate the speed knob on the FCP while keeping a close watch on your altimeter.

Maintaining your assigned cruising altitude can be accomplished using the Altitude Hold guidance function.

Flying a descent can be accomplished using the Vertical Speed function. This is true whether you are allowed to start down before, at, or after the planned top-of-descent point.

The MFD provides a very helpful bit of information that works nicely with the Vertical Speed function. Shown in the top portion of Figure 9.24, a descent rate of −1200 feet per minute is displayed for the crossing restriction of 12,000 feet at Symon intersection. This means that if you start down at the planned top-of-descent point and maintain a vertical speed of −1,200 feet per minute, you will likely remain on the planned descent path and reach Symon at 12,000 feet. The **altitude ring** that appears on the MFD just prior to Symon shows the point at which the airplane is predicted to reach the target altitude. The altitude ring can be chosen as an option to appear on the MFD on the MFD Display Menu page.

For early descent scenarios, simply monitor the vertical speed required to reach your crossing restriction and adjust your vertical speed on the FCP accordingly. You can back up the required vertical speed indication with the altitude ring.

For late descent scenarios, the same technique can be used. You must be careful not to exceed M_{MO}/V_{MO} during your descent and always have the option of using the airplane's speed brakes to control your speed.

Chapter Summary

In this chapter you were briefly introduced to the cockpit automation found in two other commercial carrier airplanes. The Boeing 747-400 was introduced to demonstrate how similar cockpit automation can be across airplanes.

Mastering the 747-400 will also allow you to practice what you have learned using a popular PC-based 747-400 simulator. The Canadair Regional Jet was introduced to provide the pilot-in-training with a look inside the cockpit of a popular airplane operated by regional airlines.

GLOSSARY

Terms and Abbreviations

ACARS: See ARINC communications and addressing system.

Active waypoint: The next waypoint that appears in the flight route. The active waypoint is the waypoint that the flight management computer is always working to achieve.

Actual navigation performance: The navigation accuracy of your navigation equipment, measured at any given time. Actual navigation performance is important when a required navigation performance must be met for a particular approach or airspace.

Alternate Destinations page: A CDU page that allows the crew to enter the names of airports that might be considered alternates in the case that a diversion is necessary. The Alternate Destinations page tracks and displays the distance and bearing to, ETA, and fuel remaining for each alternate airport.

Altitude alerter: A device that allows the flight crew to enter a target altitude and receive an alert once the aircraft reaches the vicinity of the target altitude. Designed as a backup to crew altitude awareness.

Altitude intervention: A feature that allows the altitudes associated with the waypoints that appear in the programmed flight route to be modified without the need for re-programming using the CDU. Altitude intervention allows the crew to make changes by manipulating the more "heads-up" mode control panel (MCP).

Altitude ring: A feature offered by some map displays that graphically depicts the point at which the aircraft is predicted reach a target altitude during a climb or descent. The predictions are based on the aircraft's present vertical speed and ground speed.

Altitude Select (or Altitude Hold) function: An autoflight system guidance function that allows the flight crew to capture and maintain the present altitude of the airplane.

ANP: See Actual navigation performance.

Approach function: An autoflight system guidance function that allows the flight crew to dial, capture, and simultaneously track an ILS localizer and glide slope signal.

Approach Ref page: A CDU page that displays the target speeds and flap settings for an approach. The Approach Ref page can also display other items of interest during an approach such as the predicted landing weight of the airplane and the airport elevation.

Area navigation: The ability to navigate between arbitrary points in the airspace. Compare to traditional radio navigation in which present position and bearings can only be calculated to and from a limited number of ground-based radio navigation devices.

ARINC communications and addressing system: The system that enables data transmissions between an airplane and a ground station via a VHF network. Used to exchange messages, and to automatically report flight and airplane system parameters in flight.

Armed mode: The condition in which an autoflight system mode is set to become engaged once its conditions for engagement have been met. For example, Localizer mode can be armed prior to reaching a localizer if the aircraft is set to fly an appropriate intercept heading.

Arrivals page: A CDU page that allows the flight crew to select from a list of arrival procedures. Selecting an arrival procedure causes the waypoints associated with that procedure to be inserted into the programmed flight route.

Autoflight system: The systems that allow the airplane to be automatically guided along a flight route that has been programmed into the flight management computer, or guided to simple speed, heading, course, and altitude targets entered by the flight crew. An autoflight system is typically made up of an autopilot, autothrottle, and flight director.

Autopilot: The system that automatically manipulates the roll and pitch of the airplane to help follow a route stored in the flight management computer, or to achieve simple speed, heading, course, and altitude targets entered directly by the flight crew using the mode control panel.

Autothrottle: The system that automatically manipulates the thrust setting of the airplane to help follow the route stored in the flight management computer, or to achieve simple speed and altitude targets entered directly by the flight crew using the mode control panel.

Autothrottle mode: Any one of a series of functions that can be performed by the autothrottle. Each autothrottle mode attempts to achieve a particular thrust or speed target. These speed and thrust targets can either be part of the FMC programmed route, or directly entered by the flight crew using the mode control panel.

Bottom-of-descent point: The endpoint of the descent calculated by the flight management computer. The bottom-of-descent point usually corresponds to the crossing restriction that must be met at the conclusion of a descent.

Box prompts: An array of empty boxes that can appear on a CDU page. Box prompts are used to indicate a required entry that must be made by the flight crew.

CDU: See Control display unit.

CDU page: Any one of many information displays that can appear on the CDU screen. Each CDU page has a descriptive title and presents information related to a particular topic related to your flight route.

CDU page line: One of twelve locations where information can appear on a CDU page. Six pages lines appear on the right side of the CDU and six appear on the left. Page lines are named according to their location on the CDU screen: 1L ... 6L and 1R ... 6R.

CDU screen: The small display that appears in the upper portion of the control display unit. The CDU screen serves as the monitor for the flight management computer, allowing the crew to enter information to the FMC and to view information stored in the FMC.

Climb page: A CDU page that displays the target cruising altitude, the target climb speed, and any speed and altitude restrictions that the flight management computer plans to obey during the climb.

Cockpit automation: The term that loosely refers to the entire suite of modern cockpit technology that assists the flight crew in planning and carrying out an assigned flight route.

Company route: A flight route that has been preprogrammed and stored in the flight management computer. Company routes avoid the need for the flight crew to type in a route, waypoint by waypoint. Company routes save time and reduce the likelihood of typing errors.

Conditional waypoint: A waypoint that is not geographically fixed in space, describing an event rather than a location. For example, a waypoint that describes the point at which the airplane will reach an altitude of 1,000 feet AGL is a conditional waypoint. Conditional waypoints always appear in parentheses on the Route Legs page.

Control display unit: The flight crew's interface to the flight management computer. The CDU serves as the keyboard and monitor of the flight management computer. The CDU allows the crew to input information or view information that is stored in the FMC.

Cost index: A range of numbers used to specify how the flight management computer should trade-off between time and fuel costs when planning a flight route. A low cost index results in slow speeds and fuel efficiency. A high cost index results in fast speeds and time efficiency.

Cruise page: A CDU page that displays the assigned cruising altitude and the target cruise speed. Allows the flight crew to make changes to both the planned cruising altitude and cruise speed.

DADC: See Digital air data computer.

DCP: Display control panel.

Departures page: A CDU page that allows the flight crew to select from a list of departure procedures. Selecting a departure procedure causes the waypoints associated with that procedure to be inserted into the programmed flight route.

Descent page: A CDU page that displays the descent crossing restriction, the target descent speed, and other speed and altitude restrictions that the flight management computer plans to obey during the descent.

Descent path: A geographically fixed "wire-in-the-sky" that the flight management computer constructs as the optimal means of descending down to a crossing restriction. Maintaining the airplane on the descent path at the planned descent speed is a top priority for the flight management computer and autoflight system.

Digital air data computer: Principal source of pitot and static pressure information for the flight instruments and other airplane systems. The digital air data computer receives inputs from the airplane's pitot-static systems.

Direct to page: A CDU page that allows the flight crew to enter the name of a waypoint to which they have been instructed to proceed directly. After the entry is made, the entered waypoint becomes the new active waypoint.

Display control panel: The selector switches used to control various features of the cockpit displays in the Canadair Regional Jet.

EADI: See Electronic attitude director indicator.

EFIS: See Electronic flight instrument system.

EHSI: See Electronic horizontal situation indicator.

EICAS: See Engine indicating and crew alerting system.

Electronic attitude director indicator: Combines into one display, much of the information presented by conventional flight instruments. Includes an attitude indicator, airspeed indicator, altimeter, vertical speed indicator, flight director, autoflight system modes, localizer and glide slope deviation, radio altimeter, and others.

Electronic flight instrument system: The collection of computers and electronic displays that make up the flight instruments in the modern airline cockpit. Includes the electronic attitude director indicator, the electronic horizontal situation indicator, and all of their supporting systems.

Electronic horizontal situation indicator: The map display found in the modern airline cockpit. Presents the planned flight route and the aircraft's present position with respect to the route in a graphical format. Also called a navigation display in other airplanes.

Engaged mode: An autopilot or autothrottle mode that is currently in control of the airplane and working toward a target.

Engine indicating and crew alerting system: An integrated cockpit display that combines all engine and airplane systems indications. The EICAS provides alerts and status messages to the flight crew.

Execute button: The button located on the front of the control display unit used to finalize modifications made to the route stored in the flight management computer.

FCP: See Flight control panel.

FLCH: See Flight Level Change function.

Flight control panel: Another name for a mode control panel in some airplanes.

Flight director: A cockpit display that presents guidance commands to the crew when any autoflight system guidance function is being used. Similar to following localizer and glide slope needles, the pilot flying must keep the airplane symbol aligned with the commands bars of the flight director.

Flight Level Change function: A B-747 autoflight system guidance function that provides a simple means of climbing or descending to an assigned altitude. Called Level Change in the Boeing 737 and Speed in the Canadair Regional Jet.

Flight management computer: The electronic brain of the modern airline cockpit. Used to create and store flight routes. Contains a navigation database and an airplane performance database.

Flight management computer system: Yet another name for the flight management computer or flight management system.

Flight management system: Another name used for a flight management computer that has been loaded with a current navigation database.

Flight mode annunciator: A cockpit display that presents the names of the autopilot and autothrottle modes that are engaged and/or armed. The flight mode annunciator is the only reliable source of information about what the airplane is doing now and intends to do next.

Flight Plan page: A CDU page that allows the crew to enter a planned flight route. Also called a Route page in some airplanes.

FMA: See Flight mode annunciator.

FMC: See Flight management computer.

FMCS: See Flight management computer system.

FMS: See Flight management system.

GCP: See Glare shield control panel.

Glare shield control panel: Yet another name for mode control panel (MCP) or flight control panel (FCP).

Global positioning system: A satellite-based navigation system used to determine and track the present position of an aircraft. A global positioning system (GPS) receiver must be installed on board the aircraft in order to use the satellite-based system.

GPS: See Global positioning system.

GPS unit (or receiver): A component that must be installed on board the aircraft in order to make use of the global positioning system. This unit receives satellite signals and determines and tracks the position of the aircraft.

GPWS: See Ground proximity warning system.

Great circle route: The shortest distance between two points traveling on the surface of the earth. Defined by a plane that passes through the two points of interest and the center of the earth.

Green arc: A feature offered by some map displays that graphically depicts the point at which the aircraft is predicted reach a target altitude during a climb or descent. The predictions are based on the aircraft's present vertical speed and ground speed.

Ground proximity warning system: The system that provides auditory alerts whenever the aircraft is determined to be in danger of impacting surrounding terrain.

Guidance function: Any one of many services offered to the flight crew by the airplane's autoflight system. For example, the Level Change guidance function allows the crew to receive guidance support when climbing or descending to an assigned altitude.

Heading Select (or Heading Hold) function: An autoflight system guidance function that allows the crew to dial a target heading on the mode control panel and instruct the airplane to maintain that target heading.

Heading window: Located on the mode control panel (MCP), the heading window is used by the crew to dial target headings whenever the Heading Select (or Heading Hold) guidance function is used.

Hold page: A CDU page that provides the flight crew with a simple means of programming a holding pattern.

Ident page: A CDU page that lists the software being used by the flight management computer. The most important item on the Ident page for the flight crew is the validity period for the FMC's navigation database.

Inertial reference system: Senses aircraft movement to measure aircraft attitude, heading, position, acceleration, vertical speed, wind direction and velocity, and ground track.

IRS: See Inertial reference system.

Lateral navigation function: In Boeing airplanes, the autoflight system guidance function that supports the flight crew in steering the airplane between the list of waypoints in the route stored in the flight management computer.

Level Change function: An autoflight system guidance function that provides a simple means of climbing or descending to an assigned altitude. Called Flight Level Change in other Boeing airplanes, and Speed in the Canadair Regional Jet.

Line select button (or line select key): The twelve buttons that surround the twelve CDU page lines. Typing characters into the scratch pad and then pressing a line select button causes those characters to be insert into the page line beside the line select button that was pressed. Pressing a line select button with an empty scratch pad causes the information that appears at the page line to be copied down to the scratch pad.

LNAV: See Lateral navigation function.

Map mode: One of several possible modes to which an electronic map display can be set. The map mode shows the aircraft symbol at the bottom or center of the map. A portion of the remaining flight route is shown issuing from the nose of the aircraft symbol. The map mode typically has a range setting that allows the crew to zoom in and out to see more and less of the flight route.

MCP: See Mode control panel.

Mode control panel: The device used by the flight crew to engage autoflight system guidance functions and dial heading, altitude, speed, and vertical speed targets. Also used to turn on and off the autopilot, autothrottle, and flight directors. Located just below the glare shield between the two pilot stations.

N1 Limit page: A CDU page that displays the target thrust settings that the flight management computer has calculated for takeoff, go around, climb, cruise, and descent. Also called the Thrust Limit page in some airplanes.

Navigation database: An electronic version of the paper navigation charts you use during everyday IFR flight operations. Navigation databases contain the same information as your paper charts and are published on the same 28-day schedule.

Navigation display: Another name for the map display in some airplanes.

ND: See Navigation display.

Nearest Airports page: A CDU page that lists the airports closest to the present position of the airplane. The Nearest Airports page is especially useful during emergency situations.

Overlay approach: A conventional approach procedure that relies on radio navigation equipment, but that additionally has juxtaposed on top of it another approach procedure that uses modern area navigation equipment.

Page access buttons: The buttons that appear on the front of the control display unit (CDU), and that bear the name of a CDU page. Pressing a page access buttons causes that page to appear on the CDU screen.

Perf Init page: A CDU page that allows the flight crew to enter several items of information pertaining to the performance of the airplane. The Perf Init page accepts entries for the gross weight of the airplane, the fuel on board, and the planned cruising altitude.

Performance database: An electronic database stored inside the flight management computer that details the performance characteristics of the airplane. The performance database contains all of the same information contained in the airplane flight manual (AFM).

Phantom waypoint: A waypoint that does not appear on any CDU page. Phantom waypoints are hidden cues used by the flight management computer and autoflight system to automatically initiate some action such as reducing thrust after takeoff or decelerating the airplane at the conclusion of a descent.

Pitch mode: Any one of a series of functions that can be performed by the autopilot. A pitch mode manipulates the airplane's elevators to achieve a target speed or a target path.

Plan mode: One of several possible modes to which an electronic map display can be set. The plan mode shows the entire route that has been programmed into the flight management computer. The plan mode is useful for planning purposes when it is best to have the entire route visible for review.

Pos Init page: A CDU page used to enter the present position of the airplane. The Pos Init page shows the crew estimated positions measured by all of the airplane's sensors such as the inertial reference system and global positioning system receivers.

Progress page: A CDU page that enumerates the waypoints in the planned flight route, along with an estimated time of arrival (ETA) and predicted fuel remaining for each waypoint.

QFE: Old radio "Q" code used to refer to the altimeter setting that causes the altimeter to reflect the height above airport elevation or runway threshold elevation. In other words, when set to QFE, the altimeter reads roughly "0" when the airplane is on the airport surface, regardless of the airport elevation.

QNH: Old radio "Q" code used to refer to the altimeter setting in that causes the altimeter to reflect the altitude above mean sea level. In other words, when set to QNH, the altimeter shows the airport elevation when the airplane is sitting on the airport surface. QNH is used by most every commercial carrier.

RA: See Resolution advisory.

Radio altimeter: An altitude-measuring system that makes use of reflected radio signals rather than conventional pitot-static pressure measurements. Primarily used during the final segment of an instrument approach, but also by the airplane's ground proximity warning system.

Required navigation performance: The accuracy required of any area navigation equipment when used to conduct an area navigation approach or operate in a designated airspace.

Resolution advisory: The most serious type of warning issued by the traffic collision avoidance system (TCAS). A resolution advisory takes the form of a command that instructs the pilot flying to perform a vertical avoidance maneuver to avoid impacting a nearby aircraft.

RNAV: See Area navigation.

RNP: See Required navigation performance.

Roll mode: Any one of a series of functions that can be performed by the autopilot. A roll mode manipulates the airplane's ailerons to maintain the airplane on a target heading or course.

Route Data page: A CDU page that allows the flight crew to enter predicted wind direction and velocity for each of the waypoints in the programmed flight route. Wind entries help the flight management computer fine-tune its time and fuel predictions.

Route discontinuity: A break in the programmed route stored in the flight management system. Indicates that the FMC does not know how to navigate between the two waypoints between which the route discontinuity lies. Requires crew inputs to resolve the discontinuity.

Route Legs page: A CDU page that enumerates the waypoints that make up the planned flight route. The Route Legs page lists each

waypoint in the planned route along with the distance and bearing to the waypoint, and an altitude and speed for each waypoint.

Route page: A CDU page that allows the crew to enter a planned flight route. Called a Flight Plan page in some airplanes.

Scratch pad: The area at the bottom of the CDU screen. Characters typed by either pilot using the CDU number and letter keys initially appear in the scratch pad. The scratch pad allows the flight crew to review what they have typed before finalizing the entry.

Situation awareness: Loosely refers to one's awareness of critical aspects of a flight, such as aircraft position, intended route, autoflight modes engaged, future actions required, etc.

Speed function: In Boeing airplanes, the autoflight system guidance function that allows the crew to dial simple speed targets when the Altitude Hold function is being used. In the Canadair Regional Jet, the Speed function is similar to the (Flight) Level Change function: it is used to climb and descent to target altitudes.

Speed intervention: A feature offered on many new airplanes that allows the climb, cruise, or descent speeds stored in the flight management computer to be modified without the need for reprogramming using the CDU. Speed intervention allows the crew to make changes by manipulating the more "heads-up" mode control panel.

Speed window: Located on the mode control panel (MCP), the speed window is used by the crew to dial a target speed whenever the Speed function is used.

Standalone approach: An instrument approach that relies solely on the use of area navigation equipment such as a flight management computer or global positioning system receiver.

TA: See Traffic advisory.

Takeoff/Go Around function: An autoflight system guidance function that provides guidance and thrust control during the takeoff roll and early climb out. The Takeoff/Go Around function is engaged by pressing a TOGA button located on the throttle quadrant.

Takeoff Ref page: A CDU page that allows the crew to enter an assumed temperature when a reduced thrust takeoff is desired.

TCAS: See Traffic collision avoidance system.

Thrust Limit page: A CDU page that displays the target thrust settings that the flight management computer has calculated for takeoff, go around, climb, cruise, and descent. Also called the N1 Limit page in some airplanes.

TOGA: See Takeoff/Go Around function.

Top-of-descent point: The point that the flight management computer calculates to be the ideal location to move the thrust levers back to idle and begin a descent down to the planned crossing restriction. The FMC considers fuel and time economy and prevailing winds when choosing a top-of-descent point.

Traffic advisory: A warning issued by the traffic collision avoidance system (TCAS) that alerts the flight crew to other aircraft that have moved within a prescribed "safety zone" surrounding the airplane.

Traffic collision avoidance system: The onboard system that detects the presence of some aircraft operating in the vicinity of your own airplane. TCAS works by querying the transponders of nearby aircraft and presenting their location and relative altitude on the map display. Alerts and warnings are issued to the flight crew when nearby aircraft are deemed to be a threat to safety. Two types of alerts are possible: traffic advisory and resolution advisory.

Vertical navigation function: In Boeing airplanes, the autoflight system guidance function that supports the flight crew in steering the airplane to the target altitudes, speeds, and thrusts that appear in the route stored in the flight management computer.

Vertical Speed function: An autoflight system guidance function that allows the crew to perform constant-rate climbs and descents by dialing in a vertical speed on the mode control panel.

VNAV: See Vertical navigation function.

VOR/LOC: An autoflight system guidance function that allows the crew to dial, capture, and track VOR radials and localizers.

Waypoint: A named geographical location used to define routes and terminal area procedures. Modern navigation technologies such as flight management systems are able to locate and follow courses to and from waypoints that occur anywhere in the airspace. No longer are navigation systems limited to working from a limited collection of locations such as VOR and NDB stations.

INDEX